D1423482

DISCARDED
Northamptonshire Libraries

00401203566

ALSO BY JAMES SUZMAN

Affluence Without Abundance

Work

Work

A History of How We Spend Our Time

James Suzman

BLOOMSBURY CIRCUS
LONDON · OXFORD · NEW YORK · NEW DELHI · SYDNEY

BLOOMSBURY CIRCUS
Bloomsbury Publishing Plc
50 Bedford Square, London, WC1B 3DP, UK

BLOOMSBURY, BLOOMSBURY CIRCUS and the Bloomsbury Circus logo are
trademarks of Bloomsbury Publishing Plc

First published in Great Britain 2020

Copyright © James Suzman, 2020
Illustrations © Michelle Fava, 2020

James Suzman has asserted his right under the Copyright, Designs and Patents Act,
1988, to be identified as Author of this work

Extract from 'Toads' from *The Less Deceived* by Philip Larkin, published by Faber
and Faber Ltd and used with permission. (c) Philip Larkin, 2011.

All rights reserved. No part of this publication may be reproduced or transmitted
in any form or by any means, electronic or mechanical, including photocopying,
recording, or any information storage or retrieval system, without prior permission
in writing from the publishers

Bloomsbury Publishing Plc does not have any control over, or responsibility for, any
third-party websites referred to or in this book. All internet addresses given in this
book were correct at the time of going to press. The author and publisher regret any
inconvenience caused if addresses have changed or sites have ceased to exist,
but can accept no responsibility for any such changes

A catalogue record for this book is available from the British Library

ISBN: HB: 978-1-5266-0499-6; TPB: 978-1-5266-0501-6; EBOOK: 978-1-5266-0500-9

2 4 6 8 10 9 7 5 3 1

Typeset by Newgen KnowledgeWorks Pvt., Ltd, Chennai, India
Printed and bound in Great Britain by CPI Group (UK) Ltd, Croydon CR0 4YY

NORTHAMPTONSHIRE LIBRARIES & INFORMATION SERVICES	
00401203566	
Askews & Holts	
NC	

To find out more about our authors and books visit www.bloomsbury.com
and sign up for our newsletters

Why should I let the toad *work*
Squat on my life?
Can't I use my wit as a pitchfork
And drive the brute off?

Philip Larkin, 'Toads'

Contents

Contents

Illustrations

Illustrations

Introduction

The first industrial revolution was coughed out of the soot-blackened chimneys of coal-fired steam engines; the second leapt from electric wall sockets; and the third took the form of the electronic micro-processor. Now we are in the midst of a fourth industrial revolution, born of the union of a host of new digital, biological and physical technologies, and we are told that it will be exponentially more transformative than its predecessors. Even so, no one is yet quite sure how it will play out, beyond the fact that ever more tasks in our factories, businesses and homes will be undertaken by automated cyber-physical systems animated by machine-learning algorithms.

For some, the prospect of an automated future heralds an era of robotic convenience. For others, it is another fateful step on the journey towards a cybernetic dystopia. But for many, the prospect of an automated future raises only one immediate question: what will happen if a robot takes my job?

For those in professions that have up to now been immune from technological redundancy, the rise of the job-eating robots manifests in the mundane: the choruses of robotic greetings and reprimands that emanate from the ranks of automated tellers in supermarkets or the clumsy algorithms that both guide and frustrate our adventures in the digital universe.

For the hundreds of millions of unemployed people scraping a living in the corrugated-iron margins of developing countries, where economic growth is driven ever more by the marriage of cutting-edge technology and capital and so generates few new jobs, automation is an altogether more immediate concern. It is also an immediate concern for ranks of semi-skilled workers in industrialised economies whose only option is to strike to save their jobs from automata whose principal virtue is that they never go on strike. And, even if it doesn't feel like it just yet, the writing is on the wall for some in highly skilled professions too. With artificial intelligence now designing better artificial intelligence than people can, it looks like we have been tricked by our own ingenuity into turning our factories, offices and workplaces into devil's workshops that will leave our hands idle and rob our lives of purpose.

If so, then we are right to worry. After all we work to live and live to work and are capable of finding meaning, satisfaction and pride in almost any job: from the rhythmic monotony of mopping floors to gaming tax loopholes. The work we do also defines who we are; determines our future prospects, dictates where and with whom we spend most of our time; mediates our sense of self-worth; moulds many of our values and orients our political loyalties. So much so that we sing the praises of strivers, decry the laziness of shirkers and the goal of universal employment remains a mantra for politicians of all stripes.

Beneath this lies the conviction that we are genetically hard-wired to work and that our species' destiny has been shaped by a unique convergence of purposefulness, intelligence and industriousness that has enabled us to build societies that are so much more than the sum of their parts.

Our anxieties about an automated future contrast with the optimism of many thinkers and dreamers who, ever since the first stirrings of the Industrial Revolution, believed that automation was the key that would unlock an economic utopia. People like Adam Smith, the founding father of economics, who in 1776 sung the praises of the 'very pretty machines' that he believed would in time 'facilitate and abridge labour',[1] or Oscar Wilde who a century later fantasised about a future 'in which machinery will be doing all the necessary and unpleasant work'.[2] But none made the case as comprehensively as the twentieth century's most influential economist, John Maynard Keynes. He predicted in 1930 that by the early twenty-first century capital growth, improving productivity and technological advances should have brought us to the foothills of an economic 'promised land' in which everybody's basic needs were easily satisfied and where, as a result, nobody worked more than fifteen hours in a week.

We passed the productivity and capital growth thresholds Keynes calculated would need to be met to get there some decades ago. Most of us still work just as hard as our grandparents and great-grandparents did, and our governments remain as fixated on economic growth and employment creation as at any point in our recent history. More than this, with private and state pension funds groaning under the weight of their obligations to increasingly aged populations, many of us are expected to work almost a decade longer than we did half a century ago; and despite unprecedented advances in technology and productivity in some of the world's most advanced economies like Japan and South Korea, hundreds of avoidable deaths every year are now officially accredited to people logging eye-watering levels of overtime.

Humankind, it seems, is not yet ready to claim its collective pension. Understanding why requires recognising that our relationship with work is far more interesting and involved than most traditional economists would have us believe.

———

Keynes believed that reaching his economic promised land would be our species' most singular achievement because we will have done nothing less than solve what he described as 'the most pressing problem of the human race . . . from the beginnings of life in its most primitive form'.

The 'pressing problem' Keynes had in mind was what classical economists refer to as the 'economic problem' and sometimes also as the 'problem of scarcity'. It holds that we are rational creatures cursed with insatiable appetites and that because there are simply not enough resources to satisfy everybody's wants everything is scarce. The idea that we have infinite wants but that all resources are limited sits at the beating heart of the definition of economics as the study of how people allocate scarce resources to meet their needs and desires. It also anchors our markets, financial, employment and monetary systems. To economists, then, scarcity is what drives us to work, for it is only by working – by making, producing and trading scarce resources – that we can ever begin to bridge the gap between our apparently infinite desires and our limited means.

But the problem of scarcity offers a bleak assessment of our species. It insists that evolution has moulded us into selfish creatures, cursed to be forever burdened by desires that we can never satisfy. And as much as this assumption about human nature may seem obvious and self-evident to many in the industrialised world, to many others, like the Ju/'hoansi 'Bushmen' of southern Africa's Kalahari, who still lived as hunter-gatherers through to the late twentieth century, it does not ring true.

I have been documenting their often traumatic encounter with a relentlessly expanding global economy since the early 1990s. It is an often brutal story, set in a frontier between two profoundly different ways of life, each grounded in very different social and economic philosophies based on very different assumptions about the nature of scarcity. For the Ju/'hoansi, the market economy and the assumptions about human nature that underwrite it are as bewildering as they are frustrating. They are not alone in this. Other societies who continued to hunt and gather into the twentieth century, from the Hadzabe of East Africa to the Inuit in the Arctic, have similarly struggled to make sense of and adapt to norms of an economic system predicated on eternal scarcity.

When Keynes first described his economic utopia, the study of hunter-gatherer societies was barely more than a sideshow in the newly emerging discipline of social anthropology. Even if he had wished to know more about hunter-gatherers, he would not have found much to challenge the prevailing view at the time that life in primitive societies was a constant battle against starvation. Nor would he have found anything to persuade him that, despite the occasional setback, the human journey was, above all, a story of progress and that the engine of progress was our urge to work, to produce, to build and to exchange, spurred by our innate urge to solve the economic problem.

But we now know that hunter-gatherers like the Ju/'hoansi did not live constantly on the edge of starvation. Rather, they were usually well nourished; lived longer than people in most farming societies; rarely worked more than fifteen hours a week, and spent the bulk of their time at rest and leisure. We also know that they could do this because they did not routinely store food, cared little for accumulating wealth or status, and worked almost exclusively to meet only their short-term material needs. Where the economic problem insists that we are all cursed to live in the purgatory between our infinite desires and limited means, hunter-gatherers had few material desires, which could be satisfied with a few hours of effort. Their economic life was organised around the presumption of abundance rather than a preoccupation with scarcity. And this being so, there is good reason to believe that because our ancestors hunted and gathered for well over 95 per cent of *Homo sapiens'* 300,000-year-old history, the assumptions about human nature in the problem of scarcity and our attitudes to work have their roots in farming.

Acknowledging that for most of human history our ancestors were not as preoccupied with scarcity as we are now reminds us that there is far more to work than our efforts to solve the economic problem. This is something we all recognise: we routinely describe all sorts of purposeful activities beyond our jobs as work. We can work, for instance, at our relationships, on our bodies and even at our leisure.

When economists define work as the time and effort we spend meeting our needs and wants they dodge two obvious problems. The first is that often the only thing that differentiates work from leisure is context and whether we are being paid to do something or are paying to do it. To an ancient forager, hunting an elk is work, but to many First World hunters it is an exhilarating and often very expensive leisure activity; to a commercial artist, drawing is work, but to millions of amateur artists it is a relaxing pleasure; and to a lobbyist, cultivating relationships with movers and shakers is work, but for most of the rest of us making friends is a joy. The second problem is that beyond the energy we expend to secure our most basic needs – food, water, air, warmth, companionship and safety – there is very little that is universal about what constitutes a necessity. More than this, necessity often merges so imperceptibly with desire that it can be impossible to separate them. Thus some will insist that a breakfast of a croissant served alongside good coffee is a necessity while for others it is a luxury.

The closest thing to a universal definition of 'work' – one that hunter-gatherers, pinstriped derivatives traders, calloused subsistence farmers and anyone else would agree on – is that it involves purposefully expending energy or effort on a task to achieve a goal or end. Ever since ancient humans first began to divide up the world around them and organise their experiences of it in terms of concepts, words and ideas, they have almost certainly had some concept of work. Like love, parenthood, music and mourning, work is one of the few concepts that anthropologists and travellers alike have been able to cling to when cast adrift in alien lands. For where spoken language or bewildering customs are an obstruction, the simple act of helping someone perform a job will often break down barriers far quicker than any clumsy utterances. It expresses goodwill and, like a dance or a song, it creates a communion of purpose and a harmony of experience.

Abandoning the idea that the economic problem is the eternal condition of the human race does more than extend the definition of work beyond how we make a living. It provides us with a new lens through which to view our deep historical relationship with work from the very beginnings of life through to our busy present. It also raises a series of new questions. Why do we now afford work so much more importance than our hunting and gathering ancestors did? Why, in an era of unprecedented abundance, do we remain so preoccupied with scarcity?

Answering these questions requires venturing far beyond the bounds of traditional economics and into the world of physics, evolutionary biology and zoology. But perhaps most importantly it requires bringing a social anthropological perspective to bear on them. It is only through social anthropological studies of societies who continued to hunt and gather into the twentieth century that we are able to animate the flaked stones, rock art and broken bones that are the only abundant material clues to how our foraging ancestors lived and worked. It is also only through taking a social anthropological approach that we can begin to make sense of how our experiences of the world are moulded by the different kinds of work we do. Taking this broader approach offers us some surprising insights into the ancient roots of what are often considered to be uniquely modern challenges. It reveals, for instance, how our relationships with working machines are resonant of the relationship between early farmers and the cart-horses, oxen and other beasts of burden that aided them in their work, and how our anxieties about automation are remarkably reminiscent of those that kept people in slave-owning societies awake at night, and why.

When it comes to charting the history of our relationship with work, there are two intersecting pathways that are the most obvious to follow.

The first maps the story of our relationship with energy. At its most fundamental, work is always an energy trans-action and the capacity to do certain kinds of work is what distinguishes living organisms from dead, inanimate matter. For only living things actively seek out and capture energy specifically to live, to grow and to reproduce. The journey down this pathway reveals that we are not the only species who are routinely profligate with energy; or who become listless, depressed and demoralised when they are deprived of purpose and there is no work to do. This in turn raises a whole series of other questions about the nature of work and our relationship with it. Do, for example, organisms like bacteria, plants and carthorses also work? If so, in what ways does the work they do differ from the work that humans and the machines that we build do? And what does this tell us about the way we work?

This pathway begins at the moment an energy source first somehow bound together a chaos of different molecules to form living organisms. It is also a path that widens steadily and ever more rapidly as life progressively expanded across the earth's surface and evolved to capture new sources of energy, among them sunlight, oxygen, flesh, fire and eventually fossil fuels with which to do work.

The second pathway follows the human evolutionary and cultural journey. Its early physical milestones take the form of rough stone tools, ancient hearths and broken beads. Later milestones take the form of powerful engines, giant cities, stock exchanges, industrial-scale farms, nation states and vast networks of energy-hungry machines. But this is a pathway also littered with many invisible milestones. These take the form of ideas, concepts, ambitions, hopes, habits, rituals, practices, institutions and stories – the building blocks of culture and history. The journey down this pathway reveals how, as our ancestors developed the capacity to master many new different skills, our remarkable purposefulness was honed to the point that we are now capable of finding meaning, joy and deep satisfaction in activities like building pyramids, digging holes and doodling.

It also shows how the work they did and the skills they acquired progressively shaped their experience of, and interactions with, the world around them.

But it is the points where these two pathways converge that are most important in terms of making sense of our contemporary relationship with work. The first of these points of convergence comes when humans mastered fire possibly as long as a million years ago. In learning how to outsource some of their energy needs to flames, they acquired the gift of more time free from the food-quest, the means to stay warm in the cold and the ability to vastly extend their diets, so fuelling the growth of ever more energy-hungry, harder-working brains.

The second crucial point of convergence was far more recent, and arguably far more transformative. It began some 12,000 years ago when some of our ancestors began to routinely store foods and experiment with cultivation, transforming their relationships with their environments, with each other, with scarcity and with work. Exploring this point of convergence also reveals how much of the formal economic architecture around which we organise our working lives today had its origins in farming and how intimately our ideas about equality and status are bound into our attitudes to work.

A third point of convergence occurs when people began to gather in cities and towns. This was around 8,000 years ago, when some agricultural societies started to generate big enough food surpluses to sustain large urban populations. And it too represents a major new chapter in the history of work – one defined not by the need to capture energy by working in the fields, but rather by the demands of spending it. The birth of the first cities seeded the genesis of a whole new range of skills, professions, jobs and trades that were unimaginable in subsistence farming or foraging societies.

The emergence of large villages, then towns and finally cities also played a vital role in reshaping the dynamics of the economic problem and scarcity. Because most urban people's material needs were met by farmers who produced food in the countryside, they focused their restless energy in pursuit of status, wealth, pleasure, leisure and power. Cities quickly became crucibles of inequality, a process that was accelerated by the fact that within cities people were not bound together by the same intimate kinship and social ties that were characteristic of small rural communities. As a result people living in cities increasingly began to bind their social identity ever more tightly to the work they did and find community among others who pursued the same trade as them.

The fourth point of convergence is marked by the appearance of factories and mills belching smoke from great chimneys as populations in Western Europe learned to unlock ancient stores of energy from fossil fuels and transform them into hitherto unimaginable material prosperity. At this point, which begins early in the eighteenth century, both pathways expand abruptly. They become more crowded, accommodating the rapid growth in the number and size of cities, a surge in the population of both humans and the animal and plant species our ancestors domesticated. They also become far busier as a result of the turbo-charging of our collective preoccupation with scarcity and work – paradoxically as a result of there being more stuff than ever

12

before. And while it is still too early tell, it is hard to avoid the suspicion that future historians will not distinguish between the first, second, third and fourth industrial revolutions, but will instead consider this extended moment as critical as any other in our species' relationship with work.

PART ONE

IN THE BEGINNING

1

To Live is to Work

On this particular afternoon in the spring of 1994, it was so hot that even the children with their rawhide feet winced as they darted across the sand from one patch of shade to the next. There was no breeze and the dust clouds kicked up by the missionary's Land Cruiser as it thundered up the rough sand track towards the Skoonheid Resettlement Camp in Namibia's Kalahari Desert hung in the air long after the vehicle had come to a halt.

For the nearly 200 Ju/'hoansi Bushmen sheltering from the sun, occasional visits from missionaries were a welcome break from the monotony of waiting for government food handouts. They were also far more entertaining than traipsing across the desert from one vast cattle ranch to the next in the hope of persuading a white farmer to give them some work. Over the preceding half-century of living under the whip of the ranchers who had robbed them of their land, even the most sceptical among this community – the remnants of the most enduring hunter-gatherer society on earth – had come to believe it was common sense to pay attention to the ordained emissaries of the farmers' God. Some even found comfort in their words.

As the sun dropped towards the western horizon, the missionary climbed out of his Land Cruiser, set up an improvised pulpit at the base of the trunk, and summoned the congregation. It was still meltingly hot, and they sluggishly convened in the dappled shade of the tree. The only drawback of this arrangement was that, as the sun fell lower, the congregation had to periodically rearrange itself to remain in the shade, a process that involved much getting up, sitting down, elbowing and nudging. As the service progressed and the tree's shadow lengthened, the majority of the congregation shifted progressively further and further away from the pulpit, forcing the missionary to deliver much of his sermon in a sustained bellow.

The setting added a certain biblical gravitas to proceedings. Not only did the sun provide the missionary with a squint-inducing halo, but like the moon that would soon rise in the east and the tree the congregation sat beneath, the sun had a starring role in the tale he had to tell: Genesis and the Fall of Man.

The missionary began by reminding his congregation that the reason why people came together to worship every Sunday was because God had worked tirelessly for six days to make the heavens, earth, oceans, sun, moon, birds, beasts and fish and so on, and only rested on the seventh day when his work was done. He reminded them that because humans were created in His image, they too were expected to toil for six days and on the seventh to rest, and offer gratitude for the uncountable blessings that the Lord had bestowed upon them.

The missionary's opening declaration generated some head nodding as well as an amen or two from the more enthusiastic congregation members. But most found it a challenge to identify exactly what blessings they should be grateful for. They knew what it meant to work hard, and they understood the importance of having time to rest, even if they had no idea how it felt to share in the material rewards of their labours. Over the preceding half-century, it was their hands that did the heavy lifting that transformed this semi-arid environment into profitable cattle ranches. And over this period the farmers, who were otherwise not shy of using the whip to 'cure' Ju/'hoan workers of idleness, always gave them time off on Sundays.

The missionary then told his congregation how after the Lord had instructed Adam and Eve to care for the Garden of Eden they were seduced by the serpent into committing mortal sin, as a result of which the Almighty 'cursed the ground' and banished the sons and daughters of Adam and Eve to a life of toil in the fields.

This particular Bible story made more sense to the Ju/'hoansi than many others the missionaries told them – and not just because they all knew what it meant to be tempted to sleep with people they knew they shouldn't. In it they saw a parable of their own recent history. All the old Ju/'hoansi at Skoonheid remembered when this land was their sole domain and when they lived exclusively by hunting for wild animals and gathering wild fruits, tubers and vegetables. They recalled that back then, like Eden, their desert environment was eternally (if temperamentally) provident and almost always gave them enough to eat on the basis of a few, often spontaneous, hours' effort. Some now speculated that it must have been as a result of some similar mortal sin on their part that, starting in the 1920s, first a trickle then a flood of white farmers and colonial police arrived in the Kalahari with their horses, guns, water pumps, barbed wire, cattle and strange laws, and claimed all this land for themselves.

For their part, the white farmers quickly learned that farming in an environment as hostile to large-scale agriculture as the Kalahari would take a lot of labour. So they formed commandos to capture and force into work the 'wild' Bushmen, held Bushman children hostage to ensure their parents' obedience, and meted out regular whippings to teach them the 'virtues of hard work'. Deprived of their traditional lands, the Ju/'hoansi learned that to survive, like Adam and Eve, they must toil on farms.

For thirty years, they settled into this life. But when in 1990 Namibia gained its independence from South Africa, technological advances meant that the farms were both more productive and less dependent on labour than they had been. And with a new government demanding that ranchers treat their Ju/'hoan labourers as formal employees and provide them with proper salaries and housing, many farmers simply chased them from their land. They reasoned that it was far more economical and far less trouble to invest in the right machinery and run their farms with as few staff as possible. As a result, many Ju/'hoansi had little option but to camp by the side of the road, squat in the fringes of Herero villages to the north, or move to one of the two small resettlement areas where there was little to do but sit and wait for food aid.

This is where the story of the fall ceased to make much sense to the Ju/'hoansi. For if, like Adam and Eve, they were banished by God to a life of toil in the fields, why had they now been banished from the fields by farmers who said they no longer had any use for them?

———

Sigmund Freud was convinced that all the world's mythologies – including the biblical story of Adam and Eve – held within them the secrets to the mysteries of our 'psycho-sexual development'. By contrast, his colleague and rival Carl Gustav Jung considered myths to be nothing less than the distilled essence of humanity's 'collective unconscious'. And to Claude Lévi-Strauss, the intellectual touchstone of much twentieth-century social anthropology, all the world's mythologies combined to form an immense and intricate puzzle box that if properly decoded would reveal the 'deep structures' of the human mind.

The diverse mythologies of the world may or may not offer us a window into our 'collective unconscious', explain our sexual hang-ups, or let us peer into the deep structures of our minds. But there is no doubt that they reveal some things that are universal to human experience. One is the idea that our world – no matter how perfect it was at the moment of creation – is subject to chaotic forces and that humans must work to keep these in check.

Among the missionary's congregation at Skoonheid that hot afternoon were a handful of 'old-time people'. They were the last Ju/'hoansi here to have spent much of their lives as hunter-gatherers. They bore the trauma of being violently wrenched from their old lives with the kind of stoicism that characterised traditional hunter-gatherer life, and as they awaited death they found comfort in retelling

21

one another the 'stories of the beginning' – the Creation myths – they learned as children.

Before Christian missionaries showed up with their own version of the tale, the Ju/'hoansi believed the creation of the world happened in two distinct phases. In the first phase their creator God made himself, his wives, a lesser trickster god called G//aua, the world, rain, lightning, holes in the ground that collected rainwater, plants, animals and finally people. But before completing the job, he spent time on something else, leaving the unfinished world in a state of chaotic ambiguity. There were no social rules, no customs, and people and animals alike shape-shifted from one bodily form to another, variously intermarrying and eating one another as well as engaging in all sorts of outlandish behaviour. Fortunately, the creator didn't abandon his creation for ever and eventually returned to finish the job. He did so by imposing rules and order on the world, first by separating and naming the different species and then by endowing each with its own customs, rules and characteristics.

The 'stories of the beginning' that delighted the old men of Skoonheid are all set during the period when the creator, leaving his work incomplete, took his extended cosmic sabbatical – perhaps, as one man suggested, because he needed to take a rest just as the Christian God did. Most of these stories tell of how in the creator's absence the trickster thrived, causing mayhem and chaos wherever he went. In one story, for example, G//aua cuts out, cooks and serves his own anus to his family, and laughs hysterically at the brilliance of his own joke when they compliment him on the tastiness of the dish. In others, he cooks and eats his wife, rapes his mother, steals children from their parents and callously commits murder.

But G//aua did not rest when the creator returned to finish his work, and ever since has picked mischievously and unrelentingly at the world's orderly seams. Thus where Ju/'hoansi associated the creator God with order, predictability, rules, manners and continuity, G//aua was associated with randomness, chaos, ambiguity, discord and disorder. And the Ju/'hoansi detected G//aua's devilish hand at work in all sorts of different things. They noticed it, for instance, when lions behaved uncharacteristically; when someone fell mysteriously ill; when a bowstring frayed or a spear snapped, or when they were persuaded by a mysterious inner voice to sleep with someone else's spouse while being only too aware of the discord this would cause.

The old-time people were in no doubt that the serpent who tempted Adam and Eve in the missionary's story was none other than their trickster G//aua in one of his many disguises. Spreading lies, persuading people to embrace forbidden desires and then cheerfully witnessing the life-shattering consequences play out was exactly the sort of thing G//aua liked to do.

Ju/'hoansi are but one of many peoples to have discovered their own cosmic troublemakers lurking beneath the skin of Eden's smooth-talking serpent. Tricksters, troublemakers and destroyers – like Odin's wayward son Loki, the coyote and raven in many indigenous North American cultures, or Anansi, the short-tempered, shape-shifting spider that scuttles through many West African and Caribbean mythologies – have been creating work for people to do since the beginning of time.

It is no coincidence that tension between chaos and order is a feature of the world's mythologies. After all, science also insists that there is a universal relationship between disorder and work, one that was first revealed during the heady days of the Enlightenment in Western Europe.

———

Gaspard-Gustave Coriolis loved the game of table billiards – a hobby to which he devoted many happy hours of practical 'research', the results of which he published in the *Théorie mathématique des effets du jeu de billiard*, a book still invoked with biblical solemnity by aficionados of billiards' descendants, snooker and pool. He was born in the revolutionary summer of 1792, the same year that France's Citizens' Assembly abolished the monarchy and dragged King Louis XVI and Marie Antoinette from the Palace of Versailles to await their appointment with the guillotine. But Coriolis was a revolutionary of a different sort. He was one of the vanguard of men and women who had turned their back on theological dogma and instead embraced reason, the explanatory power of mathematics and the rigour of the scientific method to make sense of the world, and who as a result ushered in the industrial age after unlocking the transformative energy of fossil fuels.

Coriolis is now best remembered for formulating the 'Coriolis Effect', without which meteorologists would have no sensible way of modelling the swirling forms of weather systems or the vagaries of ocean currents. More importantly for us he is also remembered for introducing the term 'work' into the lexicon of modern science.

Coriolis's interest in table billiards extended beyond the satisfaction he gained from the predictable click-clack of ivory balls as they collided with one another, or even the thrill he experienced when one, guided by his cue, slipped off the table into a pocket. To him, billiards revealed the infinite explanatory power of mathematics and the billiard table was a space where people like him could observe, tinker and play with some of the fundamental laws that governed the physical universe. Not only did the balls evoke the celestial bodies whose movements were described by Galileo, but every time he rested his billiard cue on his hand, he channelled the elemental principles of geometry as outlined by Euclid, Pythagoras and Archimedes. And every time his cue ball, energised by the movement of his arm, struck other balls, they diligently followed the laws on mass, motion and force identified by Sir Isaac Newton nearly a century earlier. They also raised a whole range of questions about friction, elasticity and the transfer of energy.

Unsurprisingly, Coriolis's most important contributions to science and mathematics focused on the effects of motion on rotating spheres: the kinetic energy an object like a billiard ball possesses due to its motion, and the process by which energy is transferred from an arm and through a cue to send billiard balls scuttling around the table.

It was in 1828, when describing a version of the latter phenomenon, that Coriolis first introduced the term 'work' to describe the force that needed to be applied to move an object over a particular distance.[1]

When Coriolis referred to the process of hitting a billiard ball as doing 'work', he was, of course, not focused singularly on billiards. The first economically viable steam engines had been invented a few years previously, showing that fire was capable of much more than charring meat and melting iron in a smithy's forge. Yet there was no satisfactory way of evaluating the capabilities of the steam engines that were powering Europe's Industrial Revolution. Coriolis wanted to describe, measure and compare accurately the capabilities of things like water wheels, carthorses, steam engines and human beings.

By then many other mathematicians and engineers had already arrived at concepts broadly equivalent to what Coriolis called 'work'. But none had quite found the right vocabulary to describe it. Some called it 'dynamical effect', others 'labouring force' and others still 'motive force'.

Coriolis's equations were quickly pronounced sound by his scientific peers, but it was his terminology that impressed them most. It was as if he had found the perfect word to describe a concept that had teased them for years. Over and above the fact that 'work' described exactly what steam engines were designed to do, the French word for work, *travail*, has a poetic quality that is absent in many other languages. It connotes not just effort but also suffering, and so evoked the recent tribulations of France's Third Estate – the lower classes – that had laboured for so long under the yoke of wigged aristocrats and monarchs with a taste for grandeur. And in linking the potential of machines to liberate the peasantry from a life of labour, he invoked an embryonic version of the dream, later taken up by John Maynard Keynes, of technology leading us to a promised land.

'Work' is now used to describe all transfers of energy, from those that occur on a celestial scale when galaxies and stars form to those that take place at a subatomic level. Science also now recognises that the creation of our universe involved colossal amounts of work, and that what makes life so extraordinary and what differentiates living things from dead things are the very unusual kinds of work that living things do.

———

Living things have a number of distinct characteristics that non-living things do not. The most obvious and important of these is that living things actively harvest and use energy to organise their atoms and molecules into cells, their cells into organs and their organs into bodies; to grow and to reproduce; and when they stop doing that they die and, with no energy to hold them together,they decompose. Put another way, to live is to work.

The universe hosts a bewildering array of complex and dynamic systems – from galaxies to planets – that we sometimes also describe as being 'alive'. But, besides cellular organisms, none of these purposively harvests energy from other sources and then uses that to do work to stay alive and reproduce. A 'living' star, for instance, does not actively replenish its energy from its environment. Nor does it seek to produce offspring that will in time grow up to be just like it. Rather it fuels the work it does by destroying its own mass, and 'dies' once that mass is depleted.

Life actively works to survive, grow and reproduce potentially in spite of what some physicists consider to be the 'supreme law of the universe': the second law of thermodynamics, also known as the law of entropy. The second law of thermodynamics describes the tendency for all energy to distribute itself evenly across the universe. Embodied in the many tricksters that have made mischief in the world's mythologies, entropy relentlessly unpicks whatever order the universe creates. And in time, like the malevolent trickster god Loki of Norse mythology, the second law of thermodynamics insists that entropy will bring about an Armageddon – not because it will destroy the universe but rather because, when it achieves its goal of distributing all energy evenly across the universe, no free energy will be available with the result that no work, in the physical sense of the word, can be done.

If we have an intuitive grasp of some aspects of entropy, it is because this trickster winks at us from every shadow. We see it in the decay of our buildings and our bodies, in the collapse of empires, in the way milk blends into our coffee and in the constant effort required to maintain any kind of order in our lives, our societies and our world.

For the pioneers of the Industrial Revolution, entropy revealed itself by thwarting their efforts to build perfectly efficient steam engines.

In all their experiments, they observed that heat energy inevitably tended to distribute itself evenly within boilers and then through the boilers' metal skins to the world outside. They also noticed that heat energy always flowed from hotter to colder bodies and that once the heat was distributed evenly, it was impossible to reverse the process without adding more energy. This is why once a cup of tea has reached room temperature there is no chance of it drawing some energy out of the room to warm itself up again. They also noted that in order to reverse entropy's impact, more work needed to be done using energy sourced from outside that system. Bringing your tea back to an acceptable temperature requires additional energy.

For a while, the law of entropy was considered to be a bewildering fact of existence. Then, between 1872 and 1875, an Austrian physicist, Ludwig Boltzmann, worked the numbers. He showed that the way heat behaved could be neatly described by means of the arithmetic of probability.[2] There are, he argued, infinitely more ways for heat to be spread among the trillions of molecules in a spoonful of water than for the heat to remain stored in just a few of those particles. This means that as the particles move around and interact with one another the odds are so overwhelmingly in favour of the energy being evenly distributed that it has to be considered inevitable. By extension, his mathematical model suggested that all the energy in the largest container of all, the universe, will tend to do the same.

In offering a mathematical model to describe entropy, Boltzmann simultaneously engineered its escape from the relatively narrow confines of engineering and showed us why we intuitively see entropy in decaying buildings, eroding mountains, exploding stars, spilt milk, death, cold cups of tea and even democracy.

States of low entropy are 'highly ordered', like children's bedrooms when the children are forced to tidy up and stow their toys, gadgets, clothes, books and tubs of slime in assorted drawers and cupboards. States of high entropy, by contrast, are similar to their rooms a few hours later, once they have picked up and then dropped everything they own seemingly at random. According to Boltzmann's calculations, every possible arrangement of a kid's stuff in their rooms is equally probable in a physical sense if children, as it appears is the case, are nothing more than random-stuff redistributors. There is of course a minuscule chance that, as random-stuff redistributors, they might accidentally put all their things back where they are supposed to be for the rooms to be considered tidy. The problem is that there are vastly more ways for the rooms to be messy than there are for them to be tidy, so the chances are hugely in favour of their rooms being messy until a parent demands they do the work – and so expend the energy necessary – to restore their rooms to an acceptably low state of entropy.

Even if there are many orders of magnitude simpler than a child's bedroom, the now venerable Rubik's cube gives us a sense of the mathematical scales involved. This puzzle, with its six different-coloured faces made up of nine squares and organised on a fixed central pivot that makes it possible to rotate any one of the faces independently of the others and so mix up the coloured squares, has 43,252,003,274,489,856,000 possible unsolved states and only one solved state.[3]

In 1886, four years after Charles Darwin was buried in Westminster Abbey, Boltzmann was invited to deliver a prestigious public lecture at the Imperial Academy of Sciences in Vienna.

'If you ask me about my innermost conviction whether our century will be called the century of iron or the century of steam or electricity,' Boltzmann announced to his audience, 'I answer without hesitation: it will be called the century of the mechanical view of nature, the century of Darwin.'[4]

A generation younger than Darwin, Ludwig Boltzmann's work was no less a challenge to God's authority than Darwin's proposal that it was evolution rather than God that best accounted for the diversity of life. In a universe governed by the laws of thermodynamics, there was no room for God's commandments, and the ultimate destiny of everything was pre-determined.

Boltzmann's admiration for Darwin was not based solely on their shared experience of taking wrecking balls to religious dogma. It was also because he saw entropy's hand busily shaping evolution, an idea that would only be fully fleshed out a generation later by the Nobel Prize-winning quantum physicist Erwin Schrödinger, best known for packing imaginary cats into imaginary boxes.

Schrödinger was convinced that the relationship between life and entropy was fundamental. Others before him, including Boltzmann, had made the point that living organisms were all thermodynamic engines: like steam engines they required fuel in the form of food, air and water to work, and in working they also converted some of this fuel into heat that was subsequently lost to the universe. But no one followed this idea to its inevitable conclusion until Schrödinger presented a series of lectures to an audience at Trinity College Dublin in 1943.

Schrödinger's father was an enthusiastic amateur gardener. He was especially fascinated by the way he could tip evolution's hand by carefully selecting seeds of plants with specific characteristics he found desirable. Inspired by his father's horticultural experiments, Schrödinger retained an interest in heredity and evolution that endured long after theoretical physics became the main focus of his work.

Before Schrödinger delivered his Dublin lectures, which were published a year later in the form of a short book called *What is Life?*, biology was an orphan among the natural sciences.[5] Up until then, most scientists were content to accept that life operated according to its own strange and distinctive rules. Schrödinger, however, was of the view that biology should be adopted as a fully fledged member of the scientific family. That night, he set out to persuade his audience that the science of life – biology – was just another, admittedly complex, branch of physics and chemistry. Just because physicists and chemists had not yet been able to explain life, he explained to his audience, it did not mean that there was any 'reason at all for doubting' that they could.

Schrödinger's description of what he imagined to be the extraordinary information-encoding and instruction-giving capabilities of the atoms and molecules in our cells – DNA and RNA – inspired a generation of scientists to dedicate their careers to unravelling the chemical and physical bases of biology. Among this pioneering group of molecular biologists was Cambridge's Francis Crick who, along with his partner James Watson, would reveal the distinctive double-helix shape of DNA to the world a decade later.

Schrödinger's wonder for the ability of the 'incredibly small group of atoms'[6] that comprise a genome to organise trillions of other atoms into hair, livers, fingers, eyeballs and so on was because these atoms did so in apparent defiance of the second law of thermodynamics. Unlike almost everything else in the universe, which seemed to tend to increasing disorder, life insolently gathered matter together and then organised it very precisely into astonishingly complex structures that gathered free energy and reproduced.

But as much as living organisms appeared to be only superficially accomplished and systematic violators of the law of entropy, Schrödinger recognised that life simply could not exist in violation of the second law of thermodynamics. This meant that life needed to contribute to the overall entropy in the universe, and he concluded that it did this by seeking out and capturing free energy, using it to do work, which generated heat, and thus added to the total entropy in the universe. He also noted that the bigger and more complex an organism, the more work it needed to stay alive, grow and reproduce, and that as a result, complex structures, like living organisms, were often far more energetic contributors to the total entropy of the universe than objects like rocks.

If life can be defined by the kinds of work living things do, then the process of transforming inorganic terrestrial matter into living, organic matter must have involved some kind of work – an energy-packed jump-start that set the engine of primordial life running. Precisely where this energy came from is uncertain. It may have sprung from the finger of God, but far more likely it was sourced from the geochemical reactions that made early earth seethe and fizz, or by the decay of radioactive materials in ancient earth succumbing slowly to entropy.

The fact that abiogenesis – the process by which life first appeared – involved work is perhaps the least mysterious part of it. Up until the turn of the third millennium, the balance of scientific data suggested that the emergence of life was so improbable that we were almost certainly alone in the universe. Now, for some scientists at least, the pendulum has swung the other way. They are more inclined to think that life may have been inevitable and that entropy, the trickster god, was not just a destroyer but may well have also been the creator of life. This perspective is based on the idea that biological systems might suddenly emerge because they more efficiently dissipate heat energy than many inorganic forms, so adding to the total entropy of the universe.[7]

One of the things that persuaded some of them was digital simulations that indicated that where atoms and molecules are subjected to a highly directed energy source (like the sun) and are also surrounded by an energy bath (like a sea), particles will spontaneously arrange themselves in all sorts of different formations, as if experimenting to find the arrangement that dissipates heat energy most effectively.[8] If this is the case, this model suggests, then there is a pretty good chance that one of the countless possible arrangements the atoms and molecules shuffle through might be one that transforms dead inorganic matter into a living organism.

The long history of life on earth has been described in terms of life's ability to capture energy from new sources – first geothermal energy, then sunlight, then oxygen and then the flesh of other living organisms – as well as the evolution of increasingly complex, more energy-hungry and, in the physical sense, harder working life forms.[9]

The first living creatures on Planet Earth were almost certainly simple single-celled organisms that, like bacteria, had neither nuclei nor mitochondria. They probably harvested energy from geochemical reactions between water and rock, before transducing it into a highly specialised molecule that stored the energy in its chemical bonds and released it when those bonds were broken, so enabling the organism to do work. This molecule, adenosine triphosphate, or 'ATP', is the immediate source of energy used by all cells to do work – from unicellular bacteria to multicellular anthropologists – to maintain their internal equilibrium, to grow and to reproduce.

Life has been busy harvesting free energy, storing it in ATP molecules and then putting it to work on our planet for a very long time. There is widespread fossil evidence attesting to the presence of bacterial life on earth around 3.5 billion years ago. There is also disputed fossil evidence for life dating to 4.2 billion years ago – a mere 300,000 years after the earth's formation.

The bacteria-like pioneers of life on earth had to cope with conditions that, from the point of view of most life forms now, were astonishingly hostile. Beyond the fact that early earth was seething with volcanic activity and battered by a near-continuous barrage of meteorites, the atmosphere had little oxygen, and no ozone layer to protect delicate organisms from being fried by solar radiation. As a result, earth's earliest life forms toiled far from the sun's glare.

But, over time, thanks to another characteristic unique to life, its ability to evolve, new species emerged that were capable of drawing energy from other sources, and surviving and reproducing in different conditions. At some point, probably around 2.7 billion years ago, life crept out from the shadows as a series of fortuitous genetic mutations enabled some to embrace life's old enemy, sunlight, and draw energy from it by means of photosynthesis. These organisms, cyanobacteria, still thrive today. We see them in the bacterial blooms that bubble up in ponds and lakes.

As cyanobacteria flourished, so they set to work transforming the earth into a macro-habitat capable of supporting far more complex life forms with much higher energy demands. They did so first by converting atmospheric nitrogen into the organic compounds like nitrates and ammonia which plants need for their growth. They also worked to convert carbon dioxide into oxygen and so played the critical role in inducing 'the great oxidation event' that began around 2.45 billion years ago, and which resulted in the gradual creation of the oxygen-rich atmosphere that sustains us today.

The great oxidation event not only provided an entirely new source of energy for life to exploit, but massively expanded the amount of energy available for life to work with. Chemical reactions involving oxygen release far more energy than those involving most other elements, which means that individual aerobic (oxygen-breathing) organisms have the potential to grow bigger, faster and do much more physical work than anaerobic ones.

New, more elaborate living organisms called eukaryotes evolved to exploit this energy-rich environment. Far more sophisticated and energy-hungry than their prokaryotic ancestors, eukaryotes had nuclei, reproduced by means of sexual reproduction, and could also generate all sorts of complex proteins. In time, some eukaryotes are thought to have developed mutations that enabled them to kidnap other passing life forms and plunder their energy by engulfing them through permeable outer cell membranes. The kidnapped cells had no choice but to share any energy they had captured with their jailers, one of the processes that, over time, is thought to have contributed to the emergence of multicellular life. The primitive algae, which evolved into the first plants that eventually greened early earth's barren land masses, were likely to have been the progeny of cyanobacteria-kidnapping eukaryotes.

The first creatures with both tissue and proper nervous systems are thought to have evolved in the oceans around 700 million years ago. But it was not until around 540 million years ago during the Cambrian explosion that animal life really started to flourish. The fossil record for this period shows evidence of creatures representing all the major contemporary phyla – branches on the tree of life – that populate our world today.

Additional energy from increasing atmospheric and marine oxygen certainly played a role in kick-starting the Cambrian explosion. But what likely played a more important role was that evolution began to positively select in favour of some life forms that harvested their energy from a novel, much richer source of free energy than oxygen: they consumed other living things which had already gone to the trouble of collecting and concentrating energy and vital nutrients in their flesh, organs, shells and bones.

By around 650 million years ago, enough atmospheric oxygen had accumulated in the stratosphere to form a layer of ozone sufficiently thick to screen out enough hazardous ultraviolet radiation to allow some life forms to make a living on the fringes of the oceans without being fried. Within 200 million years or so, the biosphere laid claim to much of the earth's land mass and slowly formed a series of connected, very complex marine and terrestrial ecosystems packed with all sorts of organisms diligently capturing free energy and using it to stay alive, secure more energy and reproduce.

Many of these new life forms put this energy to use in ways that far more obviously look like the kinds of behaviours we humans associate with work. While bacteria still comprised a substantial portion of the biosphere, the presence of larger land-based animals transformed the nature of work that living things did. Larger animals require lots of food but can do far more physical work than relatively immobile microorganisms. Animals variously burrow, hunt, flee, break, dig, fly, eat, fight, defecate, move things about and, in some cases, build.

The fact that from a physicist's perspective all living organisms do work, and that our planet's biosphere was constructed over millions of generations as a result of the work done by their various evolutionary ancestors, raises an obvious question. How does the work done, for example, by a tree, a cuttlefish or a zebra, differ from that which has brought our species to the cusp of creating artificial intelligence?

2

Idle Hands and Busy Beaks

Unusually for a Californian celebrity, Koko did not worry a great deal about her appearance. In 2016, when she passed away, nearly two years after delivering a special address to the UN Climate Change Conference warning of how human folly might lead us to oblivion, many prominent Californians expressed pride in the achievements of one of their state's beloved daughters.

A lowland gorilla that had known only captivity, Koko owed her celebrity to her unusual communication skills. She was a fluent and creative user of Gorilla Sign Language, a specially designed gestural language based roughly on American Sign Language. She also gave every indication of understanding around 2,000 distinct spoken English words, about 10 per cent of the active vocabulary most humans use. But Koko was terrible at grammar. Attempts to school her in the rudiments of syntax confused and frustrated her, and as a result, she often struggled to communicate with the kind of clarity or creativity her trainers believed she wanted to. Beyond her syntactical shortcomings, Koko's human trainers entertained no doubts that Koko was an emotionally and socially sophisticated individual.

'She laughs at her own jokes and those of others,' explained Penny Patterson and Wendy Gordon, two of her long-term trainers and most beloved friends. 'She cries when hurt or left alone, screams when frightened or angered. She talks about her feelings, using words such as happy, sad, afraid, enjoy, eager, frustrate, mad, shame and, most frequently, love. She grieves for those she has lost – a favourite cat that has died, a friend who has gone away. She can talk about what happens when one dies, but she becomes fidgety and uncomfortable when asked to discuss her own death or the death of her companions. She displays a wonderful gentleness with kittens and other small animals. She has even expressed empathy for others seen only in pictures.'[1]

Many others were more sceptical. Her trainers insisted her large working vocabulary was proof of her ability to see the world in terms of signs and symbols, but sceptics insisted that she (like most other famous apes, chimps and bonobos who have been hailed as skilled users of graphic symbol-based communication systems) was nothing more than a competent mimic. And that her only real social skills were used to persuade her trainers to give her occasional tickles and treats.

No one, however, disputed that she enjoyed the time she spent relaxing with her kittens, got a buzz out of going on scenic drives with her trainers, and that she sometimes got surly when she had to do more arduous tasks. But her detractors were not convinced that she thought about work and leisure in the same way that people did. Human work is purposeful, they insisted, whereas the work done by animals is only ever purposive.

It is an important distinction.

A builder working purposefully to build a wall for a garage extension has a clear idea what the finished wall will look like, and he has mentally rehearsed all the steps necessary to build it as per the architect's plans. But he is not mixing cement and laying bricks in the summer heat for this purpose alone. It is, after all, neither his wall nor his design. He is doing this work because he is motivated by a whole series of second- and third-order ambitions. If I were to interview him I might find out that he is working so diligently because he has ambitions to become a master builder, that he is a builder only because he likes to work outside or, perhaps, just because he wants to save enough money to finance his spouse's childhood dream. The list of possibilities is near endless.

Purposive behaviour by contrast is behaviour that an external observer may be able to attribute purpose to but that the agent of that behaviour neither understands nor could describe. When a tree grows to maximise its leaves' exposure to the sun so that it can harvest solar energy to convert carbon dioxide and water into glucose, it is being purposive. When during the rainy seasons what seems like thousands of moths fly fatally into the flames of a Kalahari campfire, that behaviour is also purposive. But as Koko's trainers learned, making absolute distinctions between purposeful and purposive behaviour is not always straightforward among other kinds of organisms.

When a pack of lions stalk a wildebeest, their base motivation is to secure the energy necessary to survive. But in responding to their instinct, they act far more purposefully than, for example, intestinal bacteria seeking out a carbohydrate molecule. They use cover to stalk their prey, work as a team, deploy a strategy of sorts, and make decisions throughout the process of the hunt, based on which outcome they imagine would best satisfy their purposive urge to chew on the flesh and organs of another creature.

Many researchers interested in understanding our cognitive evolution have focused their efforts on revealing whether our closest primate relatives and other obviously smart creatures like whales and dolphins are capable of purposeful behaviour in the same way that humans are. Being purposeful requires an intuitive grasp of causality, the agility to imagine an outcome arising from an action, and so also implies having 'a theory of mind'. Debates about how purposeful different animals are relative to humans remain as contested as ever.

But a number of other animal species invite us to think differently about some less obvious aspects of the way we work. Among these are creatures like termites, bees and ants, in whose ceaseless industry and social sophistication we see echoes of the extraordinary changes to the way humans worked after they became cooperative food producers and later when they moved into cities. There are also many other species who, like us, seem to spend an awful lot of energy doing work that seems to serve no obvious purpose or who have evolved physical and behavioural traits that are hard to account for because they seem so ostentatiously inefficient. Traits like the tail of a male peacock.

———

In 1859, when Charles Darwin published *The Origin of Species*, peacocks were a must-have ornament in formal gardens across Britain. They also strode imperiously across the lawns of London's grand public parks, occasionally fanning their plumage to the delight of passers-by.

Darwin was fond of birds. After all, it was the small but distinct differences he noted between closely related finch populations on each of the islands in the Galapagos that crystallised his understanding of natural selection. But he was no fan of peacocks.

'The sight of a feather in a peacock's tail, whenever I gaze at it, makes me sick!!' he wrote to a friend in 1860.[2] To him, the unblinking eyes that adorned their oversized tail feathers mocked the efficient logic of evolution. He wondered how it was possible that natural selection allowed any creatures to evolve such unwieldy, impractical and energy-expensive tails that, he was convinced, made the males easy pickings for predators.

In the end, Darwin found an answer to the problem of the peacock's tail in the similarly garish crinoline plumage of the Victorian ladies-about-town who strolled among the peacocks in the parks and the dandyish fashions of the tight-trousered men who courted them.

In 1871, he published *The Descent of Man, and Selection in Relation to Sex*, in which he explained how mate choice – sexual selection – encouraged the development of all sorts of bizarre secondary traits, from peacocks' tails to oversized horns, aimed purely at making individuals in some species irresistible to the opposite sex.

If natural selection was the 'struggle for existence', he argued, then sexual selection was the 'struggle for mates' and accounted for the evolution of a host of 'secondary sexual characteristics' that might be disadvantageous to an individual organism's chances of survival but massively boosted its chances of reproducing. Evolution, in other words, directed organisms to acquire and expend energy both on staying alive and on making themselves attractive, and where the former demanded efficiency and control, the latter tended to encourage wastefulness and flamboyance.

It is now clear that peacocks' tails are not the physical burden to peacocks that Darwin imagined. Researchers who tested the speed at which peacocks could take to the air to escape predators revealed that big tails did not make any significant difference to their ability to get airborne and out of the way in a hurry. It also turns out that peacocks' tails probably don't play a particularly important role in mate selection either.[3]

Mariko Takahashi and Toshikazu Hasegawa at the University of Tokyo in Japan were determined to better understand what features of peacocks' tails made them most irresistible to peahens. To this end, they spent seven years getting to know the flocks of peacocks and peahens in Izu Cactus Park in Shizuoka. They carefully adjudicated the different breeding males' tail feathers, taking note of the size of the display and the number of eyespots that males presented. There were clear differences among them, with some males obviously having far grander tails than others.

By the end of the project, Takahashi's team had observed 268 successful matings. To their astonishment they found no correspondence between mating success and any particular tail traits. The peahens mated as enthusiastically and frequently with males that dragged underwhelming displays behind them as they did with those that possessed the fanciest tails.[4]

It could be that Takahashi's team overlooked some feature of the tails and the way individuals displayed. Peacock tails have qualities other than eyespots and size, and we have at best only a tenuous idea of how peahens and peacocks perceive the world around them through their senses. Takahashi and colleagues think this is very unlikely though, which raises the tantalising possibility that some energy-expensive evolutionary traits like peacock tails may have less to do with the battle to survive and reproduce than may at first appear to be the case. The behaviour of some other species, like the serial builder and breaker of nests, the black-masked weaver bird of southern Africa, suggests that the need to expend energy may have played as important a role in shaping some traits as the demands of capturing it.

Untangling the nest of a black-masked weaver, one of many species of weaver birds in southern and central Africa, can be a challenge. Shaped like a gourd and not much larger than an ostrich egg, their nests are one of the avian world's many engineering wonders. Beyond the smooth woven symmetry of their ovulate grass and reed walls, masked weavers' nests are light enough to hang from a small twig, yet robust enough to shrug off the frantic winds and the pebble-heavy raindrops that test them during summer thunderstorms. For humans, at least, untangling a weaver's nest is easiest to do by stomping on it with your boots. Our fingers are too big and too clumsy. But for diminutive southern masked weaver birds, brute force is not an option.

Humans rarely have much cause to untangle weavers' nests, but for some reason male masked weavers do. Over the course of any summer, male weavers build sequences of new, structurally near-identical nests, one after the other, which they then destroy with the same diligence that they apply when building them. They do this using their small conical beaks like a pair of tweezers to first unbind the nest from the tree and then, once it plummets to the ground, to methodically unpick it, one blade of grass at a time, until nothing remains.

A male masked weaver in the final stages of completing a nest.

Breeding male masked weavers are a riot of vivid yellows and golds. This species owes its name to the distinctive patch of black plumage that extends from just above their red eyes down to the base of their throats and that resembles a bandit's mask. Female masked weavers by contrast don't build nests or have black masks. They are camouflaged from beak to claw by olive and khaki plumage that blends into a yellowish belly.

An industrious male masked weaver will build around twenty-five nests in a single season, in the hope of attracting a small harem of females to occupy some and later present him with clutches of eggs. One individual weaver's life in a garden in Zimbabwe's capital, Harare, was diligently documented over a period of several years in the 1970s. As unlucky in love as he was hard-working, he ended up destroying 158 of the 160 nests he built, one-third of them within a couple of days of weaving in the final grass thread.[5]

Masked weavers' nests are complex, energy-intensive constructions. It can take up to a week to build a nest, although some gifted builders can produce one in a day if there are enough of the right building materials nearby. Researchers trying to get to grips with the energy costs incurred in nest building by a closely related species, the village weaver in Congo, estimated that individual males fly on average thirty kilometres to gather the more than 500 individual pieces of grass and reed needed to construct a nest.[6]

During the 1970s, a long-term research project on southern masked weavers was the first to suggest that there was perhaps something more to weavers building nests than feathered automata processing genetic code.[7] This study revealed that in much the same way that an infant human will develop motor skills by manipulating and playing with objects, male weaver chicks will play and experiment with building materials soon after they emerge from their eggs and, through a process of trial and error, progressively master the threading, binding and knot-making skills necessary to build nests. Later, when researchers were able to analyse the masked weavers' endeavours by setting up a series of cameras and filming over a period of months, an even more complicated picture was revealed. It showed that weaver birds got progressively quicker and better at building nests – in other words more skilled – and that individual weavers developed idiosyncratic nest-building techniques and so were not working to a programme.[8]

Masked weavers do not conceal their nests from potential predators. If anything they draw attention to them by building them on exposed branches with the goal of catching the eye of a passing female masked weaver. And whenever a female masked weaver comes anywhere near a nest, a male will stop his work to preen and show off to try to persuade her to inspect his nest. If she does, and subsequently decides a nest is to her liking, the male will then add a short entrance tunnel at its base so the female can move in and spruce up the interior in preparation for laying a clutch of eggs.

Local folklore in much of southern Africa holds that male weavers only destroy a nest when a fussy female has inspected it and found it somehow wanting. Careful observation suggests this is not true. Not only do males habitually destroy many of their nests without any female appraisal of their workmanship, but it also seems that females make their decisions based more on the location of a nest rather than the workmanship. A poorly manufactured nest made by an indigent and clumsy male in the right place is far more likely to attract a female than a well-built nest made by a strong, skilled and energetic weaver in the wrong place.

There is no doubt these sturdy constructions improve the survival chances of masked weaver eggs and offspring. As easy as they are to spot, snakes, hawks, monkeys and crows struggle to reach them. Suspended from springy, light, leaf-stripped twigs that bend precipitously under a little additional weight, a nest is hard for any predator to reach, let alone to access the recessed central chamber through the cavity on the underside without first plummeting to the ground.

But its advantageous design offers no insights into the weaver's determination to produce near identical nests one after another, like a potter obsessively churning out the same vase again and again. Nor does it account for their single-minded determination to destroy sequences of perfectly good nests soon after completing them like a potter driven to destroy vases because of imperfections that only she can see. If the energy quest was paramount, then surely weavers would have evolved to build one or two quality nests in the right place, rather than expending huge amounts of energy building and then needlessly destroying dozens of them? And if their ability to build lots of nests was an index of their individual fitness, then why would they destroy them with such diligence?

Old Jan, a Ju/'hoan man who spent many hours idly watching weavers in the Kalahari, speculated that the reason they destroy their nests with such fierce determination is because they have very poor memories. So poor that once an individual becomes focused on building his next nest and glimpses one of his previous efforts out of the corner of his eye, he immediately concludes that it was built by a love rival trying to muscle in on his turf and destroys it to drive the phantom impostor away.

He may be right but another Ju/'hoan weaver-watcher, Springaan, expressed a far more intriguing view. He speculated that weavers were 'like my wife'. She simply couldn't bear to loiter about doing nothing in the same way her husband did. As a result, whenever she had a free moment from her chores, she would busily make pieces of beaded jewellery, one after the other, all based on a similar criss-cross design and crafted using the same set of well-practised tricks and techniques. And whenever she ran out of beads, because they rarely had money to purchase more, she would diligently unpick older completed pieces – often very beautiful ones – one bead at a time and then repurpose them into new ones. He was of the view that this was a great virtue and that he was lucky to have persuaded such a woman to marry him, a woman who, like a weaver, found pride, joy and peace in the skill, craft and artistry of making beautiful objects. She, on the other hand, was not so sure that she was lucky to have married him.

Nest-building-and-destroying weaver birds may seem unusually profligate with energy. But they are by no means the only species besides us inclined to spend energy on apparently pointless work. The avian kingdom alone is blessed with thousands of similar examples of expensive elaboration, from the grandiose plumage of birds of paradise to the over-elaborate nests of bowerbirds.

Evolutionary biologists usually take a strictly utilitarian approach to explain these behaviours. To them the history of life is basically a tale of sex and death, and all the rest is window dressing. All traits that have survived the mill of natural selection must, they insist, be accounted for ultimately in terms of the extent to which they aid or diminish an organism's chances of survival or reproducing, by offering it some kind of competitive advantage in the energy quest or the quest for a mate. They might argue that the reason why weavers build and destroy sequences of nests is to signal their fitness to prospective mates or to stay in top condition to avoid potential predators.

Strangely, however, we are reluctant to resort to similar explanations for equally energy-profligate displays by humans. After all, many of the things humans expend energy on – from building ever grander, more ostentatious skyscrapers to running ultra-marathons – are hard to reconcile with reproductive fitness or survival. Indeed, many of the things we do to expend energy risk reducing our lifespans rather than extending them. It may well be that the ultimate explanation for why weavers build with such profligacy is that, like us, when they have surplus energy, they expend it by doing work in compliance with the law of entropy.

It takes lots of energy to organise molecules into cells, cells into organs, organs into organisms, and organisms into blooms, forests, flocks, schools, herds, packs, colonies, communities and cities. Organisms that are profligate with energy, that work carelessly or inefficiently, often lose out where and when energy resources are scarce or when external conditions change suddenly as a result of climate or geology, or even an advantageous adaptation by another species that recalibrates the dynamic of an ecosystem.

There are many examples in evolutionary history of species rapidly discarding redundant, energy-expensive traits because of a change in circumstances. If, for instance, you take a population of three-spine sticklebacks – a small fish that evolved body armour to help protect them from predators – and introduce them to a predator-free lake, then within a few generations that population will cease to be armoured because building unnecessary armour is an energy-expensive business.[9]

But there are also many examples of creatures that have vestigial traits or features that have long ceased to be obviously useful but that nevertheless still exist and incur a measurable energy cost. Ostriches, emus and other flightless birds retain vestigial wings, whales have vestigial hind legs, boa constrictors retain vestigial pelvises, and humans retain a range of vestigial features, among them useless ear muscles, parts of our digestive system that no longer perform any useful function, and a coccyx optimised for tails.

It is possible that the weavers' nest-building-and-destroying habit is a vestigial trait and that it once served some easily identifiable and important purpose. A number of other closely related weaver species in Africa are similarly obsessive nest builders and they all must have inherited this trait from a common ancestor. A far more intriguing possible explanation is that they repeatedly build and destroy their nests for no other reason than the fact that they have energy to burn.

Southern masked weavers are omnivorous. They are as happy consuming a large number of different seeds and grains as they are snacking on protein-rich insects. And during the extended building season they spend hardly any time at all specifically focused on foraging. In fact, they spend so little time foraging that the research group who diligently tracked village weavers over the course of an eight-month building season observed no focused foraging behaviour by males at all, despite their unrelenting focus on nest building. They concluded that during the building season food was so abundant that the weavers foraged casually while retrieving materials for their nests by plucking[10] energy-rich insects from the air and whatever grains they encountered while scouting for building parts.

During dry late-winter months insect life all but disappears and southern masked weavers have to work a lot harder to eat than they do in the building season. How well individuals cope at this time of year determines who will live to see another season and who will not. In other words, how well or badly organisms cope during the toughest seasons is the primary and most brutal driver of natural selection. The problem is that the very traits that might benefit organisms at the toughest time of year, like being able to eat every scrap of food you find, can be problematic during times of the year when food is abundant.

Researchers curious about how the various passerine birds that regularly eat from garden bird-feeders remain slim have suggested that, despite often overeating, these birds have evolved mechanisms to manage their weight but that limiting the amount of food they eat is not one of them. They pointed out that when food is abundant passerine birds 'exercise' through upping the intensity with which they sing, fly and perform other routine behaviours, in much the same way that humans expend energy by playing sports or going for a run.[11]

One of the weaver's favourite seasonal foods also offers an oblique insight into another set of behaviours that we often imagine to be uniquely human and that are emblematic of two of the great convergences in the history of our relationship with work: the ability to grow food and to work cooperatively in big sprawling cities.

Southern Africa's Kalahari Desert is home to the most enduring population of hunter-gatherers anywhere. But it is also home to one of the world's oldest continuous farming lineages, one that has been cultivating its own food and living in cities for 30 million years longer than our species has.

The telltale signs of these ancient farming communities take the form of millions of high-rise buildings, each containing climate-controlled civic areas, urban farms, nurseries and royal quarters, all linked to one another by networks of carefully maintained thoroughfares. These cities – some of which are centuries old – are constructed from a cement of gold, white and red Kalahari sands. The tallest among them are two metres high and reach irregularly towards the sky with the same grace as the spires on the Sagrada Familia, Gaudi's famous basilica in Barcelona.

And similar to cities like Barcelona, they are also home to millions of insomniac citizens – each of whom has a specific job to do. Beyond the fact that the dwellers of these cities are much smaller than us, they are driven by a work ethic that even the most industrious and ambitious *Homo sapiens* could never dream to emulate. These termites eschew sleep in favour of labour, and work without resting until the moment they die.

Most termites are manual labourers. Blind and wingless, they maintain and build core civic structures, ensure the city-wide climate-control systems are operating optimally, and feed, water and groom those in other professions – the soldiers and the reproductives. They are also tasked with managing the inner-city fungus farms on which their colonies depend. Located just below the queen's chambers, the fungus farms are where termites produce the food that sustains a colony. Every night the workers leave the mound on foraging expeditions, returning only when their guts are packed with grass and wood chips. When they make it back to the mound they head to the farming chambers. There, they defecate the partially digested wood and grass, and set about moulding this into maze-like structures seeded with fungal spores that only thrive in the temperature-regulated darkness of the mound's bowels. Over time these fungi dissolve the tough cellulose in the wood and grass, transforming it into an energy-rich food which the termites can easily digest.

Soldier termites are no less myopically focused on job performance. The instant an intruder alarm is sounded – in the form of pheromonic signals passed from termite to termite, so creating paths for the soldiers to follow – they rush to the front and sacrifice their lives without hesitation. And these city-states have many enemies. Ants are frequent and persistent raiders. They are similarly dismissive of the

value of individual lives and their sole strategy is to overcome the much larger termite soldiers by sheer weight of
numbers. Other beasts, much bigger than ants, also test
the soldiers' mettle. These include pangolins, decked from
head to claw in armour, the long-tongued aardvarks with
almost bizarrely muscular forequarters and talons capable
of tearing the near-rock-hard walls of the mound as if it is
papier mâché, and bat-eared foxes who make use of their
super-hearing to zoom in on workers leaving the mound in
search of material for their farms at night.

And then there are the reproductives, the kings and
queens, who are as much slaves to their specialised roles as
any other termites. Both are several orders of magnitude
larger than even the soldiers and their sole job is to reproduce. Cosseted in chambers deep within the mound, theirs
is a life of sexual drudgery with the king diligently fertilising
the millions of eggs produced by a queen. Beyond the
mechanics of reproduction, biologists think it likely that
the queen has at least one slightly more regal role to play.
It is she who apportions jobs to new citizens, by secreting
pheromones that either inhibit or catalyse genes to express
in different ways for workers, soldiers and future royalty.[12]

Mound-building termite species – which are common
also in South America and Australia – are successful because
they repurpose their environments to suit them. It is difficult to be sure when the evolutionary ancestors of termites
set off down the path of sophisticated communalism. But
it is certain that they do not live as they do as a result of a
single genetic mutation that transformed them into civically
minded builders, beholden to a royal couple and protected
by soldiers who will sacrifice themselves for the good of the

mound. It was a gradual process. Just as each new significant design iteration of their mounds modified the selective pressures shaping termite evolution, so the new traits they evolved resulted in additional modifications to the mounds, creating a feedback loop that tethered the evolutionary history of termites ever closer to the work they did in modifying their environment to meet their needs.

Species that form complex, intergenerational social communities, in which individuals work together to secure their energy needs and reproduce, often do different jobs, and occasionally even sacrifice themselves for the good of the team, are described as eusocial rather than merely social. The 'eu-' is taken from the Greek εὖ, meaning 'good', to emphasise the apparent altruism associated with these species.

Eusociality is rare in the natural world, even among other insects. All termite species and most ant species are eusocial to varying degrees, but fewer than 10 per cent of bee species and only a very small proportion of the many thousands of wasp species are truly eusocial. Outside of the insect world, eusociality is even rarer. There is evidence of only one species of truly 'eusocial' marine animal – the snapping shrimp – which is more famous for the wallop it can give with its lightning-fast pincers than for its complicated social life. And while some highly social mammals, like the Kalahari's African wild dogs – who will hunt collaboratively on behalf of a breeding alpha female – flirt with eusociality, besides humans there are only two species of truly eusocial vertebrates: the naked mole rat of East Africa and the Damaraland mole rats of the western Kalahari. Both of these subterranean creatures have evolved to live in environments that they have substantially modified. And, like termites, mole rat colonies host only a single breeding pair and are hierarchical. Most eusocial mole rats are fated to be 'workers' and spend their lives foraging to feed themselves and the 'royal' reproductive couple, building and maintaining their infrastructure and driving off (or being eaten by) predators.

Humans have always found analogies for their behaviour in the natural world. And when it comes to virtuous labour, eusocial insects have proved a rich source of metaphors. Thus the New Testament instructs 'sluggardly' Christians to 'go to the ant' and 'consider her ways',[13] and it is now commonplace to invoke the industriousness of termites or the busyness of bees. But it is only from the European Enlightenment and, later, after Darwin published *The Origin of Species* in 1859 that people began to routinely invoke what they considered to be the paramount scientific laws that governed natural selection to account for or justify their behaviour. And in doing so, they elevated Herbert Spencer's eloquent but unfortunate description of natural selection as the 'survival of the fittest' into the mantra of the marketplace.

In 1879 Herbert Spencer lamented 'how often misused words can generate misleading thoughts'.[14] He was writing about the apparent hypocrisy of 'civilised men' who are so often inhuman to others, yet glibly accused others of barbarism. But he might just as easily have been writing about his most famous quote, which by then had become a popular shorthand for Darwinian evolution.

Few phrases have been so misused and generated such misleading thoughts as 'survival of the fittest', an idea that has been invoked again and again to justify corporate takeovers, genocides, colonial wars and playground spats, among many other things. Even if Spencer believed that humankind held an exalted position in the animal kingdom, what he intended when he coined the phrase was not that the strongest, the smartest and the hardest working were destined to succeed, but rather that those organisms that are best adapted by the slow mill of evolution to 'fit' into any particular environmental niche will thrive, at the expense of those that are less well adapted. Thus for Spencer, the lion along with the wildebeest, the flea that hitched a ride in the lion's ear and the grass the wildebeest consumed just before the lion, unburdened by any qualms, crushed its throat, were all equally fit in their own way.

Even if Spencer only inadvertently painted evolution as something resembling a brutal fight to the death, he was nevertheless persuaded that organisms competed with one another for energy in much the same way that shops on a high street competed with one another for customers and cash. Unlike Darwin, he also believed that the characteristics acquired by an organism during its lifetime could be passed on to its offspring, and hence that evolution was an engine for progress that resulted in ever greater complexity and sophistication, because it meant a progressive weeding out of the 'unfit' by the fit. This meant that he was as fierce an advocate for small government and free markets as he was a fierce critic of socialism and social welfare in general, which he believed stifled human flourishing and, worse still, artificially supported the 'survival of the unfittest'.[15]

Darwin also believed that the competition for energy lay at the heart of what he called 'the struggle for existence'. But he did not see it as the only driver of evolution. Beyond the fact that he insisted that sexual selection meant that many species developed ostentatious energy-inefficient traits purely for the sake of 'according to their standard of beauty',[16] he also insisted that natural selection was also shaped by co-adaptation. He noted, for instance, how most plant species depended on birds, bees and other creatures for pollination and to distribute their seeds, and how parasites depended on the health of their hosts, and how scavengers depended on hunters.

'We see these beautiful co-adaptations most plainly in the woodpecker and mistletoe,' he explained in *The Origin of Species*, 'and only a little less plainly in the humblest parasite which clings to the hairs of a quadruped or feathers of a bird.'[17]

In the 150 years since Darwin published *The Origin of Species*, our understanding of the evolutionary dance that shapes the destinies of different organisms in various ecosystems has developed considerably. When Darwin was writing, for instance, no one understood anything of the molecular mechanism of genetic inheritance; the myriad interactions occurring all the time between the near-invisible microorganisms (like bacteria) that we now know comprise a much larger proportion of all living biomass on earth than all living animals combined; or the extent to which species that seem to have at first very little to do with one another might depend on each other indirectly in order to survive or thrive.

Thus, in addition to describing species such as termites in a colony co-operate with one another, biologists' descriptions of ecosystems always reveal vast dynamic networks of interspecies interactions and dependencies. These relationships usually take the form of mutualism (symbiotic relationships where two or more species benefit), commensalism (symbiotic relationships where one species benefits but at no cost to the other) and parasitism (where one species benefits at the expense of the host). Some researchers have taken it further and suggested that the active avoidance of competition may be as important a driver of speciation in evolution as competition.[18]

Whether the avoidance of competition proves to be as important a driver of natural selection as competition, there is no doubt that Spencer's and Darwin's views were also shaped by the fact that they were both wealthy, successful males living at the heart of the largest empire the world had ever seen, and in an era when few people doubted that the human world was animated by a whole sequence of concurrent competitions between individuals, towns, businesses, races, cultures, states, kingdoms, empires and even scientific theories.

What is perhaps most strange about the invocation of competition as the primary driver of our economies is that behind the masculine bluster of ruthlessness, most businesses and business people operate in a manner far more similar to real ecosystems. This is why all big organisations, for instance, have ambitions to function with the cooperative efficiency of termite mounds; why most business leaders work to establish mutually beneficial, 'win–win' relationships with their suppliers, service providers and customers; and why, even in the countries that most enthusiastically embrace the theology of free markets, a whole battery of anti-trust laws exist to prevent excessive cooperation in the form of collusion between businesses, the creation of cartels and other 'anti-competitive behaviours'.

It is clear, however, that the version of Darwinism caricatured by economists, politicians and others in support of free markets does not have much common with the way biologists now tend to think of relationships between organisms in the natural world. It is also clear, as the busy-building weavers remind us, that while success or failure in the energy quest will always shape the evolutionary trajectory of any species, many hard-to-explain animal traits and behaviours may well have been shaped by the seasonal over-abundance of energy rather than the battle for scarce resources, and that in this may lie a clue as to why we, the most energy-profligate of all species, work so hard.

3

Tools and Skills

Neither weaver birds nor termites are especially purposeful creatures – at least as far as we can tell. It is unlikely that either species set about building their nests or constructing monumental air-conditioned mounds with clear visions of what they wish to achieve. But it is far harder to disentangle purposefulness and purposiveness among some of the many creatures that intentionally repurpose objects around them into tools, and then use those tools to perform various jobs.

Tool use has now been documented in fifteen species of invertebrates, twenty-four species of birds and four species of non-primate mammals, among them elephants and orcas.[1] It is the twenty-two species of monkey and five species of ape who routinely use tools for a variety of different tasks that have generated the most research, because in them we see more of ourselves.

Homo sapiens are by far the most prolific, expert and versatile makers and users of tools in the history of life. Almost everything we do involves a tool of some sort, and occurs in a space that we have modified in some way or another. Most of the energy humans capture now, over and above that which we use to sustain our bodies and reproduce, is expended on using tools to modify and transform the world around us.

The different things that our various evolutionary ancestors made were all important milestones in the deep history of work. But we do not have to rely on these objects alone to understand what kinds of work our evolutionary ancestors did, and how that work in turn influenced human evolution. The story of *Homo sapiens*' ability to master skills from microsurgery to masonry is written into our hands, arms, eyes, mouths, bodies and brains. It tells us not only that we are physically and neurologically the product of the work our evolutionary ancestors did, but also that, as individuals, we have evolved to be progressively remoulded over the course of our lives by the kinds of work we do. This means that the fossilised bones of our evolutionary ancestors are also important milestones in this story.

Genomic and archaeological evidence suggests that recognisably modern humans have been living in Africa for at least 300,000 years. But it is often hard to tell whether any individual set of ancient hominin bones belonged to one of our direct ancestors, or whether they came from related groups whose lineages later disappeared down evolutionary cul-de-sacs. Palaeoanthropologists are nevertheless quite confident that our species, *Homo sapiens*, as well as Neanderthals and Denisovans, descended from members of *Homo heidelbergensis*' extended family, or another, hypothesised, older lineage called *Homo antecessor*, sometime between 300,000 and 500,000 years ago. It is thought that *Homo heidelbergensis* descended from the extended *Homo erectus* family between 600,000 and 800,000 years ago, who in turn descended from a branch of the *Homo habilis* family 1.9 million years ago, who in turn descended from Australopithecenes probably around 2.5 million years ago.

Australopithecus looked like a cross between a chimp and a slouching *Homo sapiens* teenager. But if you dressed up a young adult male *Homo heidelbergensis* in jeans, a T-shirt and designer shoes, and took care to cover the pronounced ridge over his eyebrows with a generously sized cap, he wouldn't draw anything more than an occasional quizzical glance when strolling around a university campus.

Inferring how our evolutionary ancestors lived and behaved from stone tools and the other fragmented bric-a-brac they left behind requires some imagination. It also requires some imagination to infer the many cognitive and physical skills they must have acquired – skills like dancing, singing, wayfinding or tracking that leave few obvious material traces in the archaeological record. And no ancient tool worked archaeologists' imaginations more than the most widely used stone tool in human history, the Acheulean hand-axe.

The quarrymen digging out gravel in the Lower Somme Valley, not far from the town of Abbeville, had learned to listen carefully for the jingle of francs that signalled a visit from the director of Abbeville's customs bureau, Jacques Boucher de Crèvecœur de Perthes. Bored by his day job, Boucher found joy and a sense of purpose squirrelling around the gravel pits in the valley in search of interesting 'antiquarian' objects that he hoped might reveal the secrets of the ancient world.

Boucher's routine quarry visits began in 1830, after he showed a group of quarrymen a chunk of flint that he had found during his own excavations. It was twice the size of a human hand, with two symmetrical, slightly concave faces that had been roughly worked into a teardrop shape and was circumscribed by a sharp cutting edge. They recognised it instantly. It was one of the *langues de chat*, 'cat's tongues', that they occasionally found buried in the gravel, often alongside old bones, and which they usually discarded without much thought. They agreed in future to set aside any for him, as long as he was prepared to show his gratitude in the form of a few francs. It did not take long before some of them became proficient in making reasonable facsimiles of the cat's tongues themselves, to extract a few extra francs from the customs director on his visits.[2]

Over the next decade Boucher gradually built up a sizeable collection of these curious flint rocks – many of which were not forgeries – and became convinced that they had been sculpted into their near-symmetrical forms by ancient humans who lived alongside the extinct beasts whose bones also littered the gravel pits.

Boucher was not the first person to wonder about the origins of these strange objects. The ancient Greeks, for example, also recognised their artifice but, unable to establish any obvious reasons for their existence, concluded they were 'thunderstones' – the spear points of the lightning bolts dispatched to earth by their god of gods, Zeus.

In 1847, Boucher proposed his theory that cat's tongues had been manufactured by long-dead ancients in a three-volume treatise, *Les Antiquités Celtiques et Antédiluviennes*. Much to Boucher's disappointment, *Les Antiquités Celtiques* was dismissed as an amateurish hotchpotch of clumsy description and outlandish theorising. Charles Darwin, for example, thought it was 'rubbish',[3] a sentiment shared by many of the grandees of the French Académie des Sciences in Paris. But Boucher's book nevertheless persuaded some members of the Académie, most notably a young medical doctor, Marcel-Jérôme Rigollot, to investigate these cat's tongues for themselves. Over the next few years Rigollot adopted Boucher's strategy of harassing quarrymen up and down the Lower Somme Valley to alert him as soon as they discovered any of these objects. But, unlike Boucher, he insisted on digging most of them out himself.

By 1855, Rigollot had diligently documented the recovery of hundreds of cat's tongues, many from a single quarry just outside St Acheul near Amiens. Many were retrieved *in situ* from undisturbed strata that also contained ancient elephant and rhinoceros bones, leaving Rigollot in no doubt that these pieces were of ancient origin.

If Jacques Boucher de Crèvecœur de Perthes were alive today, he would probably be upset to learn that it is thanks to Rigollot's carefully documented discoveries at St Acheul that cat's tongues are now universally known as Acheulean hand-axes, Acheulean bifaces or, somewhat less inspiringly, large cutting tools. Like the one Boucher showed the quarrymen, these era-defining stone tools are typically pear-shaped or ovate, and have sharpened edges that separate two well-worked, roughly symmetrical, convex faces. Some are similar in size and shape to the space that forms between your hands when, partially cupped and with fingers extended, they are brought together as if in insincere prayer. But many are twice as large, thicker than a quarryman's clenched fist and very heavy.

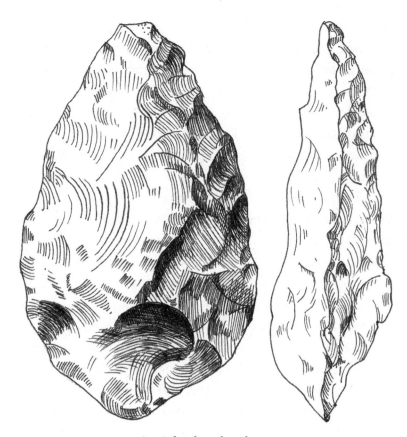

An Acheulean hand-axe

They have been confusing and frustrating antiquarians, anthropologists and archaeologists ever since.

The reason hand-axes have generated such confusion is that they almost certainly weren't ever used as hand-held axes. As robust, heavy-duty and up-to-the-job as these objects appear, holding one in your hand immediately raises a practical problem. There is no obvious way to apply significant force along any of the sharpened edges or through its point without other sharp edges cutting into your fingers or your palm. This means that if you try cleaving a log or fracturing a thick, marrow-rich bone with it, you probably won't be able to hold anything at all for some time afterwards.

As the quarrymen in Abbeville discovered by trial and error, it is not particularly hard to make a decent facsimile of an Acheulean hand-axe. Archaeologists regularly replicate the method and have found pleasure in watching generations of archaeology and anthropology students bloody their knuckles while having a go as part of their university coursework. But no one has worked out what they were used for. If hand-axes were rare then we might be content to let this mystery rest, but so many hand-axes have been found that it is hard to conclude anything other than that they were *Homo erectus*' go-to gadget.

Adding to the hand-axe's mystery is the fact that *Homo erectus* and its descendants hammered them out consistently for a period of 1.5 million years, making them arguably the most enduring tool design in human history. The oldest Acheulean hand-axes are African. These were manufactured over 1.6 million years ago. The most recent are only 130,000 years old. These were probably hammered out by remnant populations of *Homo erectus*, having been outgunned by cognitively sophisticated hominins like *Homo sapiens* and Neanderthals, who by then made use of fancy, hafted spears. While the skills of hand-axe makers improved gradually over this million-and-a-half-year period their core design and the basic techniques required to manufacture them remained largely unchanged.

Even the most basic Acheulean hand-axes are a marked step up from the clumsier efforts during the first era of widespread stone tool manufacture – a period that palaeontologists call the Oldowan. First discovered in Tanzania's Olduvai Gorge, the oldest samples of Oldowan stonework are about 2.6 million years old. *Homo habilis* ('handy' human) owes its name to the Oldowan-type tools that are closely associated with it, but making Acheulean tools appears to have been the larger-brained *Homo erectus'* gift alone. Oldowan stone tools were until recently thought to represent our evolutionary ancestors' very first systematic efforts to repurpose rocks into more immediately useful objects, but there is now some tentative evidence that suggests that *Australopithecus* were amateur stonemasons too. In 2011, researchers looking for samples of Acheulean industry around Lake Turkana in East Africa's Rift stumbled across a trove of rough stone tools, which they estimate to be 700,000 years older than any previously discovered.

There is some skill involved in making Oldowan tools. Even so, most of them look like rocks that have been optimistically beaten up in the hope of creating useful points or cutting edges. They do not look like the products of well-organised minds working to realise a clear vision. Making an Acheulean hand-axe, by contrast, is a complex, multistage process. It requires finding an appropriate rock – not just any rock will do – then hammering a workable, roughly ovulate core from it with a heavy hammer stone, before progressively smoothing and shaping its faces and edges using smaller hammer stones in combination with softer bone or horn hammers. In silent witness to the skill required to manufacture one, almost everywhere that hand-axes have been found in significant numbers, among them are the remains of hundreds of other fatally fractured hand-axes, each a casualty of an inaccurate or overpowered hammer blow.

Some anthropologists have speculated that hand-axes weren't used as tools in and of themselves but rather as solid-state toolboxes from which small, sharp rock flakes could conveniently be struck whenever a cutting edge was needed, and that over time the removal of flakes from a single rock produced the aesthetically pleasing symmetrical hand-axe shape. But the wear on hand-axe edges shows that, as unwieldy as they are, *Homo erectus* almost certainly did more with them than flake off small sharp blades. As a result, most archaeologists have half-heartedly concluded that, as unwieldy and unpractical as they seem, hand-axes were probably used for many different jobs, and so they were the Swiss army knife of the Acheulean era.

In the absence of any hand-axe-wielding *Homo erectus* to show us precisely what jobs they did with them, hand-axes are destined to remain archaeological orphans. However, a different perspective on the hand-axe conundrum may be found in the invisible archaeology of our evolutionary past: the tools and other items our ancestors made from organic materials like wood that have since decomposed and left no trace.

Hunter-gatherers need to be mobile and mobility demands not having too much heavy stuff to carry from one camp to the next. This is one of the many reasons why foragers had very frugal material cultures. Most of the tools they manufactured were made from light, organic, easily worked materials like wood, leather, sinew, rawhide, plant fibre, horn and bone. Before iron began to find its way into the Kalahari via the farming communities that settled on the Kalahari's fringes some 800 years ago, people like the Ju/'hoansi used stone flakes affixed with gum or sharpened bone as arrowheads, and stone flakes and blades for cutting. Stone, in other words, was critical, but nevertheless formed only a minor part of their inventories. Even if our evolutionary ancestors from *Australopithecus* to *Homo heidelbergensis* made far fewer tools than twentieth-century foragers did, the likelihood is that most of these were made from wood, grass and other organic materials.

One particular tool was ubiquitous among twentieth-century foragers: the digging stick. The Ju/'hoan version of this tool is made from a thick, straight branch of *grewia*, a hardwood bush that grows in abundance all through the Kalahari. These are usually a little over three feet long, sharpened into a flattened point set at an incline of about 25 degrees and then tempered in hot sand. As its name suggests, a digging stick is a very good tool for digging out roots and tubers, especially in heavily compacted sand. More than this, though, it is also a walking stick, a tool for clearing paths through thorns, a spear, a club and a projectile.

Even without archaeological evidence for it, there is a strong case to be made that this rudimentary tool – basically a sturdy, sharpened stick – rather than the hand-axe is the most enduring of all human technologies in our evolutionary history. Given that savannah chimps in Senegal use small, intentionally sharpened sticks to skewer bushbabies,

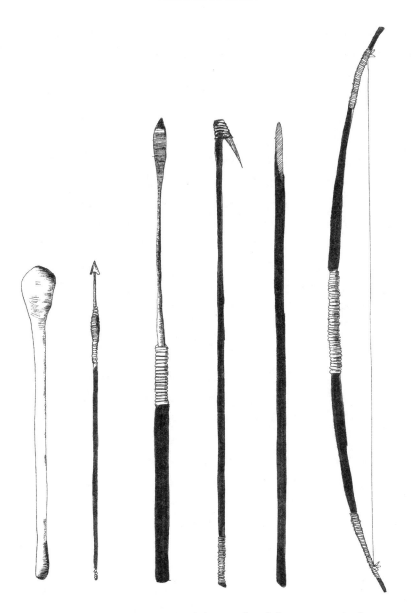

Ju/'hoan hunter's kit. From left to right, club, spear, springhare hunting hook, poison arrow, digging stick and bow.

it is almost certain that the systematic use of sharpened sticks predates the emergence of stone tools.

When exposed to the elements, organic material will decompose aerobically, a process often accelerated thanks to the attentions of various scavengers, insects, funguses and bacteria. A dead animal's soft tissue always decomposes first, and even an elephant carcass can be stripped of flesh and its bones shattered by hyena jaws in a matter of days. Lignin (the substance that gives wood its strength) might take a few hundred years to return to dust in very favourable, dry conditions, and large bones, a few thousand years. In humid conditions, though, wood and bone decompose rapidly. When dead organic material is trapped in an oxygen-poor environment, like glutinous mud, it will often take longer to decompose, but in time it will also be broken down by specialised anaerobic acid-producing microorganisms called acetogens.

On rare occasions, though, chance conspires to help organic material to survive a very long time indeed.

In 1994, archaeologists from the State Service for Cultural Heritage in Germany's Lower Saxony received a call from geologists at an open-pit coal mine near Schöningen, who reported that they had found what appeared to be a deposit of significant archaeological interest. The geologists turned out to be right. Over the following four years the cultural heritage team exhumed the bones of twenty ancient wild horses, as well as several long-extinct European bison and red deer. Some of the bones had bite marks left by some ancient predators, but of greater interest to the team was the fact that many of the bones also showed obvious evidence of butchery by human hand. Evidence of large-scale, well-organised ancient butchery is rare enough to have made this a significant discovery, but the nine uniquely well-preserved wooden spears archaeologists retrieved from among the bones, one of which was still embedded in a horse's pelvis bone, assured its fame. Alongside these they also retrieved something resembling a digging stick, a lance and a smallish trove of flint tools, several of which looked as if they were designed to be hafted onto spears.

The presence of well-preserved wooden artefacts suggested at first that these deposits were unlikely to be more than 50,000 years old. But radiocarbon dating later revealed that they were probably abandoned in the mud of an ancient lake sometime between 300,000 and 337,000 years ago, making them far older than any wooden artefact found up to then.[4] The proximity of a nearby chalk pit had meant the mud they were buried in was too alkaline for acetogenic bacteria to do their work.

Despite having partially buckled under the mud's weight they were buried in, there is no mistaking the skill and experience that went into making them. Each spear was made from a single, straight, lean spruce stem that had been carefully whittled, scraped and smoothed into a projectile with gently tapering points at each end that extended from a thicker centre. More than this, each spear had a centre of gravity in the front third of the shaft and, as a result, closely resembled the javelins used by modern athletes.

Curious about their aerodynamic properties, the archaeologists made some replicas of the Schöningen spears and asked some international-level javelinists to give them a go. The longest throw the athletes managed was seventy metres, a distance sufficient to have won a gold medal in every Olympic Games up until 1928.[5]

After four years of digging and analysis, the State Service archaeologist who led the excavation at Schöningen, Hartmut Thieme, reached the conclusion that what they had found was a large-scale hunting and carcass-processing site and, correspondingly, that the makers of these spears – most probably Neanderthals – were very socially sophisticated.

At a little over 300,000 years old, the javelins do not represent a new threshold of innovation in tool manufacture. There are plenty of contemporaneous artefacts that suggest that by then many humans had graduated from Acheulean technology. These spears are important because they tell of a highly evolved tradition of woodwork. It is for no other reason than the durability of stone that we define the longest era in human technological history by reference to lithic technologies, which at best offer no more than a half-glimpse into one aspect of our evolutionary ancestors.

Of all the organic materials that were readily available to *Homo erectus* to use as tools, only bone, ivory and shell are sufficiently hard-wearing to endure over many millennia. Clam shells were used as cutting tools by *Homo erectus* in East Asia, the only part of the world where they showed no interest in bashing out endless hand-axes. Beyond some evidence suggesting that bone tools were used to prise open termite mounds at Swartkrans, a site in South Africa, perhaps as long as 1.5 million years ago, there is surprisingly little evidence of hominins systematically repurposing bones into tools until around 300,000 years ago when people started to occasionally shape hand-axes from elephant bones.[6] This may well be because bones degrade far more easily than stone and that working them can hasten their decomposition. It may also be simply because bones were abundant and came pre-made in all sorts of shapes and sizes, so didn't need to be reworked to be particularly useful. A straight tibia from any number of species makes a handy club that can be repurposed into a simple hammer, masher or pounder; rib bones from fowl are great for prising snails from their shells; the jawbone of an ass, as the biblical Samson discovered, is useful for smiting enemies; and, as anyone who has cracked a large uncooked bone in search of marrow inside will know, when the bone fractures it almost always produces a series of lethal, very sharp, strong points and edges capable of stabbing or cutting.

———

Except on the few days a year when it is drenched by thunderstorms, everything in Kathu, a small town in South Africa's northern Cape Province, is usually coated with a fine layer of dust, much of which drifts in on the wind from massive open-pit iron mines just outside town. The miners are not the first people to have spent time and energy digging in the red soils here in search of iron-rich rocks. People were doing the same thing hundreds of thousands of years before anyone imagined that iron ore might be extracted, refined, melted and moulded into any number of useful objects. Recently, archaeologists have been digging here, too, mainly at a site they have since named 'Kathu Pan'.

Over the last four decades, Kathu Pan has yielded a sequence of startling archaeological finds. Among the most important of them is the strongest evidence yet to suggest that late *Homo erectus* or possibly *Homo heidelbergensis* made clever composite tools from both stone and wood – a technology that was until recently thought to have only been developed during the last 40,000 years.[7]

No less significant than the evidence for composite tools, though, is another, older, item recovered from this site, the unimaginatively named 'Kathu Pan hand-axe'. Found adjacent to the tooth-plates of an extinct species of elephant, it was probably made by a relative of *Homo erectus* sometime between 750,000 and 800,000 years ago. Knapped from a shimmering chunk of tiger-striped ironstone and shaped like a teardrop, this particular hand-axe is nothing like the many other well-made contemporary hand-axes found at Kathu Pan. Where the other hand-axes are solid, functional, practical and workmanlike, this one is a piece of virtuoso craftsmanship. Close to 30cm from base to tip and around 10cm at its widest point, it is a work of great symmetry, balance and precision. But, where a basic hand-axe can be fashioned by a well-practised stone-knapper with a dozen strikes, this one is the product of hundreds of precise, skilful blows.

The Kathu Pan hand-axe maintains a stony silence about why it was made and what it was used for. But, as a praise-poem to its maker's skill, it is eloquent. Each indentation in the hand-axe holds not just the memory of its maker's fingers judging the symmetry of its curved, convex faces, but also the memory of each individual stone flake and the hammer blow which cleaved them from the banded ironstone core.

No matter how much opportunity it is given to practise, a gorilla or chimp is unlikely ever to bash out a half-decent hand-axe, let alone fashion one as elegant as the Kathu Pan hand-axe. Nor is one likely to write a book or play a decent piano solo. *Homo sapiens* by contrast can master an extraordinary array of different skills, which in each case, once mastered, masquerades as instinct. An accomplished pianist will transform a melody in their mind into sound without having to consciously map out a sequence for their fingers to follow, just as a skilled footballer will hammer a ball into the top corner of a forty-metre-distant goal without any conscious thought about the complex mechanics involved in doing so.

Mastering a skill sufficiently well for it to masquerade as an instinct takes time and energy, and lots of work. The rudiments of it must first be learned, usually by means of a combination of instruction, imitation and experimentation. Then it must be practised, often for years, before it becomes second nature. Acquiring skills also requires energy, dexterity and cognitive processing power, as well as some less tangible qualities that scientists are far more wary of discussing than poets: perseverance, desire, determination, imagination and ambition.

Homo sapiens' ability to acquire and master skills as different as shooting arrows with lethal accuracy and performing microsurgery is written into our hands, arms, eyes and body shapes. Not only are we the product of the different kinds of work our ancestors did and the skills they acquired, but we are also shaped progressively over the course of our lives by the different kinds of work we do.

Over time, our evolutionary ancestors' growing dependency on tools redirected their evolutionary trajectory by progressively selecting in favour of bodies better optimised to make and use tools. Among the most obvious legacies of *Homo habilis'* determined but ham-fisted efforts to fashion rocks and other objects into useful tools are dextrous hands that can thread a needle; opposable thumbs capable of gripping and manipulating objects; shoulders and arms uniquely well designed for accurately hurling projectiles; eyes in the front of our heads that help us to judge the distance between two objects; and finely tuned motor skills that bring these qualities together.

But the most important and far-reaching physiological legacies of tool use are neurological.

The folds of white and grey matter that sit in our skulls are far more enigmatic than Acheulean hand-axes. And despite the fact that clever machines can now track, analyse and chart each electrical pulse that fires our neurons or tickles our synapses, these organs cling on to their secrets far more obstinately than, for instance, our livers, lungs and hearts. But they reveal just enough to show that the interactions between our bodies and our environments not only shape and sculpt our brains as we age, but also that the acquisition of skills like making and using tools, or reading tracks in the sand, modified the selective pressures that determined the course of our ancestors' evolution. This is made plain by the fact that the bulk of the energy surplus acquired through using tools and cooking that might otherwise have been directed towards making our ancestors grow bigger, stronger, quicker or more toothsome was instead directed towards building, remodelling and maintaining ever bigger, more complex and plastic brains, and reorganising our bodies to accommodate these exceptionally large lumps of neural tissue.

Brain size relative to body size is a useful but crude index of general intelligence, as is brain organisation. There is, for example, a broad correspondence between the general intelligence of any species and the size, shape and folding of the neocortex – a neurological feature most developed in mammals. But from the perspective of the capacity to acquire skills, what is most interesting is the series of neurological transformations that take place over the course of our childhoods, through adolescence and beyond, which enable our physical interactions with the world around us to physically reconfigure aspects of our neural architecture.

Where most animal species have evolved a series of highly specialised capabilities honed over generations of natural selection, enabling them to exploit specific environments, our ancestors short-cut this process by becoming progressively more plastic and more versatile. In other words, they became skilled at acquiring skills.

Most mammals can move independently soon after birth. Whales and other cetaceans, who have comparable lifespans to humans when not being harpooned for high-end steak and 'scientific research', are born competent swimmers; most hoofed mammals can walk, and all infant primates – save humans – are able to cling to their mother's back or neck with fierce determination from the moment they leave the womb. *Homo sapiens* newborns, by contrast, are helpless and have to be held if they demand physical contact; they are characterised by their near-complete dependency on adult care for years. Newborn chimpanzees' brains are close to 40 per cent of adult size, but grow to nearly 80 per cent of adult size within a year. Newborn *Homo sapiens'* brains are around one-quarter of the size they will achieve at adulthood and only begin to approach adult size when they reach the early stages of puberty. Partly this is an adaptation to enable them to escape their mothers' wombs through birth canals danger-ously constricted by the demands of walking upright. It is also because, to develop properly, infant *Homo sapiens'* brains depend on sensory-rich environments more than the gentle safety of the womb.

As helpless as *Homo sapiens* newborns are, their brains are all business. Assaulted by a noisy, smelly, tactile and, after some weeks, visually vibrant universe of stimuli, infancy is the period when brain development is at its most frenzied, as new neurons bind themselves into synapses to filter meaning from a chaos of sensory stimuli. This process continues all through childhood until early adolescence, by which time children have twice as many synapses as they were born with and brains fired by fantastical, often absurd, imaginations. Basic skills acquired during this period of life are unsurprisingly the ones that feel most intuitive and instinctive in later years.

At the onset of puberty, our bodies chip away at the mass of synaptic connections formed during infancy and early childhood, so that by the time we reach adulthood most of us have half the number of synapses we did when we entered puberty. This process of synaptic pruning is as critical to adult brain development as the earlier period of growth. It is during this time that the brain streamlines itself to better meet environmental requirements and focus energy resources where they are needed most, by leaving under-utilised synaptic connections to atrophy and die.

The process by which our brains are moulded by our lived environments doesn't end there. Neurological reorganisation and development continue into early adulthood and into our dotage even if as we age the process tends to be driven more by decline rather than growth or regeneration. Ironically our species' extraordinary plasticity when young and the extent to which it declines as we get older also accounts for why as we age we become more stubbornly resistant to change; why habits acquired when we are young are so hard to break when we are old; why we tend to imagine that our cultural beliefs and values are a reflection of our fundamental natures; and why when others' beliefs and values clash with our own, we slander them as unnatural or inhuman.

———

But what of our evolutionary ancestors? Were they similarly plastic when young and set in their ways when old? And might the evolution of plasticity explain why our ancestors soldiered on with their hand-axes for so long?

The fossil record shows unambiguously that in our lineage evolution consistently selected in favour of individuals with bigger brains with bigger neocortices until around 20,000 years ago when, mysteriously, our ancestors' brains began to shrink. But the fossil record is far more parsimonious about how quickly or slowly our different ancestors' brains developed over the course of their individual lifetimes. Genomic studies in the future may well offer some new insights into this. In the meantime, though, we have little option but to stare at objects like hand-axes and ask why, after making them diligently for a million years, our ancestors suddenly abandoned them 300,000 years ago in favour of more versatile tools made with a series of new techniques.

One possible answer is that our ancestors were genetically shackled to hand-axe design in much the same way that different species of birds are genetically shackled to specific designs of nest. If so, *Homo erectus* and others diligently made hand-axes while operating on instinctive autopilot with only a vague sense of why,[8] until some 300,000 years ago they suddenly crossed a critical genetic Rubicon that spontaneously ushered in a new era of innovation.

Another possible answer reveals itself if we abandon the idea that intelligence is a single generalised trait and instead view it as a collection of different cognitive traits, which evolved, initially at least, to do different jobs in response to different adaptive pressures. Thus problem solving can be thought of as one form of intelligence responsive to a particular set of adaptive pressures, abstract reasoning another, spatial reasoning another, and the ability to acquire and absorb socially transmitted information another still.

If so, then *Homo erectus* may have clung on so doggedly to the hand-axe design because the ability to learn from others was a far more beneficial adaptation at first than problem solving. Cognitively plastic creatures, like most terrestrial mammals, cephalopods and some species of birds, all learn from experience. But on its own plasticity has some obvious limitations. It requires that each individual learn the same lessons from scratch and so repeat the same energy-costly, sometimes fatal, mistakes of their ancestors.

But when they are combined with traits associated with social learning, however, the advantages of plasticity are amplified many times over, because beneficial learned behaviours – like avoiding poisonous snakes or knowing what hand-axes are useful for – can be transmitted across generations with no cost and minimal risk.

We may not know what *Homo erectus* did with their hand-axes, but they certainly did know. And they will have acquired this insight when young by watching others use them. It is inconceivable that *Homo erectus* didn't also acquire many other skills as a result of watching and imitating others. Some of these would have been technical, like fashioning a good digging stick, jointing and butchering a carcass and possibly even preparing a fire. Others would have been behavioural, like learning to track an animal or soothe others with their voices or touch.

The fact that our languages are more than a collection of words and are governed by rules of syntax that enable us to purposefully convey complex ideas may well have arisen in parallel with tool-making. To convey an idea effectively, words need to be organised into the right order. Many gorillas and chimpanzees, like Koko, who have lived in human-dominated environments, have mastered working vocabularies of several thousand words, and vervet monkeys make distinct vocal signals to warn of the presence and location of different kinds of predator. So it is reasonable to assume that *Australopithecus* had the brains to do so too. But it is a big step up from shouting accurate warnings to singing love songs, because language requires that words are organised according to a series of complex grammatical rules. This requires neural circuits that integrate both sensory perception and motor control as well as the ability to follow a hierarchy of operations. In just the same way that this sentence only makes sense because words are presented in a particular order, so the process of making tools requires that a specific hierarchy of operations is followed. You cannot make a spear without first making a spearhead, preparing a shaft and finding the materials you need to bind them together. Language processing was long thought to be the exclusive function of a highly specialised and anatomically discrete module within the brain – Broca's area – but it is now clear that Broca's area also plays a substantial role in non-linguistic behaviours, like tool-making and tool use,[9] which means it is possible that selective pressures associated with making and using tools may have been instrumental in language's early development.

———

George Armitage Miller lived in a world of words. Every object that fell into his vision and every word he heard instantly set off a cascade of associations, synonyms and antonyms that flashed through his mind. A psychologist with an interest in understanding the cognitive processes behind language and information processing, he founded the Center for Cognitive Studies at Harvard. And, in 1980, long before digital networks were part of everyday life, he was the driving force behind the development of Wordnet, a still functioning online database that details the myriad lexical relationships between most words in the English language.

But for a while in 1983 he was stuck looking for a word to describe the relationship between living organisms and information. A fan of Erwin Schrödinger's *What is Life*, Miller was certain that Schrödinger had left something important out of his definition of life. In order for living organisms to consume free energy per entropy's demands, Miller insisted, they had to be able to find it, and to find it they had to have the ability to acquire, interpret and then respond to useful information about the world around them. It meant, in other words, that a significant proportion of the energy they captured was expended seeking out information using their senses and then processing it in order to find and capture more energy.

'Just as the body survives by ingesting negative entropy [free energy],' Miller explained, 'so the mind survives by ingesting information.'[10]

Miller didn't find the word he was looking for to describe organisms that ingest information, and so he coined a new one, 'informavores'. He originally intended it only to apply to 'higher organisms' like us, with energy-hungry nervous systems and brains, but it is now clear that all living things, from prokaryotes to plants, are informavores. Thus, for example, bacteria in a puddle may not even have the physical apparatus with which to think, but like a plant bending its leaves to catch sunlight, they are able to respond to stimuli signalling the proximity of energy sources around them, and if there aren't any, to seek them out.

Much of the energy captured by complex organisms with brains and nervous systems is used to filter, process and respond to information acquired through their senses. In all cases, though, when the information is deemed irrelevant it is usually instantly disregarded. But when it is not, it is usually a trigger for action. For a cheetah, the sight of easy prey switches it into hunting mode in just the same way that the sight of a cheetah's tail will send a gazelle running. Many species, however, have the ability not just to respond instinctively to acquired information, but to learn, like Pavlov's dogs, to respond quasi-instinctively to specific stimuli. And some also have the ability to choose how to respond on the basis of a combination of instinct and learned experience. Thus when a hungry jackal encounters lions resting near a recent kill it will calculate the risks of robbing a bone of meat from the carcass by cautiously testing the lions' vigilance and mood before making a decision on whether or not to dive in.

With our super-plastic neocortices and well-organised senses, *Homo sapiens* are the gluttons of the informavore world. We are uniquely skilled at acquiring, processing and ordering information, and uniquely versatile when it comes to letting that information shape who we are. And when we are deprived of sensory information, like a prisoner in solitary confinement, we conjure sometimes fantastical information-rich worlds from the darkness to feed our inner informavore.

It does not require a great deal of brain to keep our various organs, limbs and other bodily bits and pieces running as they should. The vast majority of the energy-expensive tissue in our skulls is devoted to processing and organising information. We are also almost certainly unique in terms of the amount of heat-generating work these otherwise immobile organs do, by generating electric pulses when mulling over the often trivial information our senses gather. Thus when we sleep we dream; when we are awake we constantly seek out stimulation and engagement, and when we are deprived of information we suffer.

Large primates are already outliers in the animal world in terms of the amount of raw physical work their brains do, just by processing and organising information. And in our lineages' evolutionary history, each surge in brain growth signalled a surge in our ancestors' appetite for information and the amount of energy they expended in processing it.

Because of how much urban-dwelling *Homo sapiens* interact with other humans, the bulk of research into the implications of plasticity in the human evolutionary story has focused on its role in the development of skills like language, which enable the transmission of cultural knowledge and help individuals navigate complex social relationships. Surprisingly, however, given the fact that our ancestors may well have only became highly skilled language users relatively late in our evolutionary history, far less attention has been given to the skills they developed to process non-linguistic information. These would have been acquired and developed through observing, listening, touching and interacting with the world around them.

Hunter-gatherers in the Kalahari did not doubt the importance of culturally transmitted information. Knowing, for example, which plants were good to eat and when they were ripe, or which tubers and melons contained sufficient liquid to sustain a hunter were essential to survival. When it came to matters like hunting, some important knowledge could be transmitted using words – like where one might find some *diamphidia* larvae to poison an arrowhead, or which animal sinews made the best bowstrings. But the most important forms of knowledge could not. This kind of knowledge, they insisted, could not be taught because it resided not just in their minds but also in their bodies, and because it found expression in skills that could never be reduced to mere words.

We can of course only speculate what these individual skills were. Wayfinding and navigation were very likely among them. As was the ability to read the behaviour of potentially dangerous animals and situations, and to calculate and manage risk. And for hunters it almost certainly involved the ability to infer detailed information from nothing more than animal tracks in the sand, and use this to put meat in their bellies.

———

For a few hours after dawn, animal tracks decorate the sand in the Kalahari Desert like letters typed in a hundred different fonts and sizes, arranged into a chaos of continuous intersecting lines. For all but a few species, night is the busiest time in the Kalahari and each morning the stories of their nocturnal adventures are written briefly in the sand for those who know how to read them.

When the sun gets higher and the shadows shorten, the tracks become much harder to see, and harder still to recognise. For a skilled tracker, though, it makes little difference. Like reading a sentence in which a few letters or words have been blacked out, or listening to familiar words in an unfamiliar accent, they use their intuition to first infer and then find hard-to-see tracks from those that came before.

To foraging Ju/'hoansi, tracks are an endless source of amusement, and human footprints are observed as carefully as animal ones – something that in Ju/'hoansi communities continues to make life as tricky for clandestine lovers as it does for thieves.

Adults often shared the stories they read in the sand with children, but they did not make any special efforts to teach their children tracking. Instead they quietly encouraged children to acquire these skills by observing and interacting with the world around them. Armed with mini sets of bows and arrows, boys would spend their days stalking and hunting the various insects, lizards, fowl and rodents that scurried invisibly through their camps. This, adults explained, taught the boys to 'see' and so prepared them for adolescence when they would begin to gradually master the more rarefied skill of entering the perceptive universe of any animal they tracked – the difference between a successful hunt and failure.

Ju/'hoansi hunters experience the desert as a vast inter-active canvas animated by the tales of different animals who inscribe their comings and goings in the sand. Like poetry, tracks have a grammar, a metre and a vocabulary. But also like poetry, interpreting them is far more complex and nuanced than simply reading sequences of letters and following them where they lead. To unpack the layers of meaning in any individual set of tracks and establish who made it and when, what the animal was doing, where it was going and why, hunters must perceive the world from the perspective of the animal.

Among Ju/'hoansi, a hunter's skill is not only measured by his perseverance or his accuracy with his bow. It is measured by his ability firstly to find an animal – often by tracking it for miles – and then to be able to approach close enough to ensure a decent shot. Doing so, they insist, is only possible if you enter the mind of the animal and perceive the world through its senses, and the way to do this is through its tracks.

In most of the Kalahari, there are no hills or elevated points from which to spot game grazing on the plains below, and the bush is often too thick to see much further than a few metres ahead. Here you can hunt the big meat-animals – like eland, oryx or hartebeest – without any weapons or tools at all, but not without being able to read stories written in the sand.

No Ju/'hoansi still regularly practise persistence hunts any more. Of the slowly shrinking group of active hunters in Nyae-Nyae today, all prefer to hunt big meat-animals with their bows and poison arrows. Most of them are now well into their middle age, but as fit as they may be, persistence hunts are for younger, 'hungrier' men. Back in the 1950s, several Ju/'hoansi in Nyae-Nyae were still masters of persistence hunts, an art that may well be as old as our species and possibly much older still. It is also an art that reminds us how much of the work done by our evolutionary ancestors in the course of meeting their basic energy needs was cerebral, and involved gathering, filtering, processing, hypothesising and debating sensory information from the world around them.

The evolutionary arms race in the Kalahari has made most of the important meat-animals quick and agile, and most of the predators that hunt them sharp-clawed, a little bit quicker and a lot stronger. But, with a few exceptions, neither predator nor prey has much stamina. Unable to sweat, it takes time for animals like lions or wildebeest to reduce the body heat they generate when trying to make or escape a kill. When a kudu is charged by a lion or a springbok by a cheetah, the outcome of a hunt is always determined in a few energy-sapping seconds. If the escape is successful, both predator and prey will need some time to rest, cool down and regather their wits.

Humans never win in a short sprint when they are charged by a lion or pursue an antelope. But they are hairless and can sweat. As bipeds with long, easy strides, they are capable of running far and of keeping a steady, unrelenting pace for hours if necessary.

A persistence hunt is simple in theory. It involves finding a suitable animal, ideally one weighed down with heavy horns, and then pursuing it relentlessly, offering it no opportunity to rest, rehydrate or cool down, until eventually the dehydrated, overheating and delirious animal freezes, a ghost of itself, and invites the hunter to walk up casually and take its life.

In the 1950s, the Ju/'hoansi only hunted this way alongside a set of shallow depressions, in which the summer rains gathered and which were bordered by a sticky mucous of grey soft mud that when dry sets hard like a brittle cement. For eland, the largest of Africa's antelope, and the Ju/'hoansi's favourite meat, the mud is a problem. When drinking at the pans the mud gathers in the bored cleft between their hooves, and later, when drying, expands and splays the hoof apart, making it painful for them to run. Scouting in the dry sand beyond the pan, it is easy enough to recognise the distinctive prints of eland with mud-gunked hooves.

Persistence hunts were only ever initiated on the hottest days, when temperatures soared close to or beyond 40 degrees Celsius, and all sensible meat-animals thought only of finding shade and doing as little as possible. Then the hunters would take the eland's spoor, following it at a gentle rhythmic trot. Unlike hunting with a bow, which requires a careful, silent stalk, persistence hunters want the eland to panic and to tear off into the bush as fast as it can. Then, perhaps after running a couple of kilometres, the eland, confident that it has escaped any imminent threat, seeks out shade in which to catch its breath and ride out the pain in its hooves. But before long the hunters, following steadily in its tracks, come back into view again and hound it into another sprint. Within three or four hours, and after thirty or forty kilometres, the eland, tortured by its glued-up toes, crippled by cramps and delirious with exhaustion, meekly offers itself up to the hunters, who by then are able to approach it unhidden and suffocate it by lying on its neck while holding its nostrils and mouth shut with their hands.

This method of hunting was not unique to southern Africa. Paiute and Navajo Native Americans used to run down pronghorn antelope in this way; Tarahumara hunters in Mexico ran down deer that, once exhausted, they suffocated with their bare hands; and some Australian Aboriginals occasionally made use of this technique when hunting kangaroo.

Because this method of hunting leaves no obvious material trace, there is no hard archaeological evidence that our evolutionary ancestors hunted in this way. But if technologically limited *Homo erectus* and others hunted plains game in addition to scavenging, it's hard to think of them doing it in any other way. And if they had the smarts to imagine a hand-axe buried in a lump of nondescript rock, there is no reason to believe that they should not also have been able to conjure the form of a familiar living animal from its tracks. For some anthropologists, most notably Louis Liebenberg, an accomplished tracker himself, the tracks in the archaeological and fossil records are clear. He is of the view that *Homo erectus* must have hunted in this way and that this form of hunting must also have played a part in making us bipedal – in moulding our bodies for long-distance running, in developing the ability to cool our bodies with sweat, and adapting our minds to the challenges of inferring meaning from this, the most ancient form of writing.

He is almost certainly right. The skills required to infer complex meaning from sandy tracks are not only indicative of the kind of purposefulness we associate now mainly with humans, but also the cognitive traits necessary to use grammar and syntax in a more sophisticated manner than Koko did. In other words, hunting was almost certainly among the selective pressures that encouraged the development of our ancestors' ability to develop complex language. Equally importantly, hunting in this way may have played an important role in shaping their sociality and social intelligence as well as building up the perseverance, patience and sheer determination that still characterises our approach to work.

Other skills that leave no obvious archaeological traces must also have played a role in increasing the efficiency of our ancestors in their food quest. And arguably the most important of all these skills was the one that not only helped provide the nutrition necessary to feed their big brains but that also kick-started the most important and far-reaching energy revolution in human history: mastery of fire.

4

Fire's Other Gifts

For the Ju/'hoansi fire is the great transformer. It is generated by the gods through lightning, but can be made by anyone with two dry sticks or a flint once they know how. It transforms the raw into the cooked, makes cold bodies warm, tempers wet wood until it is as hard as bone and can melt iron. More than that, it transforms darkness into light and dissuades curious lions, elephants and hyenas from harassing people while they sleep. And every dry season wildfires blaze through the Kalahari, scouring the land of dead grass and inviting the first summer rains to fall, so ushering in a new year and new life.

Ju/'hoansi shamans also insist that fire provides the energy that transports them to the shadow world of spirits during healing-dances as they dip and dive through roaring hot flames and bathe in coals to ignite their *n/um*, the healing force that resides deep in their bellies and that, when heated, assumes control of their bodies.

Were fire capable of transporting these shamans into the ancient past, they would see in its flames a vision of how by mastering it our ancestors reduced the amount of time and effort they had to dedicate to the food quest, and how this in turn helped stimulate the development of language, culture, stories, music and art, as well as shifting the parameters for both natural and sexual selection by making us the only species where brains might be more sexually beneficial than brawn. Then they would see how, in providing our ancestors with leisure time, language and culture, fire also summoned into existence leisure's odious opposite: the concept of 'work'.

Knocking fruit from a tree with a stick involves less work and is less risky than climbing up into a tree to pluck fruit from its branches, just as slicing through a dead mastodon's hide by concentrating force in the cutting edge of an obsidian flake requires less effort than gnawing at its carcass with teeth better suited to mashing soft fruit and grinding vegetables into a digestible pulp. The habitual use of tools vastly expanded the range of foods available to our evolutionary ancestors, helping to establish them as versatile generalists in a world where most other species were specialists who had evolved to exploit often narrow ecological niches to secure their basic energy needs. But in terms of energy, no physical tool holds a torch to the most important tool in all of human evolutionary history: fire.

Around 2 million years ago, *Australopithecus* could only extract energy from the world by proxy. Like many other species, they did this by eating plants that had captured, stored and repackaged mainly solar energy into more conveniently edible forms like leaves, fruits and tubers by means of photosynthesis. Then around 1.5 million years ago *Homo habilis* extended the energy-by-proxy model by developing a taste for more complex organisms that had already gone to the trouble of concentrating the nutrients and energy in plants by converting them into flesh, organs, fat and bone. This was our lineage's first energy revolution, because the additional nutrition and energy that flesh, fat and bone provided helped *Homo habilis* to grow much bigger brains. It also reduced the extent of their dependency on less energy-dense gathered foods and so reduced the total hours they needed to dedicate to the task of finding food. But raw flesh, fat and bone was not enough on its own to grow and maintain brains as big and energy-hungry as *Homo sapiens'*. To do that they needed to cook their food, and to cook it, they needed to master fire, a process that kicked off the second, and arguably the greatest, energy revolution in our history.

It is impossible to know what first persuaded our evolutionary ancestors to master fire. Maybe they were intoxicated by the smells of burnt meat as they scavenged their way through lands scorched by wildfires, or perhaps they were hypnotised by the dangerous beauty of the flames. Neither do we know which of our evolutionary ancestors first mastered fire or when they did it.

It's one thing to grab a glowing ember from the path of a wildfire with the ambition of making a smaller, controlled fire to cook meat on or keep warm by. But being able to conjure it at will and so access a near-limitless supply of energy is something altogether more special. And mastery of fire would not have been possible if, at some point in the distant past, our ancestors had not begun to fiddle with, manipulate and intentionally repurpose objects around them. The discovery of how to make fire must have happened more than once, and in each event it was almost certainly a fortunate accident, one that occurred while using or making other tools with an entirely different goal in mind. Some populations may have discovered how to make fire when knapping flakes off an iron-rich stone like pyrite that produces sparks when struck. But a more likely scenario is that our ancestors discovered the secret of making fire while crafting something that involved creating friction between pieces of wood.

Conjuring fire from two sticks is a complex process. Beyond requiring some dexterity, it also requires a lightness of touch and a much more sophisticated understanding of causality than that needed to knock a fruit from a tree with a stick or persuade termites from a mound using a twig. These are traits we associate with modern *Homo sapiens*, but there is good reason to think that our evolutionary ancestors made use of fire long before our species appeared 300,000 years or so ago.

Wonderwerk Cave, which means 'Miracle Cave' in Afrikaans, is located on top of a dolomite hill just north of the small town of Kuruman in South Africa's semi-arid Northern Cape. It owes its name to a desert-parched group of Afrikaner travellers who found a pool of life-saving water in the cave's interior some two centuries ago. Geologists prefer to credit this particular miracle to natural processes, but this does not discourage members of local apostolic churches from trying to plunder the cave's 'holy' water.

If Wonderwerk inspires talk of miracles among the godly, it inspires equal wonder among palaeoarchaeologists, who are the latest in a long procession of humans to find hope and inspiration in its interior.

The cave extends nearly 140 metres into the hill. Its walls and ceiling join together to form a smooth arc that runs the length of the cave, giving the appearance of a rock-hewn aircraft hangar. Even on the brightest days natural light only penetrates fifty or so metres into the interior; beyond this the darkness is absolute. On entry, the first obvious sign of the cave's historical importance is the gallery of finger-painted elands, ostriches, elephants and enigmatic geometric patterns that decorate the walls as far as the natural light reaches. They were painted by the ancestors of southern Africa's indigenous foragers 7,000 years ago. But Wonderwerk Cave holds far more important clues to unravelling the history of work than the finger-paintings of relative newcomers.

A five-metre-tall stalagmite shaped like a clenched fist stands guard at the cave's mouth, and also marks the starting point of archaeological excavations. These stretch into the bowels of the cave where archaeologists have dug several metres below the level of the cave floor. Each layer of sediment archaeologists have exposed has revealed another chapter in the long history of our species from around 2 million years ago.

By far the most important finds in Wonderwerk date to about 1 million years ago. These include fire-charred bones and plant ash, indicating the oldest good evidence for systematic fire use by a human population anywhere. Most likely the bones and ash were left behind by one of the many *Homo erectus* – the first humans that walked upright and also had limbs in recognisably *Homo sapiens*-like

101

proportions. But the Wonderwerk ashes don't reveal how the fire was made or what it was used for.

If Wonderwerk was the only place offering evidence for controlled use of fire beyond half a million years ago it could be dismissed as a one-off, but there are other tantalising indications of use of fire elsewhere, some well over a million years old. In the Sibiloi National Park, adjacent to Lake Turkana in Kenya, archaeologists have found a clear association between the presence of hominins and what appear to be controlled fires dating from roughly 1.6 million years ago, but in the absence of other examples it is hard to say whether this was systematic.

There is, however, plenty of evidence for the systematic use of fire in the more recent past. Archaeologists have found lots of evidence for the sustained use of fire by early humans who lived in Qesem Cave in Israel 400,000 years ago. This data is supplemented by the dental remains of the cave's hominin inhabitants from around the same period. These suggest that they all had horrendous coughs as a result of inhaling too much smoke.[1] Archaeologists have also found compelling evidence suggesting controlled fire use at another Israeli site. This excavation on the shores of the palaeo-Lake Hula, in the northern Dead Sea Rift Valley, revealed a series of what archaeologists think are hearths containing ash from wild barley, olives and grapes alongside burnt flint fragments. These are speculated to be 790,000 years old.[2]

But finding definitive proof for the controlled use of fire by our early ancestors is near impossible. The first problem is that the evidence of the use of fire is always, somewhat inconveniently, burned, and ashes are easily dispersed by gusts of wind or a rainstorm. Generally for evidence of fire to be found, fires would have needed to be made repeatedly in the same spot to steadily build up a supply of ash large enough to leave a trace that would distinguish it from that left by a wildfire.

The other problem is that many 'cavemen' tended not to live in caves, the only places where ashes and burnt bones stand a good chance of being preserved beyond a few months. As savannah dwellers, most would have slept under the stars with little more than a simple shelter to protect them from the elements, just as many hunter-gatherers still did in the twentieth century. As we know from communities like the Ju/'hoansi, a good fire is all you need to keep even the hungriest nocturnal predators at bay. Another obvious problem – as the former residents of Qesem Cave would tell you – is that fires in confined spaces risk suffocating you, if the smoke doesn't drive you to distraction first.

Besides ancient embers from places like Wonderwerk, by far the most compelling evidence indicating that some hominins at least mastered fire perhaps as long as a million years ago is the fact that it marked the beginning of a period of sustained and rapid brain growth, an idea championed by the Harvard-based evolutionary archaeologist Richard Wrangham.

Until 2 million years ago our *Australopithecus* ancestors' brains fell well within the size range of those occupying the skulls of modern-day chimpanzees and gorillas. They were between 400 and 600 cubic centimetres in volume. *Homo habilis*, the first official member of our genus *Homo*, appeared around 1.9 million years ago. Their brains, though, were only a little larger than those of

Australopithecus, averaging a little over 600cm³ in volume. But fossil evidence suggests that they were organised somewhat differently to *Australopithecus*, brains and had more highly developed forms of some of the features we now associate with modern humans' neuroplasticity and higher cognitive functions (like unusually large neocortices).

The oldest fossil skulls of *Homo erectus* are 1.8 million years old. Their brains were significantly larger than *Homo habilis'* suggesting that something that happened around that time catalysed the rapid growth of *Homo erectus'* brains. *Homo erectus'* million-year reign as cleverest primate, however, was marked by very little in the way of brain growth. But then, beginning 600,000 years ago, there was another surge in brain growth that saw the emergence of *Homo heidelbergensis*, and then a few hundred thousand years later the emergence of archaic *Homo sapiens* and Neanderthals, many of whom had brains larger than most of us do now.

A host of different theories have been proposed to explain the two surges in brain-size growth, but only one accounts for the outsized energy demands associated with building and maintaining big brains with big neocortices.

Our brains only constitute 2 per cent of our total body weight but they consume around 20 per cent of our energy resources. For chimpanzees, whose brains are roughly one-third the size of our own, the energy used is closer to 12 per cent and for most other mammals it is between 5 and 10 per cent.[3]

Building and maintaining such big brains on the basis of a foraged raw-food, vegetarian diet would have been impossible. Even if they were to eat constantly, every waking minute of every day, gorillas and orang-utans would not be able to meet the outsized energy requirements of running a brain the same size as ours based on a diet of wild fruits, leaves and tubers alone. To do this requires eating more nutritionally dense foods. The transition from *Homo habilis* to *Homo erectus* is marked by good archaeological evidence for the more frequent consumption of just such a food source. Based on the scant archaeological evidence for fire use until half a million years ago, it seems likely that cooking spurred the next big period of brain growth.

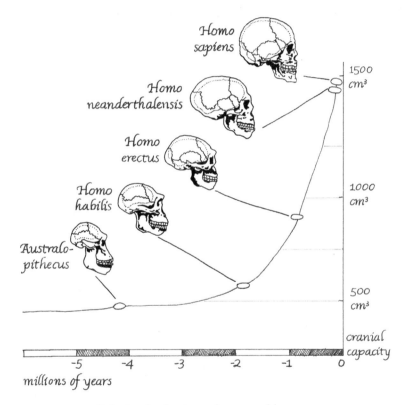

Relative brain sizes of ancestral humans

Meat, flesh and organs may be a rich store of calories, amino acids and other nutrients, but they are also slimy, tough, and hard to chew and digest when raw. Though now many in the industrialised world display a preference for lean cuts of meat, this is more an index of the astonishing productivity of the modern food industry than the base nutritional value of those cuts. Hunter-gatherers – and indeed most human populations before the twentieth century – eschewed lean cuts like fillets in favour of the fattier, gnarlier, offalier cuts because these were far more nutritious. And, as any hunter-gatherer will tell you, trying to swallow a long, stringy, fatty tendon or extract every last bit of marrow from a buffalo's shin bone is an awful lot easier if you cook it first.

Cooking not only makes meat more palatable; it also vastly extends the range of plant foods that we can eat.[4] Many tubers, stalks, leaves and fruits that are indigestible – or even poisonous – raw are both nutritious and flavoursome when cooked. Eating uncooked nettles, for example, is a recipe for pain. Eating boiled nettles is a recipe for a healthy, surprisingly tasty, soup. Thus in environments like the Kalahari, where most wild herbivores depend on eating large qualities of a handful of related plant species, the Ju/'hoansi were able to use fire to make use of over a hundred different plant species (in addition to eating the meat of pretty much anything that moved), and by cooking them extract far more energy with far less effort.

If fire helped once mostly vegetarian hominids to access the nutritional treasures of meat and to grow big brains, then it almost certainly contributed to shaping other aspects of our modern physiology too. Primates like chimpanzees and gorillas have much larger long intestines than humans. They need this additional colonic real estate to squeeze nutrition from their fibrous, leafy diets. By 'predigesting' foods through the process of cooking, fire made a significant proportion of this digestive plumbing redundant. Cooking also helped redesign our faces. Eating softer, cooked foods meant that having big-muscled jaws ceased to be a selective advantage. So as our ancestors' brains grew, their jaws shrank.[5]

Perhaps it is because so many see cooking as hard work that we have paid so little attention to what may be among the most important of fire's many gifts: the gift of free time. For fire was not only the first great energy revolution in our species' history, it was also the first great labour-saving technology.

Because their diet is not particularly nutritious, gorillas have to eat around 15 per cent of their bodyweight in food per day to stay healthy. This does not leave much time for fighting, sex or play. This is why large-primate researchers are forced to spend endless hours sitting around watching their subjects methodically foraging and eating if they are ever to witness them doing something more interesting. We know that most of the larger primates spend between eight and ten hours per day foraging and eating. This equates to something between a fifty-six- and seventy-hour working week. Chewing, digesting and processing the leaves, pith, stalks and roots is also time-consuming and energy-intensive. They spend most of what's left of their time sleeping and lazily grooming one another.

Life for our last distinctly simian-looking ancestor, *Australopithecus*, was probably not very different.

When confronted by an all-you-can-eat buffet it sometimes feels like we can match our primate cousins' appetites. But we can thrive by consuming only 2 or 3 per cent of our bodyweight per day (based on hunter-gatherer diets). And, if groups like the Ju/'hoansi are anything to go by, then we know that for much of the year, a group of economically active *Homo sapiens* adults living in a relatively hostile environment can typically feed themselves and an equal number of unproductive dependants on the basis of between fifteen and seventeen hours' work per week. This translates into one to two hours' work per day, a fraction of the time spent on the food quest by other large primates and a fraction of the time most of us spend at work.

If by mastering fire and cooking, *Homo erectus* secured greater energy returns for less physical effort, then as their brains grew so did the amount of time available to them to apply their intelligence and energy to activities other than finding, consuming and digesting food.

The archaeological record doesn't leave us too many clues indicating what our ancestors did with the free time their cooked food bought them. We know that as their brains grew they got measurably better at making tools, and they probably also had much more time for sex. But for the rest we have to speculate.

———

In mapping the evolution of *Homo sapiens'* intelligence, many researchers have zeroed in on how activities like hunting cooperatively were likely to have been instrumental in honing our problem-solving and communication skills. They almost certainly were, but the emphasis afforded activities like these may be more a reflection of the cultural importance we now ascribe to economic activities than the reality of day-to-day life for our evolutionary ancestors.

How *Homo habilis* and *Homo erectus* spent their free time from the food quest must have also played some role in shaping their evolutionary journey. This raises the tantalising prospect that in evolutionary terms we may well be as much a product of our leisure as our labour.

Boredom is not a uniquely human trait but it manifests in different ways for different species. This is why some philosophers like Martin Heidegger insisted that to claim under-stimulated animals are bored is pure anthropomorphism. To be properly bored, they argue, requires self-awareness and most animals are not self-aware.

Dog owners whose pets' tails wag optimistically at the prospect of a walk would dispute this. As do the animal behaviourists who work hard to find ways to alleviate the miseries of captivity experienced by many under-stimulated zoo animals. Where we obviously differ from numerous other species is in the extent to which boredom spurs creativity. We play, we fiddle, we experiment, we talk (even if only to ourselves), we daydream, we imagine and, eventually, we get up and find something to do.

Surprisingly little scientific research has been done on boredom, given how much time many of us spend bored. Historically, boredom has only proved of sustained interest to those in solitary professions, like philosophers and writers. Some of Newton's, Einstein's, Descartes' and Archimedes' greatest insights have all been attributed to boredom. As Nietzsche (who also credited boredom with breathing life into some of his most influential ideas) put it, 'for thinkers and sensitive spirits, boredom is that disagreeable windless calm of the soul that precedes a happy voyage and cheerful winds'.

Nietzsche was almost certainly right. The only obvious adaptive advantage of boredom is its ability to inspire the creativity, curiosity and restlessness that motivates us to explore, seek novel experiences and take risks. Psychologists also remind us that boredom is a more fertile mother of invention than necessity, and that it can stimulate very un-Nietzschean pro-social thoughts as well as a heightened sense of self-awareness, a perspective that is theologised in Zen Buddhism.[6] Beyond this, boredom drives our species' purposiveness and makes it possible for us to find satisfaction, pride and a sense of achievement in pursuit of hobbies that serve no immediate purpose other than keeping us busy. If it were not for boredom, we would live in a world with no train-spotters, no part-time Jedi Knights, no stamp collectors, no wood whittlers and very possibly none of the inventions that have changed the course of history. It is far more likely to have been boredom rather than an instinct for physics that taught *Australopithecus* that cracking rocks together might produce sharp flakes that could cut. It was also possibly boredom that inspired our ancestors' interest in fire and their bored fidgeting hands that discovered that rubbing sticks together might generate enough heat to ignite a small fire.

Boredom's ability to induce fidgeting, ferreting and creativity must also have played a role in persuading our ancestors to make art, an activity that is simultaneously work and leisure, that is emotionally, intellectually and aesthetically functional, but of no practical value to foragers in terms of the food quest.

Evidence of purely representational art appears quite late in the archaeological record. The oldest high-quality rock paintings that survive have been dated to around 35,000 years ago, some 265,000 years after the first signs of *Homo sapiens* in the archaeological record. The oldest obviously representational sculptures, slabs of ochre with neat geometric patterns engraved into them, have been dated to between 70,000 and 90,000 years ago. But defining art in terms of symbolism alone is to close our eyes and hearts to half the world. If we include careful, deliberate, aesthetically charged craftsmanship then we can push these dates back to long before *Homo sapiens* appeared on the scene.

The Kathu Pan hand-axe shows us that not only did some *Homo erectus* have an eye for aesthetics, but also that they must have had the energy, time and desire to spend on activities that were not directly related to the food quest. In other words, it shows us that they almost certainly had some concept of work.

It is also likely that our evolutionary ancestors' artistic sensibilities predate their ability to manufacture objects like the Kathu Pan hand-axe and long predate the first unambiguous evidence of symbolic art. Song, music and dance leave no trace other than in the memories of those that performed, heard or watched it. Nor does by far the most important medium of symbolic expression: spoken language.

―――――

The most complex entities that any individual *Homo erectus*, *Homo habilis*, *Homo heidelbergensis* or archaic *Homo sapiens* had to deal with were others of their own species. And with some leisure time at their disposal, humans that mastered fire must have spent a lot more time in each other's company without much of an idea about what to do with the excess energy their cooked food gave them – a state of affairs that would have placed far greater emphasis on managing social relations.

Being good at fighting is an important skill for keeping order in complex social groups. Many primate species keep the peace by establishing and then enforcing hierarchies with demonstrations of aggression and, when push comes to shove, physical power. When these hierarchies are contested – as they often are – life in primate groups gets distinctly edgy and unpleasant. But quite how important this was for early and then later hominins would hinge on where they sat on the spectrum between aggressive hierarchical primates and fiercely egalitarian, hyper-cooperative hunter-gatherers. As our ancestors gained more free time, making or keeping peace by humouring, entertaining, persuading and engaging others – rather than beating them into submission – will have become an ever more important skill. To do this would have required emotional engagement, empathy and, above all, the ability to communicate.

It is unlikely – but not impossible – that our species' unique communication skills would have evolved as they did were it not for our vocal abilities.

Early attempts to assess the linguistic capabilities of other higher primates failed mainly because researchers had not yet realised that these creatures simply did not have the physical apparatus necessary to make the same range of vocalisations that we can. Assessments of the skull morphology of various ancient hominins indicate a strong link between our vocal capabilities and our upright posture, such that it may well be the case that the morphological changes to our mouths, throats and larynxes enabled by eating cooked foods also provided us the hardware with which to talk.

But having versatile vocal cords and speech-optimised larynxes are not on their own enough to make language. That requires a level of cognitive processing power well beyond other primates.

Interest in understanding the emergence of language now attracts researchers from a wide range of disciplines – anthropology, neuroscience, linguistics, comparative anatomy, archaeology, primatology, psychology and more besides. This is important because no single approach can adequately account for the emergence of our remarkable linguistic skills. But that doesn't stop experts in different disciplines from trying. Hypotheses put forward include Grammaticalisation theory, which suggests the rules of languages grow incrementally from the use of a few basic verbal concepts over a long period of time, and Noam Chomsky's Single Step theory, which proposes that our ancestors' ability to use language came about near instantly after a single evolutionary step completed the circuitry needed to switch on a cognitive grammar-forming apparatus that we all share.

Most of the competing theories are nevertheless compatible to some degree with the idea that increased leisure time was one of the selective pressures that advanced the development of our linguistic capabilities, none more so than the Gossip and Grooming hypothesis advanced by primatologist Robin Dunbar. He has proposed that language had its origins in the affectionate grooming we see among primate groups as they gently scour each other's hides for parasites, and suggests that our language skills evolved as a form of vocal grooming that enabled hominids to touch and soothe others at a distance and groom more than a single individual at a time. The gossip part of the thesis comes from the fact that, as complex social beings, our favourite thing to do is to gossip with others about others.

The idea of language emerging as an extension of grooming behaviour is persuasive. Not only does it recognise that language has a strong emotional component, it also suggests that females probably played a far more important role in the development of our language capabilities than males. 'If females formed the core of these earliest human groups and language evolved to bond these groups,' Dunbar argues, 'it naturally follows that the early human females were the first to speak.'[7]

Humans are unique in their ability to be passively engaged by words, images, sounds and actions. We can get lost in music and transported into other worlds by doing little more than listening to someone speak, even if that person is a disembodied voice on the radio or a low-resolution, electronically generated, two-dimensional facsimile on a screen.

The need to occupy ever more restless minds during free time was an evolutionary pressure that likely selected in favour of those who could liberate others from the burden of boredom: the socially able, the articulate, the imaginative, the musical and the verbally astute – those who could use language to tell stories, entertain, charm, calm, amuse, inspire and seduce. Seduction is a particularly important part of this equation because natural selection not only weeds out the unfit, it is also a positive process in which traits are selected by sexual partners. In many primate social groups, high-ranking, physically dominant individuals typically monopolise sexual access to lower ranks.

But when the food quest became less time-consuming, less physically robust males who nurtured their skills as linguists may well have found themselves becoming increasingly successful in the competition for sexual partners, so ensuring that their genes made it through to the next generation. In other words, when our ancestors outsourced some of their energy requirements to fire, they took the first steps towards creating a world where the physically powerful sometimes play second fiddle to the articulate and charismatic.

Mastery of fire also made it easier for some members of early human communities to feed those unable to feed themselves and perhaps even those who provided value in non-material forms, like gifted storytellers and shamans. Among other species the only widespread non-reciprocal sharing relationships are those between mothers (and less frequently fathers) and their offspring before they are weaned. There are of course the eusocial species like termites where workers support soldiers and reproductives. There are also species where more productive individuals 'share food' with other, less productive, often dominant individuals, most famously female lions who 'share' their kills with dominant males. But there are no unambiguous examples in the animal kingdom of animals systematically and routinely caring for those too old to feed themselves, although instances of this kind of care have occasionally been recorded among some highly social species like the matriarchal African wild dogs of the Kalahari. Systematic well-organised non-reciprocal sharing outside of a parental context, in other words, is a uniquely human trait, one that would not be possible without fire.

We do not know the extent to which the likes of *Homo habilis* and *Homo erectus* cared for non-productive members of their species – in other words, the extent to which they were willing to do work on behalf of others. There is good evidence that *Homo heidelbergensis*, a likely ancestor of the Neanderthals who lived around half a million years ago, did.[8] But if *Homo habilis* or *Homo erectus* had fire, this means that it was not beyond their economic abilities to do so. Caring for the elderly would suggest empathy, sympathy and a sense of self sufficiently evolved to fear death. The most obvious evidence for this level of cognitive and emotional awareness is mortuary rituals like burying the dead.

There is little clear evidence of ritual burial among our distant evolutionary ancestors until 30,000 years ago, but strangely there is for another small-brained hominin, *Homo naledi*, a contemporary of later *Homo erectus* and early *Homo sapiens*. Researchers in southern Africa found evidence of the intentional, likely ritualised, placing of *Homo naledi* corpses in a difficult to access chamber of a vast cave complex between 236,000 and 335,000 years ago.[9] If *naledi* did this, then there is good reason to assume that more cognitively developed hominids also feared death, cared for the elderly and mourned their dead. This in turn means that they must have had the conceptual apparatus to divide up the world around them and their experiences of it, and so also had culture and language, even if in rudimentary form. If so, then they would almost certainly have categorised some activities as 'work' and others as 'leisure'. This is important because work is not only something that we do, it is also an idea represented in our languages and cultures, and to which we attribute all sorts of different meanings and values.

When the sewers were working and the rubbish had been collected, the smells that percolated from the market stalls, cafes and restaurant kitchens that made Paris the post-Second World War gastronomic capital of the world ensured that when most Parisians were not eating they were either thinking or talking about food. Just like many other intellectuals haunting the Left Bank of the Seine in those years, fire, food and cooking feature often in the work of Claude Lévi-Strauss, who for much of the second half of the twentieth century was the most admired public intellectual in France. 'Cooking,' Lévi-Strauss explained, 'is a language through which society unconsciously reveals its structure.'

An anthropologist who disliked rubbing shoulders with 'natives' in strange lands, Lévi-Strauss synthesised other anthropologists' fieldwork to produce an entirely new way of interpreting culture that he called 'structuralism'.

Lévi-Strauss's structuralist method was spelled out in a series of weighty tomes, none more important than his four-volume magnum opus, *Mythologiques*. And reflecting the importance of fire and food in his thinking, three of the four volumes of *Mythologiques* made explicit reference to cooking and fire in their titles. The first, *The Raw and the Cooked*, was published in 1964, the second, *Honey and Ashes*, in 1966, and the third, *The Origin of Table Manners*, in 1968. For Lévi-Strauss, cooking was the very essence of what it meant to be human.

For a Parisian, Lévi-Strauss's writing about cooking is surprisingly joyless. And as with much of the rest of his work, it was easy for his critics to argue that the ideas proposed in *Mythologiques* offered a far greater insight into the carefully ordered, highly technical, dour but very clever world inside the head of Claude Lévi-Strauss than the world that lay beyond it.

As complex as some of Lévi-Strauss's writing may be, his grand 'structural' theory of culture was based on a very simple premise: that the individual beliefs, norms and practices that make up a culture are on their own meaningless but are meaningful when viewed as part of a set of relationships.

He took his lead from linguists, who by then had established that there was no organic relationship between what a word in any given language referred to and the word itself. The letters 'd-o-g' have no organic relationship with the creatures that many of us share our homes with, which is why the same creatures are represented by different, ultimately arbitrary sounds in other languages, like 'chien' in French or 'gǂhuin' in the Ju/'hoansi's click language. To understand what the sound 'dog' meant, the linguists explained, required putting it in the context of the language as a whole. Thus the sounds made by the letters d-o-g made sense in the broader set of words that comprise English, and in which phonemically similar terms like h-o-g or j-o-g had radically different meanings.

Lévi-Strauss's exploration of the ever-expanding ethnographic record persuaded him that just as physical sounds are arbitrary, so are our cultural norms, symbols and practices. This is why gestures that may be considered polite in one culture – such as greeting a stranger with a kiss – may be considered grossly offensive in another and completely without meaning in a third. Therefore, he argued, individual cultural practices could only be made sense of by looking at their relationship with other practices in the same culture. In this way a *bisou* on the cheek in France could be understood to be equivalent to shaking hands in Britain or rubbing noses among Inuit in the Arctic.

Lévi-Strauss was also of the view that our cultures are a reflection of the way our minds work. And as far as he was concerned humans are hard-wired to think in terms of opposites. Good, for example, only makes sense by reference to its opposite, bad. Left to right, dark to light, raw to cooked, work to rest, and so on. This persuaded him that for anthropologists to understand any particular culture they had to identify these oppositions and map out the intersecting webs of relationships between them.

The oppositions between the raw and the cooked appeared again and again in the myths and cultural practices of different peoples across the globe. 'All cultures have to manage this struggle between nature and culture,' he wrote. 'Nature ("raw") is associated with instinct and the body, while culture ("cooked") is associated with reason and the mind, among other things.'

What also particularly interested him about this opposition was that it implied a transition. Where left can never become right, something that is raw can become cooked.

119

'Not only does cooking mark the transition from nature to culture,' he argued, 'but through it and by means of it the human state can be defined with all its attributes.'

Early in his career, Lévi-Strauss was intrigued by the idea of identifying the point of transition from pre-human to human, the point we went from animal to human, from nature to culture. But by the time he came to develop structuralism this was not what preoccupied him.

Trying to make sense of humankind was like 'studying a mollusc', he explained, because it is 'an amorphous, glutinous jelly that secretes a shell of perfect mathematical form, just as the chaos of humanity produced structurally perfect cultural artefacts'. He believed it was the ethnographer's job to study the structurally perfect external form while others prodded and poked around in its slippery interior.

Even if he meant it as a grand metaphor rather than a statement of historical fact, cooking symbolised perhaps more eloquently than anything else the emergence of complex culture in our evolutionary history, because a defining attribute of culture is the ability to purposefully and imaginatively transform objects from a 'raw' natural state into a cooked, cultural state.

And this, of course, is a defining trait of work. Just as raw food is 'worked' by a combination of human agency and fire into a meal, so a carpenter transforms trees into furniture; a manufacturer of plastic cutlery works to mould chemical compounds into plastic knives; a teacher works to transform students from a state of ignorance to one of enlightenment; and a marketing executive works to transform accumulated stock into profitable sales.

Few, if any, anthropologists follow Lévi-Strauss's structural method now. Advances in cognitive sciences have shown that our minds – and our cultures – are far more than a mollusc shell of oppositions and associations. We also know that not all cultures distinguish between nature and culture in the way Lévi-Strauss assumed, and that our cultures are far more the product of what we do with our bodies than the likes of Lévi-Strauss ever realised. But the idea of understanding cultures as systems still shapes much modern anthropological inquiry, as does the idea that to make sense of any individual cultural action, belief or norm requires understanding what they are not.

And this is where Lévi-Strauss's structural model adds another critical dimension to the history of work, because it suggests that by giving our ancestors more leisure time, fire simultaneously breathed life into leisure's conceptual opposite, work, and set our species off on a journey that would lead us from foraging in forests to the factory floor.

PART TWO

THE PROVIDENT ENVIRONMENT

5

'The Original Affluent Society'

By the dawn of the third millennium, even though there was good archaeological evidence to show that anatomically modern *Homo sapiens* may have been around for at least 150,000 years, most anthropologists believed that our ancestors only became 'behaviourally modern' much more recently. They were convinced that up until around 50,000 years ago our ancient ancestors languished on the wrong side of a critical cognitive evolutionary threshold and so lacked the ability to muse about the mysteries of life, praise gods and curse spirits, tell funny stories, paint decent pictures, reflect on a day's events before drifting off into dream-filled sleep, sing love songs or make clever excuses to get out of a chore. Similarly they were convinced that until *Homo sapiens* crossed this threshold our ancestors were not intellectually nimble enough to creatively apply skills acquired in one context to other, different contexts with the fluidity that we do today. In short, they were convinced that our ancestors only very recently became capable of working with the purposefulness and self-awareness that we do today.

They believed this because, up to then, the earliest unambiguous evidence for this kind of cleverness – in the form of skilled rock paintings and engravings, symbolic sculptures, complex and diverse tool-making traditions, elegant jewellery and ritualised burial – was 40,000 years old. Given that there were no obvious physical changes to *Homo sapiens* at this time, they hypothesised that this 'great leap forward' occurred when an invisible genetic switch was thrown, perhaps around 60,000 years ago. As a result, they argued, human populations across Africa as well as those that had crossed into Europe and Asia simultaneously became 'behaviourally modern' around this time and, inspired by their new-found abilities, promptly set off to colonise the rest of the world, leaving signs of their ingenuity, creativity and intelligence wherever they went, when they weren't too busy wiping out the local megafauna and picking fights with distantly related humans like Neanderthals.

The broken skulls of Neanderthals and other early humans stored in museum basements and university archives across the world don't care what anyone says about them now. But it is hard to ignore the obvious problems that arise when adjudicating the cognitive sophistication of a people based mainly on the kinds of things they made. After all, many indigenous people the world over were until recently deemed subhuman by others on the basis of their simple material culture, none more so than Tasmanian Aboriginals in the eighteenth century, who were such efficient foragers that they acquired all the food they needed using a set of tools so basic that they would make a *Homo erectus* hand-axe look like cutting-edge technology.

Now a rapidly growing body of data indicates that not only were early *Homo sapiens* every bit as self-aware and purposeful as we are now, but also that *Homo sapiens* have been around far longer than was ever imagined before. As new archaeological discoveries in southern Africa and beyond also show, people were already making all sorts of clever things tens of thousands of years before the supposed cognitive revolution. And, taken together with research conducted by anthropologists among geographically isolated peoples who continued to make a living as foragers in the twentieth century, this data suggests that for 95 per cent of our species' history, work did not occupy anything like the hallowed place in people's lives that it does now.

For more than a century after Darwin published *The Origin of Species*, academic debates about the genetic affinities of ancestral populations hinged as much on moments of inspiration, imagination, Aristotelian reasoning, and rhetorical skills honed in the debating chambers of the Oxford and Cambridge Unions, as they did on actual hard evidence. There was simply no absolute way of establishing the genetic relatedness of individuals purely on the basis of physical resemblance.

Palaeogenetics – the science of distilling deep human history from ancient genomes – is a science in its infancy. But it is a whale of an infant. Over the past two decades, as technologies have advanced and scientists have become more adept at prising genetic information from ancient bones and teeth to compare with living populations, so they have generated a flurry of new insights into and questions about our species' evolution, expansion and interactions over the past half-million or so years.

A human genome can now be sequenced in any one of thousands of different laboratories in an afternoon and at a price that will give you some change from $500 (£400). And with economy has come scale. Now an army of algorithms trawl day and night through almost unimaginably large databases packed with high-resolution data on the DNA of millions of individuals both living and dead. Most of these algorithms have been designed to find, compare and interrogate interesting patterns either within individual genomes or across sets of genomes for medical and epidemiological research. But some of them have been designed specifically to ferret out the mysteries of our evolutionary history, by untangling the affinities between ancestral DNA recovered from well-preserved ancient bones and DNA from contemporary human populations. These have yielded data that has forced us to completely reimagine much of our species' deep history.

Now, new evidence-based discoveries come so frequently and are often so surprising that genetic historians rarely hold on to any single interpretation of the data because they have learned to expect that at any moment something new will be revealed that will turn their thinking on its head.

Some of these discoveries – like the unambiguous evidence showing that most of us have recent Neanderthal ancestry – ask new questions about our sense of what it means to be human. Some also demand that we abandon the well-established visual metaphor of portraying evolutionary history as a tree, with a discrete trunk, branches and twigs representing the distribution of genetic information across generations and between the different kingdoms, clades, orders, families, genera and species that make up all living things. Because when we zoom in tighter on the tree we see that it better resembles an inland river delta comprised of thousands of intersecting channels that variously merge with and split from one another.

But among the most intriguing of all the discoveries thus far is that the neat story of *Homo sapiens* evolving from a single small distinct lineage of archaic humans somewhere in Africa and then spreading out to conquer the world is almost certainly wrong. Instead it now seems likely that several distinctive *Homo sapiens* lineages that shared a common ancestor around half a million years ago evolved in parallel with one another, and appeared near-simultaneously around 300,000 years ago in North Africa, southern Africa and the East African Rift Valley, and that all people today are made up of a mosaic of genetic features inherited from all of them.[1]

The new genomic data is illuminating, but the archaeological record for the first quarter-million years of *Homo sapiens'* history is too fragmented and incomplete to offer us anything more than glimpses into their lives. It shows that also around 300,000 years ago, early *Homo sapiens* (and Neanderthals) across Africa gave up on their hand-axes in concert with one another in favour of making and using a variety of other tools: smaller, more regularly shaped stone flakes that were then individually customised for doing different jobs.

Occasionally stone flakes reveal much more about their makers' lives than how technically skilled they

129

were. Among the most revealing stone tools from this era are some 320,000-year-old obsidian and chert flakes recovered from Olorgesailie in southern Kenya. These flakes are not especially interesting or unusual. By then many populations were making similar tools and knew all too well that obsidian flakes have finer cutting edges than a surgeon's scalpel, and that chert – a sedimentary rock composed of tiny quartzite crystals – is the next best thing. What was special about these flakes was that the unworked obsidian and chert were sourced from quarries nearly a hundred kilometres distant[2] from where they were chiselled into a variety of different-sized and -shaped blades and points. This may signify the existence of complex exchange and social networks spread over hundreds of square kilometres. This is what the archaeologists that discovered the pieces have hypothesised. At the very least it reveals that the makers of the flakes were sufficiently purposeful and determined to trek very long distances to specific sites to acquire the best possible materials with which to make their stone tools.

It is likely that other very old sites like Olorgesailie will be found in future, adding texture to our understanding of early human life in Africa. But this optimism is tempered by the knowledge that environmental conditions in much of the continent are far less suitable for preserving bones and other organic artefacts than the frost-bitten provinces of Europe and Asia. For now the most vivid and surprising evidence of how some early *Homo sapiens* in Africa spent their time comes from a sequence of coastal caves in southern Africa.

Blombos Cave overlooks a quiet bay not far from where the Indian and Atlantic Oceans merge on Africa's south-east coast. From the cave's mouth it is easy to see the southern right whales that sometimes winter in the waters below.

Today, some thirty-five metres below the cave's mouth lies a series of exposed rock, filled with fry, winkles, mussels, octopus and crabs. For much of the last 200,000 years, though, these rock pools were dry. Then trillions of metric tonnes of water were bound into the ice caps, the ocean here was only visible as a black greasy slick on the distant horizon, and getting to the beach from the cave involved a long trek over an undulating expanse of grassy dunes and an ever-shifting web of river estuaries and knee-deep coastal lagoons.[3] But for a 30,000-year period, beginning around 100,000 years ago, sea levels along this coastline were as high as they have been at any point in the last half-million years and so were not much different to what they are today.

Back then, southern right whales in the bay may have occasionally noticed people watching them breach and tail-bob from the cave above, or glimpsed them gathering molluscs and bivalves in the rock pools by the beach. For the people, the cave not only granted them a good view of the bay and easy access to beaches further to the east and west, but also shelter from the winter storms that barrelled into this coast from the south over the winter months. But perhaps the most appealing thing about this cave was the excellent surf-and-turf dining opportunities it offered, one of the highlights of which was the punchy meat and energy-rich blubber of the whales who ran foul of the shifting dune beds in the shallower bays, and perished on nearby beaches.

Fossil remains inside the cave show that its occupants ate much more than whale steak. In addition to snacking on limpets, winkles and mussels alfresco on the beach, they dragged hauls of shellfish up the hill to eat in the comfort of the cave. To add variety to their diets, they hunted seals, penguins, tortoises, meaty hyraxes and less-meaty mole rats. Archaeologists have also recovered fish bones from the cave. Fish bones decay quickly so it is hard to draw firm conclusions about how much fish Blombos' various residents actually ate, and how much was left by owls, but the bones are of sufficient variety and quantity to suggest that some of the cave's occupants knew a thing or two about catching fish.

Plant remains don't endure nearly as well as mollusc shells. But this was a rich landscape. Their food almost certainly included vegetables, tubers, fungi and fruits gathered inland and on beach margins.

The cave was also packed with stone points and shards, among them some finely edged, razor-sharp lance heads to show that they made sophisticated composite tools that resemble some of those still used by Ju/'hoansi hunters today. But Blombos Cave is most famous for what its occupants did when they were not foraging.

A clutch of 75,000-year-old sea-snail beads with holes bored into them, and which were probably bound together on strings made from sinew, leather or plant fibres, shows that people who stayed there were interested in making jewellery to adorn themselves with. In the upper excavated layers of the cave, archaeologists also retrieved two chunks of ochre. Each was engraved with a scruffy, but obviously intentional, diamond pattern. A fragment of smoothed rock onto which a similar design had been drawn with an ochre crayon was found as well. These pieces are estimated to have been made between 73,000 and 77,000 years ago. And while none of these items are particularly impressive artistically, and were clearly made by much less practised hands than those that made the Kathu Pan hand-axe, they are now described by many as the oldest pieces of representational art yet discovered.

The oldest finds were unearthed from the deepest layers in the cave. These are around 100,000 years old. They comprise two pigment-making 'toolkits' of abalone-shell paint-bowls containing a mix of powdered ochre, charcoal and other binding agents; matching grindstones to pound them into powder; and bone stirrers to mix them into a paste. The ochre and charcoal may have been used as a glue or, more likely, mixed with fat to produce a decorative all-in-one sunscreen and insect repellent. Arranged as if they had been put to one side by someone midway through mixing a paste, these abandoned toolkits hint at sophisticated lives suddenly and mysteriously interrupted.

There are several other sites in southern Africa that, like Blombos, are so rich in similar artefacts that many of the archaeologists have been persuaded to abandon their customary caution when it comes to imagining complete and complex lives on the basis of a few material scraps. Further north and a little way inland from Blombos, for instance, there is Sibudu Cave. Between 77,000 and 70,000 years ago, its ancient residents busily made pretty ornaments from seashells, and slept on mattresses of sedge and other aromatic herbs. There is also evidence to suggest that they took care to work and decorate leather using awls and needles carved from bone, and that one of the reasons they could afford to spend time on such activities was that they had cracked the principles of archery some 60,000 years before any *Homo sapiens* population in Europe or Asia did.[4]

Reconstruction of a 70,000–75,000-year-old Nassarius *shell necklace recovered from Blombos Cave in South Africa*

There is also some tantalising evidence that indicates this kind of sophistication was not confined to southern Africa. At a site near the Semliki River in the Congo, an area not well suited to preserving ancient artefacts and where political instability has made long-term exploration near impossible, archaeologists retrieved a set of 90,000-year-old bone harpoon-heads.[5] These were carefully notched along one edge with sequences of precisely sized barbs, making them perfect for spearing the fat, nutritious catfish whose bones were found alongside the harpoon-heads. Further to the north, in several sites across North Africa,[6] there is also good evidence that, like the residents of Blombos, people there also routinely made jewellery from the shells of *Nassarius* mud snails.

Genomic data suggests that through much of their history ancient African forager populations were characterised by a surprising level of demographic stability. This in turn implies that they lived very sustainably. Indeed, it suggests that if the measure of a civilisation's success is its endurance over time, then the direct ancestors of southern Africa's Khoisan are the most successful civilisation in human history – by a considerable margin. Genetic diversity in Africa as a whole is much higher than anywhere else in the world, and the genetic diversity of the now tiny 100,000-strong population of Khoisan is higher than that of any other regionally established population anywhere in the world. Some of this diversity can be accounted for by a brief injection of genes from adventurous migrants from East Africa around 2,000 years ago, but much of it can also be accounted for by the relative infrequency of famines and other catastrophes that occasionally wiped out foraging populations that expanded into Europe and beyond over the course of the last 60,000 years.

The new finds in southern Africa are compelling, but it is hard to infer much detail from them about how hard these foragers worked or indeed what they thought about work. But they offer enough to show that in terms of their economic practices, material culture and social organisation, they had a great deal in common with the members of the small-scale foraging populations who largely through isolation had continued to hunt and gather well into the twentieth century.

———

In October 1963, Richard Borshay Lee, a doctoral student enrolled in the anthropology programme at the University of California, set up a makeshift camp near a waterhole in the remote desert in north-east Botswana. He was there to spend time among one of the last of the world's few largely isolated hunting and gathering societies, the northern Ju/'hoansi, or as he referred to them at the time, the '!Kung Bushmen'. They formed part of the same broad language community that included the southern Ju/'hoansi in places like Skoonheid. Crucially though, in the 1960s these Ju/'hoansi were still free to forage in their traditional lands among the lions, hyenas, porcupines, aardvarks and myriad other animals that their ancestors had lived among for possibly 300 millennia.

Like many other anthropology students at the time, Lee was frustrated by the fact that the fragmented archaeological record offered no real sense of how even our recent hunting and gathering ancestors had actually lived. As far as he was concerned, broken arrowheads, long-abandoned hearths and the crumbling remains of gnawed animal bones, which were the palaeoanthropologist's stock-in-trade, raised many more questions than they answered. How large, for example, were hunter-gatherer group sizes? he wondered. How were they organised? Did they differ markedly from one ecosystem to another? And was life really as tough for them as everyone imagined?

136

Lee speculated that studying the handful of societies that continued to hunt and gather into the twentieth century might help anthropologists and archaeologists alike shed light on a way of life that was 'until 10,000 years ago a human universal'.[7] As novel as Lee's approach was, the most surprising thing about it was that no one else had thought of doing it before. It had been widely believed for some decades that people like the BaMbuti Pygmies or the Ju/'hoansi Bushmen were living fossils who, by dint of geography, circumstance and just plain bad luck, had been left languishing in the Stone Age when the rest of humankind embarked on its epic journey to scientific enlightenment.

Above all, Lee wanted to understand how well hunter-gatherers coped with scarcity and took the view that the best way to do this was to document how much time they spent procuring what he expected would be their meagre rations. The scientific consensus at the time was that hunter-gatherers lived permanently on the edge of starvation, were plagued by constant hunger and counted themselves lucky to survive into their thirties. Outside of academia, most people's views on hunter-gatherers were shaped by a patchwork of grisly tales about elderly 'Eskimos' unable to pull their weight being abandoned on ice floes, and of mothers in remote tribes throwing newborn infants to the hyenas because they knew they could not feed them.

Lee chose to go to the northern Kalahari instead of Australia or South America – both of which had well-established hunter-gatherer populations – because he believed that the bands of Ju/'hoansi Bushmen were likely to offer the best insights into Stone Age life anywhere. He understood that while Bushmen elsewhere in

137

southern Africa had been partially 'acculturated', the northern Ju/'hoansi living beyond the white cattle ranches had remained largely isolated from agricultural societies because of the raw hostility of the Kalahari environment, which, incidentally, he also suspected resembled the 'actual floral and faunal environment occupied by early man'.[8]

Lee's desire to experience hunter-gatherer life was not shaped solely by academic curiosity. Like many others whose earliest childhood memories were forged during the Second World War, Lee struggled to buy wholeheartedly into the narrative of progress that had shaped his parents' and grandparents' attitudes to life, work and well-being. He wondered whether a better understanding of how our hunter-gatherer ancestors lived might offer some insights into the fundamental nature of our species 'stripped of the accretions and complications brought about by agriculture, urbanisation, advanced technology, and national and class conflict'.

'It is still an open question,' wrote Lee, 'whether man will be able to survive the exceedingly complex and unstable ecological conditions he has created for himself' and whether 'the efflorescence of technology' that followed the agricultural revolution would lead us to Utopia or 'to extinction'.[9]

While settling into the rhythms of Kalahari life, Lee impressed his hosts with how quickly he came to grips with their complex click language. They also appreciated his generosity and easy-going manner, even if their near-constant demands on him for gifts of food and tobacco began to exhaust him. And so in addition to politely answering the hundreds of often tedious questions that anthropologists like to ask their hosts, the Ju/'hoansi put up with him shadowing them as they went about their daily chores while he checked his watch and weighed every morsel of food they got their hands on.

Eighteen months after arriving in the Kalahari, Lee gathered up his notebooks, packed up his camp and returned to the United States. Once he returned home he presented the results of his research at the 'Man the Hunter' conference, which he convened in April 1966 with his long-term research partner, Irven DeVore, at the University of Chicago. Word had got out that some surprising new insights would be shared at this conference, with the result that a few anthropological grandees, including the great Claude Lévi-Strauss, crossed the Atlantic to attend.

Lee's revelations set the tone for what would become one of the most talked-about conferences in the history of modern anthropology. In a now famous presentation, Lee explained how the Ju/'hoansi had persuaded him that, contrary to received wisdom, 'life in a state of nature is not necessarily nasty, brutish and short' as was widely believed until then.[10]

Lee told his audience that despite the fact that he conducted his research during a drought so severe that most of rural Botswana's farming population only survived courtesy of emergency food-aid drops, the Ju/'hoansi needed no external assistance and sustained themselves easily on wild foods and hunting. He said that each individual in the band he followed consumed an average 2,140 calories per day, a figure close to 10 per cent higher than the recommended daily intake for people of their stature. What was most remarkable was that the Ju/'hoansi were able to acquire all the food they needed on the basis of 'a modest effort' – so modest, in fact, that they had far more 'free time' than people in full-time employment in the industrialised world. Noting that children and the elderly were supported by others, he calculated that economically active adults spent an average of just over seventeen hours per week on the food quest, in addition to roughly an additional twenty hours per week on other chores like preparing food, gathering firewood, erecting shelters and making or fixing tools. This was less than half the time employed Americans spent at work, getting to work and on domestic chores.

The data Lee presented wasn't a surprise to everyone at the conference. In the audience were several others who had spent the last few years living and working among groups of foragers elsewhere in Africa, in the Arctic, Australia and South East Asia. While they hadn't conducted detailed nutritional surveys, they noted that, like the Ju/'hoansi, people in these societies were also remarkably relaxed about the food quest, typically met their nutritional requirements with great ease and spent most of their time at leisure.

———

When Richard Lee convened the 'Man the Hunter' conference, many other social anthropologists were struggling to reconcile the often bewildering economic behaviours of 'tribal' peoples with the two dominant competing economic ideologies of the time: the market capitalism embraced in the West and the state-led communism embraced by the Soviet

Union and China. By then economics had emerged as one of the main specialisms in social anthropology, and resolving this problem had split economic anthropologists into two warring tribes, the 'formalists' and the 'substantivists'.

The formalists took the view that economics was a hard science and based on a series of universal rules that shaped all peoples' economic behaviours. They argued that 'primitive' economies, like those of the Ju/'hoansi and various Native American peoples, were best understood as unsophisticated versions of modern capitalist economies, because they were shaped by the same basic desires, needs and behaviours. Culture, they acknowledged, played an important role in determining what people in different societies considered valuable. This was why, for instance, a host of pre-colonial eastern and southern African civilisations measured wealth and status in terms of the number, size, colour, horn shape and temperament of their cattle, and north-west-coast Native American civilisations like the Kwakwaka'wakw and Coast Salish did so in terms of their ability to lavish gifts of hides, canoes, woven cedar blankets, slaves and beautifully carved bentwood boxes on others. But the formalists insisted that deep down all people were economically 'rational' and that, even if people in different cultures valued different things, scarcity and competition were universal – everyone was self-interested in their pursuit of value and everyone developed economic systems specifically to distribute and allocate scarce resources.

The substantivists, by contrast, drew inspiration from some of the more radical and original voices in twentieth-century economics. The loudest voice among this chorus of rebels was that of the Hungarian economist Karl Polanyi, who insisted that the only thing universal about market capitalism was the hubris of its most enthusiastic advocates. He argued that market capitalism was a cultural phenomenon that emerged as the modern nation state replaced more granular, diverse, socially grounded economic systems based mainly on kinship, sharing and reciprocal gift-exchange. The substantivists insisted that the economic rationality the formalists believed was part of human nature was a cultural by-product of market capitalism, and that we should be far more open-minded when it came to making sense of how other people apportioned value, worked or exchanged things with one another.

One of the attendees of the 'Man the Hunter' conference, Marshall Sahlins, was steeped in the intricacies of this particular debate. He was also plugged into the broader social and economic questions booming post-war America was asking of itself at the time. Like Claude Lévi-Strauss, Marshall Sahlins had done some fieldwork but was more at ease wrestling with theory than doing battle with blowflies and dysentery in some distant land. With a reputation for being as immodest as he was gifted,[11] he was able to see the bigger picture a little more vividly than some of his sunburnt colleagues, and declared that to his mind, foragers like the Ju/'hoansi were 'the original affluent society'.

Sahlins was not surprised by the revelation that hunter-gatherers like the Ju/'hoansi did not endure a life of material deprivation and endless struggle. He'd spent several years previously focused on questions about the evolution and emergence of complex societies from simple ones. While Lee and others were plucking scorpions from their boots in deserts and jungles, he'd been ferreting through anthropological texts, colonial reports and other documents that described encounters between Europeans and hunter-gatherers. From these he had concluded that at the very least the stereotypical image of hunter-gatherers enduring life as a constant struggle against scarcity was far too simplistic. What interested Sahlins the most was not how much more leisure time hunter-gatherers enjoyed compared to stressed-out jobsworths working in agriculture or industry, but the 'modesty of their material requirements'. Hunter-gatherers, he concluded, had so much more free time than others mainly because they were not ridden with a whole host of nagging desires beyond meeting their immediate material needs.

'Wants may be easily satisfied,' Sahlins noted, 'either by producing much or desiring little.'[12] Hunter-gatherers, he argued, achieved this by desiring little and so, in their own way, were more affluent than a Wall Street banker who, despite owning more properties, boats, cars and watches than they know what to do with, constantly strives to acquire even more.

Sahlins concluded that in many hunter-gatherer societies, and potentially for most of human history, scarcity was not the organising feature of human economic life and hence that 'the fundamental economic problem', at least as it was described by classical economics, was not the eternal struggle of our species.

6

Ghosts in the Forest

To the thirty-eight-year-old Joseph Conrad, the Congo rain-forest was a cauldron of nightmares. In 1895, slumped on a deckchair beneath the smokestack of a rickety fifteen-tonne steamer, the *Roi des Belges,* as it shuttled between ivory- and rubber-trading stations on the banks of the Congo River, the author of *Heart of Darkness* imagined this jungle to incubate 'forgotten and brutal instincts' in everyone it drew to 'its pitiless breast'. And, to him, nothing evoked this more than the heady 'throb of drums' and the 'weird incantations' that drifted through the humid night air from the villages concealed beyond the tree line, and which 'beguiled the soul beyond the bounds of permitted aspirations'.

Conrad's haunting description of Africa's greatest forest was textured by the repeated bouts of malaria and dysentery he suffered, which left him delirious and hallucinating over the course of his six-month adventure in the eastern Congo. But more than anything, it was a reflection of his bearing direct witness to what he later described as 'the vilest scramble for loot that ever disfigured the history of human conscience and geographical exploration', as the Belgian King Leopold's Force Publique paid for the rubber, ivory and gold they demanded from Congolese villagers in the currency of fear, by chopping off the hands of those who failed to meet their quotas and taking the heads of anyone who argued.

The same 'weird incantations' that were the soundtrack to Conrad's ghoulish nightmares persuaded the British anthropologist Colin Turnbull, then aged twenty-nine, to visit the Ituri Forest in northern Congo six decades later, in 1953. An aficionado of choral music, Turnbull was intrigued by recordings he heard of the complex, cascading, poly-vocal harmonies in the songs of the local BaMbuti Pygmies. He wanted to hear them performed live.

Between 1953 and 1958, Turnbull made three long trips to the Ituri. But where Joseph Conrad found only 'vengeful darkness' in the forest's ceaseless 'cascade of sounds', Turnbull was enchanted by a 'lusty chorus of praise' that celebrated a 'wonderful world'. He described how for the BaMbuti there was nothing dark, depressing or forbidding about this forest; how they insisted the forest was a 'mother and a father' to them; how it was generous with 'food, water, clothing, warmth and affection'; and how it also occasionally indulged them, its 'children', with sweet treats like honey.

'They were a people who had found in the forest something that made their life more than just worth living,' explained Turnbull, 'something that made it, with all its hardships and problems and tragedies, a wonderful thing full of joy and happiness and free of care.'[1]

On his return, he produced the mandatory academic and technical pieces. But his most important work, *The Forest People: A Study of the People of the Congo*, was anything but the studious tome the subtitle suggested. His lyrical description of BaMbuti life lifted the gloomy veil that Conrad had draped over the forest, struck a chord with the American and British reading public and was, for a while, a runaway bestseller. Its success propelled Turnbull briefly into the world of glossy magazine profiles and daytime television chat shows, but it did not win him the adulation of many fellow anthropologists. Some resented his commercial success and declared him a crass populist. They whispered among themselves that Turnbull was a romantic whose work told us more about his inflamed passions than it did about the BaMbuti's forest world. Others commended him for being a sensitive and empathetic chronicler of BaMbuti life, but they were not persuaded that his work was of tremendous academic merit. This didn't bother Turnbull particularly. He didn't care a great deal more about his colleagues' criticism than he did about some of his neighbours' gossip when he settled into a new home, as part of an openly gay, interracial couple, in one of the most conservative small towns in Virginia.

Turnbull's descriptions of BaMbuti life evoked something of the deep logic that shaped how foragers thought about scarcity and about work. First, they revealed how the 'sharing' economies characteristic of foraging societies were an organic extension of their relationship with nurturing environments. Just as their environments shared food with them, so they shared food and objects with one another. Second, they revealed that even if they had few needs that were easily met, forager economies were underwritten by the confidence they had in the providence of their environments.

———

The BaMbuti were not the only twentieth-century foragers who saw generous and affectionate parents lurking among the shadows of their forest. Hundreds of miles to the west in Cameroon, other Pygmy peoples like the Baka and Biaka did so too, as did forest-dwelling foragers like the Nayaka of Kerala Province in India and the Batek of central Malaysia.

Hunter-gatherers living in more open, less womb-like environments than tropical forests did not always describe themselves as the 'children' of nurturing landscapes that loved them, fed them and protected them. But in their environments they saw what they imagined to be the hands of spirits, gods and other metaphysical entities sharing food and other useful things with them. Many of Australia's Aboriginal peoples, for instance, still insist that sacred rivers, hills, forests and billabongs are populated by primal spirits who 'sang' the land into existence during the 'Dream Time', the Creation. Northern nomadic peoples, among them the many Inuit societies, some of whom continue to carve out a living hunting on the rapidly melting fringes of the Arctic, believed that the moose, reindeer, walrus, seals and other creatures they depended on not only had souls, but also selflessly offered their flesh and organs to humans as food and their skins and furs to keep them warm.

By hunter-gatherer standards, Kalahari foragers had an usually profane view of their environment, one that mirrored the mixed feelings they had about their gods, who they did not think of as particularly affectionate, generous or even interested in human affairs. But, even so, the

Ju/'hoansi maintained sufficient confidence in the providence of their environment never to store food or gather more than was necessary to meet their immediate needs on any particular day.

Almost all well-documented small-scale hunter-gatherer societies living in temperate and tropical climates were similarly uninterested in accumulating surpluses and storing food. As a result, when one or another species of wild fruit or vegetable came into season they never harvested more than they could eat in a single day, and were happy enough to leave whatever they didn't need in the short term to rot on the vine.

This behaviour perplexed farming peoples and later colonial and government officials as well as development workers who came into regular contact with hunter-gatherers. To them, growing and storing food was something that set humans apart from other animals. Why, they wondered, if there was a temporary surplus, wouldn't hunter-gatherers capitalise on the opportunity and work a little bit harder now to make their future more secure?

These questions would finally be answered in the early 1980s by an anthropologist who had spent the preceding two decades living and working among another group of twentieth-century hunter-gatherers, the Hadzabe, who lived near Lake Eyasi on the Serengeti Plateau in East Africa's Rift Valley.

———

Some Hadzabe elders insist that their most ancient ancestors descended to earth from a heavenly realm in

the sky. But they are not certain whether they made land-
fall as a result of sliding down the neck of a particularly
tall giraffe or by scrambling down the meaty boughs of a
giant baobab tree. They don't care a great deal one way or
another, and archaeologists and anthropologists are similarly uncertain as to the origins of this ancient population
of East African foragers. Genomic analyses indicate that
they are regional outliers and form part of a continuous
ancient lineage of hunter-gatherers going back tens of
thousands of years. They are also linguistic outliers in a
region where most people speak the languages associated
with the first farming populations that expanded into
and beyond East Africa around 3,000 years ago. Theirs is
a phonemically complex language that includes some of
the click consonants that are otherwise unique to Khoisan
languages, and which suggests a direct but very ancient
linguistic connection between them and southern Africa's
indigenous people. The Hadzabe's savannah environment
is also somewhat less spartan than the northern Kalahari
and water more plentiful. They nevertheless traditionally
organise themselves in similar-sized bands and, like the
Ju/'hoansi, move between seasonal camps.

In contrast to southern Africa's foragers like the Ju/'hoansi,
Hadzabe still retain access to enough land to stick a collective finger up at government officials who want them to
abandon foraging and assimilate into Tanzania's mainstream
subsistence and market farming economy. As a result, many
today still depend primarily on hunting and gathering, and
Lake Eyasi has become a magnet for scientists curious to
find out more about the relationship between nutrition,
work and energy in our evolutionary history.

In the summer of 1957, James Woodburn scrambled up the Serengeti Plateau to reach the shores of Lake Eyasi, where he became the first social anthropologist to develop a long-term relationship with the Hadzabe. In the 1960s, he was also was one of the most influential among the cohort of young anthropologists who spearheaded the resurgence in hunter-gatherer studies. And just like Richard Lee, he was struck by how little effort it took for the bow-hunting Hadzabe to feed themselves. In the early 1960s, he described the Hadzabe as irrepressible small-stakes gamblers who were far more preoccupied with winning and losing arrows from one another in games of chance than with wondering about where their next meal would come from. He also noted that, like the Ju/'hoansi, they met nutritional needs easily, 'without much effort, much forethought, much equipment or much organisation'.[2]

Up until his retirement in the early 2000s, Woodburn spent nearly half a century commuting between Lake Eyasi and the London School of Economics, where he taught social anthropology. One of the many things that intrigued him about the Hadzabe was not just how little time they spent on the food quest, but the fact that, again like the Ju/'hoansi, they were never inclined to harvest more than they needed to eat that day and never bothered storing food. And the more time he spent there the more convinced he became that this kind of short-term thinking was the key to understanding how societies like theirs were so egalitarian, stable and enduring.

'People obtain a direct and immediate return from their labour,' he explained. 'They go out hunting or gathering and eat the food obtained the same day or casually over the days that follow. Food is neither elaborately processed nor stored. They use relatively simple, portable, utilitarian, easily acquired, replaceable tools and weapons made with real skill but not involving a great deal of labour.'[3]

Woodburn described the Hadzabe as having an 'immediate return economy'.[4] He contrasted this with the 'delayed return economies' of industrial and farming societies. In delayed-return economies, he noted that labour effort is almost always focused primarily on meeting future rewards, and this was what differentiated groups like the Ju/'hoansi and the BaMbuti not only from farming and industrialised societies, but also from the large-scale complex hunter-gatherer societies like those living alongside the salmon-rich waters of the Pacific North West Coast of America.

Woodburn was not especially interested in trying to understand how some societies transformed from having immediate-return economies to delayed-return ones, or how this transition may have shaped our attitudes to work. But he was intrigued by the fact that all immediate return societies also spurned hierarchy, did not have chiefs, leaders or institutional authority figures, and were intolerant of any meaningful material wealth differentials between individuals. He concluded that foragers' attitudes to work were not purely a function of their confidence in the providence of their environment, but were also sustained by social norms and customs that ensured food and other material resources were evenly distributed. In other words, that no one was able to lord it over anyone else. And among them, one of the most important was 'demand-sharing'.

For many of the anthropologists living among the remnants of the world's foraging cultures in the second half of the twentieth century, the unselfconscious requests by their hosts for food or gifts, tools, pots, pans, soaps and clothing was at first reassuring. It made them feel useful and welcome as they tried to adjust to life in what at first felt like a very alien world. But it wasn't too long before it began to set their teeth on edge as they witnessed their food supplies disappearing into their hosts' bellies; their medical boxes rapidly emptying of pills, plasters, bandages and ointments; and as they noticed people wearing clothing that had until a few days earlier been theirs.

The usually temporary sense that they were somehow being exploited by their hosts was often amplified by their sense that the flow of material traffic was mainly in one direction – away from them. It was also often sharpened by the absence of some of the social niceties they were accustomed to. Foragers, they learned quickly, did not bracket requests for food or items from one another with the 'pleases', 'thank-yous' and other gestures of interpersonal obligation and gratitude that in most other places are part and parcel of asking, giving and receiving.

Some struggled to settle into the rhythms of forager life and so never quite escaped the feeling that they were being taken advantage of. But most soon gained a more intuitive sense of the logic that governed the flows of food and other things between people, and relaxed into a world where the social rules governing giving and receiving were in some respects a polar opposite to those they had grown up with. It became clear that no one considered it at all impolite to straightforwardly ask for things from someone else, but that it was considered extremely rude to turn down requests for something and that doing so would often result in bitter accusations of selfishness and could even lead to violence.

They also quickly learned that in foraging societies anyone who had anything worth sharing was subject to similar demands and the only reason that they received so many requests was because, even with their meagre research budgets, they were immeasurably wealthier in material terms than any of their forager hosts were. In other words, in these societies the obligation to share was open-ended and the amount of stuff that you gave away was determined by how much stuff you had relative to others. As a result, in forager societies there were always some particularly productive people who contributed more than others, and also people who (in the language of finger-pointing politicians and perplexed economists) are often referred to as 'freeloaders' or 'scroungers'.

Nicolas Peterson, an anthropologist who spent time living among Yolngu Aboriginal foragers in Australia's Arnhem Land in the 1980s, famously described their redistributive practices as 'demand sharing'.[5] The term has since stuck. It is now used to describe all societies where food and objects are shared on the basis of requests by the receiver rather than offers made by the giver. It may only be in hunter-gatherer economies that demand sharing is the principal means through which objects and materials flow between people, but the phenomenon of demand sharing is not unique to their societies. It is an important redistributive mechanism for food and other objects in specific contexts in all other societies too.

But not all anthropologists at the time agreed that 'demand sharing' was the best term to describe this model for redistributing goods in a community. Nicholas Blurton-Jones was one of a platoon of social anthropologists who parachuted in and out of the Kalahari in the 1970s and 80s to conduct a series of short-term research projects. He suggested that it might be better to think of demand sharing as 'tolerated theft'.[6]

'Tolerated theft' is what many people think when they scowl at their salary slips and note how much of it has been appropriated by the taxman. But even if formal taxation serves a similar redistributive purpose to demand sharing, 'consensus-based command sharing' is probably a better description of state-level taxation systems – at least in functioning democracies. Unlike demand sharing, where the link between giver and receiver is intimate, state taxation systems are shrouded in institutional anonymity and backed by the faceless power of the state, even if they draw their ultimate authority from governments mandated by their citizens to take their money.

The Ju/'hoansi were horrified when I asked whether demand sharing could be described as a form of 'theft'. As far as they were concerned, theft involved taking without asking. They also pointed out that back when they still foraged freely there was simply no point pilfering from one another. If you wanted something, all you had to do was ask.

We sometimes use the terms 'tolerated theft' or 'freeloaders' to describe those who make a living in the parasite economy: the rentiers, moneylenders, slum landlords, ambulance chasers and others who are often caricatured as pantomime villains picking the pockets of ordinary folk. It is not a new phenomenon. The equation of taxation and theft is as old as extortion. And while it is hard to avoid the idea that taxation is a form of theft when revenues are misappropriated to sustain the lavish lifestyles and egotistical ambitions of kings and kleptocrats, it is a far harder accusation to make stick in places where people have assumed the collective responsibility for the common good to ensure a society in which inequality doesn't fester.

Market capitalists and socialists are both equally irritated by 'freeloaders' – they just zero in their animosity towards different kinds of freeloaders. Thus socialists demonise the idle rich, while capitalists tend to save their scorn for the 'idle poor'. That people of all political stripes now distinguish between the makers and takers, producers and parasites, even if they define the categories somewhat differently, might suggest that the conflict between the industrious and idle in our societies is a universal one. But the fact that among demand-sharing foragers these distinctions were considered to be relatively unimportant suggests that this particular conflict is of a far more recent provenance.

Foraging societies like the Ju/'hoansi also pose a problem for those who are convinced that material equality and individual freedom are at odds with one another and irreconcilable. This is because demand-sharing societies were simultaneously highly individualistic, where no one was subject to the coercive authority of anyone else, but at the same time were intensely egalitarian. By granting individuals the right to spontaneously tax everybody else, these societies ensured firstly that material wealth always ended up being spread pretty evenly; secondly that everyone got something to eat regardless of how productive they were; thirdly that scarce or valuable objects were circulated widely and were freely available for anyone to use; and finally that there was no reason for people to waste energy trying to accumulate more material wealth than anyone else, as doing so served no practical purpose.

The norms and rules that regulated demand sharing varied from one hunter-gatherer society to the next. Among foraging Ju/'hoansi, for instance, demand sharing was moderated by a subtle grammar of reasonability. No one would expect someone to surrender more than an equal share of the food they were eating and no one would reasonably expect to have the shirt off someone's back if it was the only shirt they had. They also had a long series of proscriptions and prescriptions regarding precisely who could ask for what from whom, when and under what circumstances. And, because everyone understood these rules, people rarely made unreasonable requests. As importantly, no one ever resented being asked to share something even if they may have regretted it.

The Ju/'hoansi had another, far more formal system of gift giving as well, for objects like jewellery, clothing or musical instruments, which operated according to a different set of rules. These bound people into networks of mutual affection that extended far beyond any individual band or family group. Significantly, nobody ever held on to any gifts they were given under this system for too long. The important thing was the act of giving and part of the joy of the system was that any gifts received would soon be re-gifted to someone else who in turn would inevitably pass it on. The net result was that any individual gift – for instance an ostrich-eggshell necklace – might end up being gifted back to its maker after journeying through other people's hands over the course of several years.

Envy and jealousy have a bad reputation. They are, after all, 'deadly sins', and according to Thomas Aquinas in the *Summa Theologiae* are 'impurities of the heart'. It is not just Catholicism that has it in for these most selfish of traits. All major religions seem to agree that a special place in hell awaits those in thrall to the green-eyed monster.

Some languages distinguish between jealousy and envy. In most European languages envy is used to describe the feelings that arise when you covet or admire the success, wealth or good fortune of others, whereas jealousy is associated with the overwhelmingly negative emotions that inspire us to protect from others what we already have. In practice, though, most of us use the terms interchangeably. Unsurprisingly, the two also don't translate straightfor-wardly into many other languages. In Ju/'hoan, for instance, there is no distinction between the two, and Ju/'hoansi who are also fluent in English or Afrikaans use the term 'jeal-ousy' to refer to both.

It is not hard to see why evolutionary psychologists struggle to reconcile selfish traits like jealousy with our social ones. It is also not hard to see why Darwin considered the cooperative behaviour of highly social insect species to be a 'special difficulty' that he worried might be potentially 'fatal' to his theory of evolution.[7]

At an individual level, the evolutionary benefits of our selfish emotions are obvious. In addition to helping us stay alive when things are scarce, they energise us in the quest to find sexual partners, so enhancing our chances of survival and of successfully passing on our individual genes. We see this play out among other species all the time, and it is fair to assume that something akin to the emotions stimulated in us by envy and jealousy floods through the synapses of other animals when beating each other up to establish social hierarchies, or to gain preferential access to food or sexual partners.

But *Homo sapiens* are also a social and highly collaborative species. We are well adapted to working together. We also all know from bitter experience that the short-term benefits of self-interest are almost always outweighed by the longer-term social costs.

Unravelling the mysteries of the conflict between our selfish and social instincts has not been the sole preserve of evolutionary psychologists. It has been a near-universal preoccupation of our species ever since any of our evolutionary ancestors had second thoughts about stealing the food from the mouth of a smaller sibling. It has found expression in every imaginable artistic medium, and has generated endless debate and discussion among theologians and philosophers. This conflict also lies behind the convoluted theorems, spidery graphs and sinewy equations that are the stock-in-trade of the modern economist. For if economics deals principally with the systems we develop to allocate scarce resources, resources are only ever scarce because individuals want them for themselves and because to maintain functioning societies we need to agree social rules in order to allocate them fairly. And even if very few contemporary economists make explicit reference to this very fundamental conflict in their work, it was at the front of his mind when the Enlightenment philosopher Adam Smith set out to write what would later be recognised as the founding document of modern economics.

Ever since Adam Smith's death in 1790, historians, theologians and economists have trawled through his writings trying to establish whether he was a religious man or not. Most agree that if Smith was a man of faith he was probably at best a lukewarm believer, one who always looked first to reason rather than dogma to make sense of the world around him. Even so, it is clear that he was convinced that there were certain mysteries one could describe and analyse, but not fully explain.

Smith took the view that people were ultimately selfish creatures. He believed that 'Man intends only his own gain'. But he also believed that when people acted in their own self-interest somehow everybody benefited, as if they were guided in their actions by 'an invisible hand' to promote the interests of society more effectively than 'man' could, even if he had intended to. Smith's points of reference for this were the market towns of eighteenth-century Europe, where the traders, manufacturers and merchants all worked to make their own personal fortunes, but where collectively their effort had helped to enrich their towns and communities.

This led Smith to conclude that free enterprise unburdened by regulatory interference would inadvertently create wealth for all and so ensure 'the same distribution of the necessaries of life, which would have been made, had the earth been divided into equal portions among all its inhabitants'.

Adam Smith was neither the unapologetic champion for selfishness nor the apostle for unregulated markets that he is portrayed as by his fiercest critics and most ardent fans alike. And even if Smith's hidden hand is still solemnly invoked by some as gospel, few would defend an inflexible interpretation of it now. Smith himself would almost certainly be among the first to acknowledge that the contemporary economic world, with its convoluted financial derivatives and ever-inflating asset values, is a very different place from the one populated by the 'merchants and mongers' he had in mind when he mused on the unintended benefits of self-interested commerce. Indeed, based on his philosophical writings, it is hard to imagine that he would not, for instance, have supported the Sherman Act, which was passed unanimously by the US Congress in 1890, a century after Smith's death, with the aim of breaking up the railway and oil monopolies that by then were slowly but surely throttling the life out of American industry.

But ironically, the social role of selfishness and jealousy in foraging societies suggests that, even if Smith's hidden hand does not apply particularly well to late capitalism, his belief that the sum of individual self-interests can ensure the fairest distribution of the 'necessaries of life' was right, albeit only in small-scale band societies. For in societies like the Ju/'hoansi's, envy-fuelled demand sharing ensured a far more an equitable 'distribution of the necessaries of life' than is the case in any market economy.

The 'fierce egalitarianism' of foragers like the Ju/'hoansi was, in other words, the organic outcome of interactions between people acting in their own self-interest in highly individualistic, mobile small-scale societies with no rulers, no formal laws and no formal institutions. And this was because in small-scale foraging societies self-interest was always policed by its shadow, jealousy, which, in turn, ensured that everyone got their fair share and individuals moderated their desires based on a sense of fairness. It also ensured that those with natural charisma exercised any natural authority they acquired with great circumspection. For beyond demand sharing, the most important weapon hunter-gatherers deployed to maintain their fierce egalitarianism was mockery. Among Ju/'hoansi, and among many other well-documented hunter-gatherer societies, mockery was dished out judicially to anyone and everyone. And while it was often cutting and close to the bone, it was rarely if ever malicious, spiteful or mean.

In hierarchical societies, mockery is often associated with bullies whose power exceeds their moral authority. But it is also a tool of the weak, a means to pillory those in power and hold them to account. In the Ju/'hoan case this is best reflected in the traditional practice of 'insulting the hunter's meat'.

Ju/'hoansi foragers considered fat, marrow, meat and offal to be the 'strongest' of all the foods. Rich in energy, vitamins, proteins and minerals that were in short supply in the nuts, tubers and fruits they gathered, meat – and its absence – was one of the few things that could cause even the calmest among them to lose their cool.

It also meant that hunters never expected nor received praise when they brought meat back to the camp. Instead they expected to be mocked for their efforts, and for those due a share of the meat to complain that the kill was scrawny or that there wouldn't be enough meat to go around no matter how impressive it was. For his part, the hunter was expected to be almost apologetic when he presented the carcass and to be unfailingly humble about his achievements.

The Ju/'hoansi explained that the reason they did this was 'jealousy' of the hunter and concern that someone might gain too much political or social capital if they were in charge of distributing meat too often.

'When a young man kills much meat, he comes to think of himself as a chief or a big man, and he thinks of the rest of us as his servants or inferiors,' one particularly eloquent Ju/'hoan man explained to Richard Lee. 'We can't accept this . . . So we always speak of his meat as worthless. This way we cool his heart and make him gentle.'[8]

Being insulted, even if only light-heartedly, was not the only price good hunters had to pay for their hard work and their skill.

Because meat provoked such strong emotions, people took extraordinary care in distributing it. Where a kill was so big that there was more than enough meat for everybody to eat as much as they wanted, this was not a problem. But where there wasn't enough to go round, who got what cut and how much was a challenge. While hunters always distributed meat according to well-established protocols, there was the chance that someone would be disappointed with their share, which they expressed in the language of jealousy. As much as meat generated great ecstasies when it was eaten, hunters often considered the pressures of distributing it to be more trouble than it was worth.

The Ju/'hoansi had another trick to deal with this. They insisted that the actual owner of the meat, the individual charged with its distribution, was not the hunter, but the person who owned the arrow that killed the animal. More often than not this was the individual hunter. But it was not unusual for keen hunters to borrow arrows from less enthusiastic hunters precisely so that they could avoid the burden of having to distribute the meat. This also meant that the elderly, the short-sighted, the clubfooted and the lazy got a chance to be the centre of attention once in a while.

Not all well-documented hunting and gathering societies had the same aversion to hierarchy as the Ju/'hoansi or Hadzabe.

Around 120,000 years ago, some *Homo sapiens* ventured across the land bridge between Africa and Asia, now bisected by the Suez Canal, and established themselves in the Middle East. It is uncertain when these populations later expanded beyond these warm latitudes into central Europe and Asia. Genomes prised from ancient bones and teeth indicate that the wave of modern humans that accounts for much of the genetic make-up of all major non-African populations today began around 65,000 years ago. This was during the depths of the last glacial period when global temperatures were on average five degrees lower than they are now and winter ice sheets were rapidly expanding southwards, progressively swallowing up all of Scandinavia, much of Asia and northern Europe – including all of Britain and Ireland – with the result that the tundra in some places extended into the south of France, and much of modern Italy, the Iberian Peninsula and the Côte d'Azur better resembled the cold steppes of eastern Asia than the sun-baked destinations they are today.

The same genomic data also suggests that the vanguard of this wave of expansion headed first towards the sunrise, eventually making it as far as Australia sometime between 45,000 and 60,000 years ago. The expansion westwards and northwards into an icebound mainland Europe was far slower, indicating that the Iberian Peninsula was occupied exclusively by Neanderthals until around 42,000 years ago.[9] Just as it was for European immigrants over the last three centuries, the Americas were very much a new world for our *Homo sapiens* ancestors too. By the time the first modern humans crossed to North America 16,000 years ago, modern humans had been living and foraging continuously in southern Africa for more than 275 millennia. And just like many later arrivals to the new world, the first Americans probably arrived by boat.[10]

Some of the foragers that established themselves in the more temperate parts of Europe, Asia and beyond lived, worked and organised themselves in broadly similar ways to their African cousins. But not all of them.

Those who settled in frostier climates, where seasons were more starkly pronounced than they were for African and other foragers in the humid tropics and subtropics, had to take a different approach to work, at least for part of the year. Some anthropologists have argued that in some ways they must have better resembled the 'complex' hunter-gatherer societies of America's Pacific North West Coast, like the Kwakwaka'wakw and Coast Salish and Tsimshian that began to emerge around 4,400 years ago and who thrived until the late nineteenth century. Their elegant cedar longhouses and villages were often home to hundreds of individuals, and once dotted the bays and inlets of the Pacific West Coast from Alaska in the north, through British Columbia and Washington State to Oregon, and their imperious carved totems guarded the network of waterways that separate the patchwork of islands from the continental mainland. Beyond the fact that these societies fed themselves by means of hunting, gathering and fishing, and were similarly convinced of the generosity of their environments, they had very little obviously in common with foragers like the Ju/'hoansi. Described variously as 'complex hunter-gatherers' or 'delayed return hunter-gatherers', they better resembled some of the most productive *farming* societies anywhere. They lived in large permanent settlements, stored food on a large scale and were deeply preoccupied with achieving social rank, which they did through lavish discharges of gifts. They did so because they lived in places that were astonishingly rich in seasonal food sources, like the berries, mushrooms and cattails that flourished from spring through to the autumn. But it was their taste for seafood and their skills as fisher-people that made all the difference.

Over the course of any year they dined on black cod, ling cod, dogfish, flounder, snapper, shellfish and sole pulled from the sea, as well as trout and sturgeon from inland rivers and lakes. But it was the teeming schools of oily fish like herring and eulachon that swam a few miles offshore, and the five species of salmon that migrated annually up local rivers in their teeming millions to spawn every year from early summer through to autumn, that enabled them to abandon the austere approach taken by foragers like the Ju/'hoansi. These were harvested in such prodigious quantities that over the course of a few short weeks people could catch and preserve enough salmon to sustain them through to the following year.

Their fisheries were so seasonally productive that for much of the year people in these societies spent most of their time and energy developing a rich artistic tradition, playing politics, holding elaborate ceremonies and hosting sumptuous ritual feasts – potlatch ceremonies – in which the hosts attempted to outdo each other with acts of generosity. Reflecting their material affluence, these feasts were also often characterised by lavish displays of wealth and sometimes even the ritual destruction of property, including the burning of boats and the ceremonial murder of slaves. When the guests headed home in canoes heavy with gifts of fish oil, exquisite woven blankets, bentwood boxes and copper plates, hosts would often begin to tally up the sometimes considerable debts they incurred to supply lavish enough gifts to merit the status they sought.

There is no suggestion that the foragers who settled into central and northern Asia and Europe beginning around 50,000 years ago were anything near as materially sophisticated as the civilisations that flourished on the Pacific North West Coast between 1500 BC and the late nineteenth century. Nor is there any question that the environments they lived in were large permanent communities. But there is a good case to make for critical elements of the seasonal nature of their work being similar to the Pacific North West Coast peoples, and that this represented a significant departure from the way small-scale foragers in warmer climates organised themselves.

For a start, populations who settled, for instance, on the frosty steppes of Asia had to do more work than African foragers just to stay alive. They could not roam naked or sleep under the stars throughout the year. Enduring long winters demanded that they make elaborate clothing and sturdy footwear and gather far more fuel for their fires. They also needed to find or build shelters robust enough to withstand winter blizzards.

Unsurprisingly, the oldest evidence for the construction of near-permanent structures and dwellings comes from some of the coldest places where humans settled during the frostiest years of the last glacial period —roughly between 29,000 and 14, 000 years ago. They take the form of sturdy domes constructed from hundreds of heavy, dry mammoth bones that have been discovered at sites across Ukraine, Moravia, the Czech Republic and southern Poland. When in use, these domes were likely shrouded with animal hides to make them windproof and watertight. The largest of them have diameters in excess of six metres, and the sheer effort involved in their construction suggests that their makers returned to them annually. The oldest excavated have been dated to 23,000 years ago, but there is good reason to believe that similar structures were built elsewhere, possibly using less enduring material than mammoth bone, like wood.

Living in these environments not only demanded that people did more work but also that they organised their working lives differently, for part of the year at least.

Preparing for winter required significantly more planning for them than it did for African foragers. Building a mammoth-bone house and binding skins to it with raw-hide is not something that can be done after the first winter storms have blown through. Nor is hunting and preparing skins and furs for winter clothing. It was also not always practical or even possible to find fresh food on the basis of a few hours of spontaneous effort all year round. For the several months when the landscape was blanketed in snow and ice, gathering was near impossible and hunting far more treacherous. But living in a vast deep-freeze for months on end had some benefits. It meant that food didn't decay and that meat butchered when the first heavy frosts fell might still be good to eat months later when the snows began to thaw. It is hard to make sense of the evidence for their routinely hunting animals as big and dangerous as mammoths if it wasn't to create a surplus.

During the depths of winter, the pace of life and work will have fallen into step with the more glacial tempo of the season. Besides occasional hunting, or expeditions to refresh stocks of firewood, many hours would have been spent huddled close to the fire. Busy minds would entertain and be distracted by stories, ceremonies, songs and shamanic journeys. Agile fingers would have found purpose in developing and mastering new skills. It is unlikely to be a coincidence that the efflorescence of artwork in Europe and Asia that archaeologists and anthropologists once assumed indicated *Homo sapiens* crossing a crucial cognitive threshold may well have been the progeny of long winter months. It is also unlikely to be a coincidence that much of this art, like the 32,000-year-old frescoes of mammoths, wild horses, cave bears, rhinos, lions and deer that decorate the walls of Chauvet Cave in France, was painted in the light of fires illuminating the interior of weatherproof caves, while most rock in places like Africa and Australia tended to be on more exposed surfaces.

Evidence of how these populations busied themselves around their fires in winter take the form of ancient bone, antler and mammoth ivory carvings, and precise, clever jewellery recovered from sites across Europe and Asia. Among the most famous of these is the world's oldest representational sculpture, the *Löwenmensch*, 'Lion Man', of Hohlenstein-Stadel. Carved between 35,000 and 40,000 years ago, the mammoth ivory statue reminds us that not only did foragers see the relationship between themselves and their animal neighbours as ontologically fluid, but also that they had developed and mastered a whole range of techniques and tools to handle the idiosyncrasies of ivory as a medium to work with.

But it is an archaeological site called Sunghir, discovered in the 1950s on the muddy banks of Klyazma River on the eastern fringes of the Russian city of Vladimir, that hints at how these populations busied themselves while waiting for the worst of winter to pass. Included among the stone tools and other more conventional bits and pieces, archaeologists there discovered several graves. None were more remarkable than the elaborate shared grave of two young boys who, sometime between 30,000 and 34,000 years ago, were buried together alongside a straightened mammoth-tusk lance in clothing decorated with nearly 10,000 laboriously carved mammoth-tusk beads, as well as pieces including a belt decorated with teeth plucked from the skulls of over a hundred foxes.

With archaeologists estimating it took up to 10,000 hours of work to carve these beads alone – roughly equivalent to five years' full-time effort for one individual working forty hours a week – some have suggested that these boys must have enjoyed something resembling noble status, and as a result that these graves indicate formal inequality among these foragers.[11] It is at best tenuous evidence of institutional hierarchy; after all, some egalitarian foraging societies like the Ju/'hoansi made similarly elaborate items. But the amount of time and skill involved in manufacturing the mammoth beads and other items suggests that, like the indigenous people of the Pacific North West, the annual work cycle for them was seasonal and that in the winter months people often focused their energies on more artistic, indoor pursuits.

In occasionally storing food and organising their working year to accommodate intense seasonal variations, European and Asian foraging populations took an important step towards adopting a longer-term, more future-focused relationship with work. In doing so, they also developed a different relationship with scarcity, one that resembles that which shapes our economic life now in some important respects. But even if they needed to plan ahead more than foragers in warmer climates, they remained largely confident in the at least seasonal providence of their environments. Somewhat ironically, it was only when the earth began to warm 18,000 years ago that anyone would take the first fateful steps towards food production, and so lay the foundations of our species, increasing energy footprint and obsession with work.

PART THREE

TOILING IN THE FIELDS

7

Leaping off the Edge

On the evening of Saturday 19 October 1957, hikers negotiating the cliffs near Govett's Leap in Australia's Blue
Mountains found a pair of spectacles, a pipe, a compass
and a hat, all neatly arranged on top of a folded mackin-
tosh raincoat. It was later established that these belonged to
Professor Vere Gordon Childe, the recently retired, world-
famous and notoriously eccentric archaeologist. He was
booked in as a guest at the nearby Carrington Hotel and had
been reported missing earlier that day by his driver when
he failed to show up to be ferried to a lunch appointment
after a morning hiking in the mountains. The search party
that was dispatched to investigate the rocks 500 feet below
Govett's Leap returned with the professor's lifeless body.
After a brief investigation, the local coroner concluded
that the short-sighted professor had lost his footing after
abandoning his spectacles and fallen to his death in a hor-
rible accident.

Twenty-three years later the coroner's verdict was
proved wrong.

A year before Childe checked into the Carrington
Hotel, the sixty-four-year-old had bid farewell to a long

and distinguished career, first as Professor of Archaeology at Edinburgh University and later as the director of the University of London's Institute of Archaeology. Several days before plunging from Govett's Leap, Childe wrote to Professor William Grimes, his successor at the institute. Childe requested that Grimes kept the contents of the letter to himself for at least a decade in order to avoid any scandal. Grimes did as he was asked. He only revealed Childe's secret in 1980, when he submitted the letter to the leading archaeology journal, *Antiquity*, who published it in full.[1]

'Prejudice against suicide is utterly irrational,' Childe wrote to Grimes. 'To end his life deliberately is in fact something that distinguishes *Homo sapiens* from other animals even better than ceremonial burial of the dead. An accident may easily and naturally befall me on a mountain cliff,' he said, and added that 'life ends best when one is happy and strong'.

Having remained resolutely single throughout his life, the prospect of a lonely retirement on an inadequate pension played some role in Childe's decision to end his life. But his letter to William Grimes was, above all, an unemotional meditation on the meaninglessness of a life without useful work to do. In it he expressed the view that the elderly were no more than parasitic rentiers who leeched off the energy and hard work of the young. He also expressed no sympathy for the elderly who continued to work, determined to prove that they were still useful. He insisted that they were obstacles in the path to progress and robbed 'younger and more efficient successors' of the opportunity for promotion.

Born in Sydney in 1892, Childe was the foremost prehistorian of the interwar years, publishing hundreds of influential papers and twenty books over the course of his career. But at the age of sixty-four he had reached the dismal conclusion that he had no 'further useful contributions to make' and that much of his work, in hindsight, had been in vain.

'I actually fear that the balance of evidence is against theories that I have espoused or even in favour of those against which I am strongly biased,' he confessed.

Childe's suicide was a final revolutionary act in a life in which revolutions played a big role. An avowed Marxist, his youthful hopes that the carnage of the First World War might accelerate the end of the imperial era and inspire a global communist-style revolution saw him ostracised by many in Australia. The same views also resulted in him later being barred from travelling to the United States, and Britain's secret service, MI5, declaring him a 'person of interest' and routinely monitoring his written correspondence. But his most revolutionary work was in the far less politically incendiary field of prehistory. He was the first to insist that our ancestors' transition from hunting and gathering to farming was so profoundly transformative that it should be thought of as a 'revolution' rather than merely a transformation. This was an idea he nurtured and expanded throughout his career, but which found its clearest expression in his most important book, *Man Makes Himself*, published in 1936.

For most of his career, the principal tools used by archaeologists were trowels, brushes, buckets, sieves, panama hats and their imaginations. Towards the end of his life Childe grew increasingly worried that many of his best ideas would be proved worthless. By then archaeologists had begun to work far more with geologists, climatologists and ecologists, and their discoveries were revealing that the story of the transition to agriculture was far more complex than that which he described in *Man Makes Himself*. It also now seems increasingly likely that some of what he thought were consequences of the adoption of agriculture – like people living in permanent settlements – were actually among its causes. But where Gordon Childe was absolutely right was in his assessment that in broad historical terms the transition to agriculture was as transformative as any other that came before or after it. If anything, he underestimated its significance. For while previous and later technologically driven transformations – from the mastering of fire to the development of the internal combustion engine – also dramatically increased the amount of energy humans were able to harness and put to work, the agricultural revolution not only enabled the rapid growth of the human population but also fundamentally transformed how people engaged with the world around them: how they reckoned their place in the cosmos and their relationships with the gods, with their land, with their environments and with each other.

Gordon Childe was not especially interested in culture, at least not in the same way that his colleagues in the Social Anthropology Department were. Also, just like most of his contemporaries, he had no reason to believe that small-scale hunter-gatherers like Australia's Aboriginals might have enjoyed lives of relative leisure or imagined their environments to be eternally provident. As a result, he never made the connection between the profound hollowness he felt when he believed he was no longer able to contribute usefully through his work with the cultural and economic changes that arose organically out of our embrace of agriculture.

Nor did he imagine that the assumptions underwriting the economic system that left him anxious about how he would fund his retirement, ideas that claim idleness is a sin and industry is a virtue, were not part of humankind's eternal struggle. They were also by-products of the transition from foraging to farming.

To the MI5 employees who rifled through archaeological field reports in search of conspiratorial code in Gordon Childe's mail, the word 'revolution' conjured images of treasonous plots. But to Childe's colleagues at the university, it invoked the gentler image of an established theory quietly buckling under the weight of its own contradictions and so clearing the ground for new ways of trying to solve old problems.

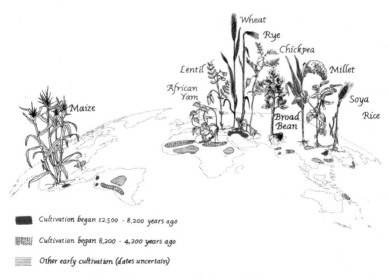

Wheat
Rye
Chickpea
Lentil
Millet
African Yam
Soya
Maize
Broad Bean
Rice

■ Cultivation began 12,500 - 8,200 years ago

▨ Cultivation began 8,200 - 4,200 years ago

▤ Other early cultivation (dates uncertain)

Independent centres of plant domestication

When viewed against the backdrop of millions of years of human history, the transition from foraging to food production was as revolutionary as anything before or since. It transformed how people lived, what they thought about the world, how they worked, and rapidly increased the amount of energy people could capture and put to work. It also happened in the blink of an evolutionary eye. But none of those who were part of this revolution thought of themselves as doing anything particularly remarkable. After all, viewed against the span of a single human lifetime or even against that of several consecutive generations, the adoption of agriculture was a gradual transition during which people and a whole series of plants and animals slowly but inexorably bound their destinies ever closer to one another, and in doing so changed one another forever.

Over a 5,000-year period beginning a little over ten millennia ago, a sequence of unrelated populations in at least eleven distinct geographical locations across Asia, Africa, Oceania and the Americas began cultivating some crops and rearing a variety of domesticated animals. Quite why or how this happened nearly simultaneously remains something of a mystery. It may have been an astonishing coincidence. It is far more likely, though, that this at first apparently unlikely convergence was catalysed by a series of climatic, environmental, cultural, demographic and possibly even evolutionary drivers.[2]

The oldest clear evidence for plant domestication occurs in the gentle valleys and rolling hills of the Levant, a region that extends across modern Palestine, Lebanon, Syria and Turkey. People there started to experiment with cultivating wild wheat and legumes like chickpeas from around

12,500 years ago, and from around 11,000 years ago some domesticated strains of wheat begin to appear in the archaeological record. Besides dogs, whose association with humans stretches back at least 14,700 years, if not a whole lot earlier,[3] the oldest evidence of systematic animal domestication comes from the Middle East where there is good evidence of people rearing and herding goats and sheep from around 10,500 years ago. Another truly ancient crucible of agriculture was mainland China, where communities in the floodplains of the Yangtze, Yellow and Xiliaohe Rivers cultivated millet and reared pigs from around 11,000 years ago. A few thousand years later they also began to farm with primitive variants of what are now the most important regional staples in East Asia, among them soya beans and rice.[4]

It took four millennia before agriculture was established as the principal subsistence strategy for people settled across the Middle East. By then several important plant and animal species including barley, lentils, peas, broad beans, chickpeas, wheat, pigs, cattle, goats and sheep had bound their destinies to the women and men that reared, nurtured and consumed them.[5] It was also around this time that agriculture began to take off in other places, with the result that by 6,000 years ago farming was a well-established subsistence strategy across many parts of Asia, Arabia and North, South and Central America.

The Natufians are thought to be the first people anywhere to experiment systematically with farming. But we have no

181

idea what languages they spoke, or what they called themselves. This population, who are associated with parts of the Middle East from 12,500 to 9,500 years ago, owe the suitably ancient-sounding name to the imagination of a far more recent pioneer in the world of work, Dorothy Garrod, an archaeologist and a contemporary of Vere Gordon Childe. She named the Natufians after one of the archaeological sites where she found evidence of this culture, the Wadi al Natuf, in what was then British Palestine.

In 1913, Garrod became the first woman to graduate from Cambridge University with a degree in history. Several years later, after taking a break from her studies to assist the British war effort, she acquired a postgraduate qualification in archaeology and anthropology from Oxford University, and determined it was her destiny to be a field archaeologist. Unsurprisingly, she struggled to persuade anyone to recruit her on an important dig. Back then archaeological field sites were the preserve of gin-soaked men with pipes clenched in their teeth, who believed that women were not built to cope with the rigours of excavating remote sites in alien lands.

As quietly spoken as she was unflappable, Garrod did not consider herself a feminist, but she was convinced that women were every bit as capable of roughing it in the field as their male peers. So was the French archaeologist Abbé Breuil, with whom she studied in Paris for a couple of years after leaving Oxford. In 1925 and 1926, he sent her to lead a series of minor digs in Gibraltar on his behalf. After she returned to Paris, having successfully retrieved and reassembled a now-famous Neanderthal skull known as the 'Devil's Tower Child', her male colleagues had little choice but to reluctantly acknowledge her skills.

In 1928, with her reputation as a no-nonsense excavator firmly established, Garrod was invited to lead a series of new excavations on and around Mount Carmel, on behalf of the American School of Prehistoric Research and the British School of Anthropology in Jerusalem. Defying convention, she assembled an almost entirely female team for the Mount Carmel Project, a good number of whom were recruited from local Palestinian villages. Over a five-year period, beginning in 1929, she led twelve major digs in and around Mount Carmel, and in the process pioneered the use of aerial photography as an aid to excavation. The results of her efforts were published in a 1937 book, *The Stone Age of Mount Carmel*, which she co-authored with another gender-stereotype-busting archaeologist, Dorothea Bates.

The Stone Age of Mount Carmel was groundbreaking. It was the first study of any place to chart a continuous archaeological sequence spanning nearly half a million years of human history. It was also the first to include sequences of material from both Neanderthal and *Homo sapiens* populations. But most importantly of all it was the first to propose that the area around Mount Carmel was home to a distinctive regional culture around 12,000 years ago, and that that culture was responsible for the invention of agriculture.

No one in the Archaeology Department at Cambridge University now remembers whether or not Dorothy Garrod, who held a professorship there from 1939 through to her retirement in 1952, liked to end her days with a sherry

183

or a gin and tonic in the senior fellows common room at Newnham College where she lived. It was customary to do so before dinners in college, and as the first woman ever to be appointed to a full professorship at Cambridge, she must have often needed a drink after spending a day suffering the snide comments of some of her male colleagues. But the ever-expanding wealth of new material, supporting her theory that the Natufians played a pivotal role in the transition to agriculture, includes evidence that they may well have also been the first people anywhere to relax with an alcoholic drink after a day's work. Analysis of microscopic chemical residues retrieved from the stone pestles and mortars used by Natufians reveal that these were not only used to pound wheat, barley and flax into flours to bake simple unleavened breads,[6] but also that they were also used for fermenting grains and brewing beer.

The researchers who established that the Natufians were enthusiastic home-brewers are almost certainly right to believe that the discovery of beer hastened the Natufians' embrace of agriculture and hence a regular supply of grains to ferment. They may also be right that the beer was used mainly for ritual purposes.[7]

But archaeologists and anthropologists alike are often too quick to find the sacred in the profane, especially when it comes to sex and drugs. In the same way that some of the famous frescoes were ultimately soft porn, the Natufians may have drunk beer for the same reasons most of us do now.

The Natufians' foraging ancestors were almost certainly not beer drinkers. But they were versatile and skilful foragers, who routinely made use of more than a hundred individual plant species, among them wheat, barley,[8] wild grapes, almonds and olives. They were also probably not as singularly focused on only meeting their immediate needs as people like the Ju/'hoansi. The sharper transitions between seasons in the Levant during the last glacial period meant that even if they lived from hand to mouth for much of the year, they no doubt spent some periods in the year working harder than others in order to acquire small surpluses to help tide them over through cold, dark winters.

Some tentative and surprising new evidence suggests that at least one, presumably very innovative, community who lived near the Sea of Galilee some 23,000 years ago conducted some early experiments with cultivation. This supports the idea that foragers in the Levant had a considerably more delayed-return mindset than others like the Ju/'hoansi. Sadly for this group, the archaeological evidence also suggests that all they succeeded in doing was hastening the evolution of some of the weed species that to this day still frustrate wheat farmers.[9]

Early experiments with growing food notwithstanding, grains aren't thought to have formed a major part of the Natufians' ancestors' diets before the current warm interglacial period began. Back then, wild stands of wheat, barley and rye that grew in the Levant were not especially prolific. They also only ever produced measly grains that sometimes must have been barely worth the trouble of collecting and then threshing. It would take a significant, and relatively abrupt, change in climate before these particular plants would become sufficiently productive to bind their destiny to that of the humans who occasionally harvested them.

Some more established theories linking climate change to the adoption of farming are broadly based on the hypothesis that the slow transition from the last cold glacial period to the current warm, interglacial period, between 18,000 and 8,000 years ago, catalysed a whole series of ecological changes that in turn created terrible hardships for some established hunter-gatherer populations. They suggest that necessity was the mother of invention and that foragers had little option but to experiment with new strategies to survive as familiar staples were replaced by new species. Newer research in a series of related fields has since reaffirmed that climate-change-induced scarcity played an important role in pushing some human populations down the path towards being food producers. But they also suggest that periods of climate-change-induced abundance played an important role in the process too.

The earth is currently in the grip of its fifth major ice age, known as the Quaternary Ice Age. The Quaternary Ice Age began around 2.58 million years ago when the Arctic ice caps began to form, but it has been characterised by periodic swings between briefer warm 'interglacial' and cool 'glacial' periods. During glacial periods average global temperatures are roughly 5 degrees Celsius cooler than during interglacial periods and, because lots of water is locked up in ice sheets, they are also considerably drier. Glacial periods typically last around 100,000 years, but interglacial periods – like the one we are in now – are fleeting, lasting only between 10,000 and 20,000 years. It also often takes up to ten millennia from the end of a glacial period for global temperatures to climb to levels historically associated with warmer interglacial periods.

Sunspot activity, cosmic radiation, volcanic eruptions and celestial collisions have all played a role in shifting the delicate balance of earth's climate in the past. Fossil-fuel-fixated humans are by no means the first or the only living organism to have substantially changed the atmospheric composition sufficiently to radically transform the climate. We still have a long way to go before we make an impact comparable to that made by carbon dioxide-eating cyanobacteria during the great oxidation event that preceded the efflorescence of oxygen-breathing life forms on early earth. But the main reasons that the earth fluctuates between frosty glacial and milder interglacial periods are shifts in the alignment of the earth's axis – the earth's tendency to wobble slowly as it spins – and changes in the path of its orbit around the sun as a result of being nudged back and forth by the gravitational pull of other big celestial bodies.

The earth entered the current warmer period as a result of a convergence of these cycles some 18,000 years ago. But it was not until 3,300 years later that anyone would have noticed that anything fundamental had changed. Then, in the matter of a few short decades, temperatures in Greenland suddenly soared by a glacier-melting 15 degrees Celsius and in southern Europe by a more modest, but still utterly transformative, 5 degrees Celsius. This period of rapid warming, and the two millennia that followed, is called the Bolling Allerød Interstadial. Over this brief period, the Middle East was transformed from a chilly dry steppe ecosystem into a warm, wet, temperate Eden, hosting forests of oak, olive, almond and pistachio, and grasslands replete with wild barley and wheat, where vast herds of contented gazelle grazed while keeping a watchful eye for lions, cheetahs and hungry Natufians.

But it wasn't only the warmer, wetter conditions that inspired the Natufians to embrace something resembling a form of proto-agriculture during this period. Coincident with the retreat of the ice sheets, a small but significant change in the composition of gases in the earth's atmosphere created conditions that enabled cereals, like wheat, to thrive at the expense of some other plant species.

Not all plants do the work of transforming the inorganic carbon in carbon dioxide into the organic carbon-based compounds in their living cells in the same way. Some, such as wheat, beans, barley, rice and rye, deploy an enzyme – rubisco – to kidnap passing molecules of carbon dioxide and then metabolise them into organic compounds. Rubisco, though, is a clumsy kidnapper and is in the habit of occasionally taking the oxygen molecules hostage by mistake – a process called photorespiration. This is a costly error. It wastes the energy and nutrients that went into building the rubisco and also causes the plant to incur an opportunity cost in terms of its growth. The frequency with which the rubisco binds with oxygen is more or less proportional to the amount of oxygen relative to carbon dioxide in the air. As a result, these 'C_3' plants, as biologists refer to them, are particularly responsive to changes in atmospheric carbon dioxide, because increasing the proportion of CO_2 in the atmosphere increases the photosynthesis rate and decreases the photorespiration rate. By contrast, C_4 plants like sugar cane and millet, which comprise nearly a quarter of all plant species, metabolise carbon dioxide in a far more orderly fashion. They have evolved a series of mechanisms that ensure they don't waste energy on photo-respiration. Consequently they are relatively indifferent to small increases in carbon dioxide levels but then outperform C_3 plants when carbon dioxide levels decline.

Analysis of Greenlandic ice cores shows that the end of the last glacial period was marked by a surge in atmospheric carbon dioxide. This process stimulated increased photo-synthesis in C_3 plants by between 25 and 50 per cent, so encouraging them to grow bigger and outmuscle C_4 plants in the competition for soil-based nutrients.[10] This in turn stimulated higher levels of nitrogen in the soil, giving C_3 plants a further push.[11] As the Middle East warmed, several species of C_3 plants – most notably various grains, legumes, pulses and fruiting trees including wheat, barley, lentils, almonds and pistachios – thrived, while a whole range of other plant species that were better adapted to colder conditions fell into decline.

With a warming climate and a more carbon dioxide-rich atmosphere causing some familiar food species to dis-appear while simultaneously ratcheting up the productivity of others, local populations, through no fault of their own, became increasingly dependent on far fewer but much more prolific plants.

Foragers are opportunists, and, to the Natufians, the warm Bolling Allerød period was an opportunity to eat well for much less effort. Their summers became balmier, their winters lost their brutal edge, it rained more frequently, and food yields increased so much that over the following centuries many Natufians cheerfully abandoned their ancestors' once necessarily mobile existence in favour of a far more sedentary life in small, permanent villages. Some Natufians even went to the trouble of building sturdy drystone-walled dwellings with carefully cobbled floors surrounding inset stone hearths – the oldest intentionally built permanent structures discovered anywhere. And if graveyards adjacent to these villages are anything to go by, these settlements were occupied continuously over many consecutive generations. Being sedentary also meant that the Natufians were happy to spend far more time and energy than anyone before them on building and using unwieldy tools that could not be easily carried from one camp to the next. Most important among these are the very heavy limestone and basalt pestles that they used to powder grains, pulp tubers and, it seems, make beer.

With so much food about, the Natufians were also able to develop other skills. Beautifully decorated stone and bone tools, erotically charged stone sculptures and elegant jewellery recovered from Natufian archaeological sites suggest they were happy to spend time making their tools, homes and selves look good. We know nothing of the songs they sang, the music they made or what they believed, but if the care they took to ensure that their dead ventured into the afterlife adorned in finery is anything to go by, they had a rich ritual life too.

Natufian graveyards tell another important story about their lives. Osteological analyses of Natufian bones and teeth show that they rarely suffered from systematic dietary deficiencies, or endured the sustained periods of dietary stress comparable with early farming communities. They also indicate that Natufians did not have to cope with too much in the way of arduous physical labour, especially when compared to later farming populations. Even so, it appears that the Natufians must have endured some difficulties. The osteological evidence shows that few Natufians in the permanent settlements lived much beyond thirty years old, perhaps because they had not yet come to grips with some of the very specific hygiene-related requirements necessary to live in a permanent village.

The Natufians remained keen hunters during this period and routinely ate aurochs (the oversized ancestors of modern cattle), wild sheep, ibexes and wild asses. They consumed snakes, pine martens, hares and tortoises as well, pulled freshwater fish from the river Jordan and trapped waterfowl along the river's banks. But the piles of gazelle bones that litter Natufian archaeological sites suggest that these were by far their favoured source of protein. And in conjunction with grooved stones that have no obvious purpose other than to straighten wooden arrow shafts, the Natufian appetite for gazelles also suggests that they had mastered archery in order to bring down these animals, among the swiftest and most alert of all ungulates. As foragers in southern and eastern Africa know all too well, it is near impossible to hunt creatures like gazelles without good projectile weaponry.

Wild wheat generates much lower food yields than modern domesticated variants, which is why consumers who eat loaves baked from 'ancient grains' need deep pockets. But compared to most other wild plant foods, wild cereals are almost uniquely high-yielding. One of the ancient ancestors of modern wheats, emmer wheat, can achieve yields of up to 3.5 metric tonnes per hectare in the right conditions, but yields of between 1 and 1.5 metric tonnes per hectare are more common. Einkorn, another ancestor of some modern wheats, can generate yields of up to 2 metric tonnes per hectare.

In the 1960s, Jack Harlan, a plant agronomist and an early cheerleader for the importance of maintaining plant biodiversity, was inspired to conduct a couple of experiments when, while travelling in south-eastern Turkey, he stumbled across 'vast seas of primitive wild wheats' on the lower slopes of Karacadag, a volcanic mountain. How much wheat might an ancient Middle Eastern hunter-gatherer have been able to harvest from a field like this in an hour? he wondered.

In one experiment, Harlan measured how much wild wheat he could harvest by hand. In another he measured how much he could harvest using a flint and wood sickle similar to those retrieved by Dorothy Garrod some thirty years earlier. Using just his hands, he was able to recover a couple of kilograms of grain in an hour. Using the sickle to cut the wheat before hand-stripping the grains, he was able to increase that yield by a further 25 per cent. Doing so, he noted, resulted in less wastage but most importantly helped him to spare his soft 'urbanised hands' from being rubbed raw. On the strength of this experiment, he concluded that a 'family group, beginning harvesting near the base of Karacadag and working upslope as the season progressed could easily harvest . . . over a three-week span or more and, without working very hard . . . more grain than the family could possibly consume in a year'.[12]

Reconstruction of a Natufian stone sickle

If foragers like the Ju/'hoansi enjoyed a form of affluence without abundance because they had modest desires that were easily met, and lived in an environment that was only ever capable of sustainably meeting those modest desires, the Natufians enjoyed a form of affluence based on far greater material abundance. For a while their landscape was nearly as spontaneously productive per hectare as those of the later agricultural societies with much bigger populations that followed in their wake. But importantly the Natufians didn't have to work nearly as hard. Where future grain farmers would be held captive to an agricultural calendar, with specific seasons for ploughing, preparing, planting, irrigating, weeding, harvesting and processing their crops, all the Natufians had to do was wander out to established fields of wild stands of wheat, harvest and process them. But this abundance was seasonal. They needed to prepare for future lean seasons, with the result that some periods spent harvesting and storing additional food were far busier than others. The same archaeologists who found the evidence for the Natufians' beer brewing also found micro-botanical traces in some large stone mortars used by Natufians, which indicate that these were used for storing grains as long as 13,000 years ago, and that their discovery of beer was probably a food-storage-related accident.[13]

This may be the only indisputable evidence for food storage by early Natufians, but this does not mean that the Natufians did not find other ways of storing and preserving food. There is evidence to suggest, for example, that they made baskets from jute, kenaf, flax and hemp plant fibres that have long since decayed into dust. It is also possible that the distinctive pits found in the cobbled floors of some stone Natufian dwellings were larders of a sort. And given the prolific numbers of gazelle they killed, it is almost certain that they occasionally preserved meat, probably by drying it.

Cereals and legumes were by no means the only floral beneficiaries of a warming climate. Many other plants prospered too, and during this period of abundance Natufians dined on a host of different tubers, fungi, nuts, gums, fruits, stalks, leaves and flowers.[14] But what likely nudged the Natufians further down the line from being casual consumers of grains with a taste for sour beer into intensive managers of wild cereals and accumulators of big surpluses was another, far less cheerful period of climatic upheaval.

Over the course of the first 1,800 years of the Bolling Allerød, the climate cooled gradually but never to the extent that anyone would have noticed much of a difference from one year to the next. Then, sometime around 12,900 years ago, temperatures suddenly plunged. In Greenland average temperatures fell by as much as 10 degrees Celsius over two decades, with the result that glaciers that had been in full retreat began to rapidly advance again, tundra refroze and the ice caps began to muscle their way rapidly southwards. Outside of the polar regions, temperature declines were less severe but no less transformative. Across most of Europe and the Middle East, it must have seemed to many that they had returned to a glacial period almost overnight.

It is uncertain what caused this sudden cold snap, referred to by palaeoclimatologists as the Younger Dryas. Explanations have ranged from cosmic supernovae that messed with the earth's protective ozone layer to a massive meteor impact somewhere in North America.[15] They are also unclear as to how severe the ecological impact was in different locations. There is, for example, no evidence to indicate that the levels of atmospheric carbon dioxide declined during the Younger Dryas, or that it had much impact at all in places like southern and eastern Africa. It is also uncertain whether during this period the Levant was cold and dry like the preceding glacial period or whether it was cold but still relatively wet.[16] But there is no doubt that the sudden and unwelcome return of long, freezing winters and abbreviated cool summers caused substantial declines in the yields of many of the key plant foods the Natufians had grown used to over preceding millennia, and that as a result they will have simultaneously lost faith in both the providence of their environment and their ability to spend most of the year focused only on meeting their immediate needs.

We know that not long after the temperatures plummeted, the Natufians were forced to abandon their permanent villages because the immediate environments were no longer sufficiently food-dense to support them year-round. We also know that after 1,300 long years of miserable weather, temperatures suddenly surged upwards again, just as abruptly as they had fallen.

But beyond this we can only speculate as to how they coped with these changes and, more importantly, how their efforts to make sense of them changed their relationships with their environments. If the archaeological record for the period immediately following the Younger Dryas is anything to go by, these changes were profound.

The first obvious indication that by then foragers in the Levant had lost confidence in the eternal providence of their environment are the broken remains of purpose-built granaries, the most impressive of which had storage areas sufficient to store up to ten tonnes of wheat. These were excavated by archaeologists near the banks of the Dead Sea in Jordan and have been dated to when the Younger Dryas came to an abrupt end 11,500 years ago.[17] They were not just simple chambers; these mud, stone and straw buildings had elevated wooden floors that were cleverly designed specifically to keep pests at bay and prevent damp. Tellingly, they were located adjacent to what appear to have been food-distribution buildings. It is also clear that these were not spontaneous designs; even if archaeologists have not yet found evidence for older, more primitive granaries, the ones they excavated were the product of many generations of experimentation and elaboration.

But by far the most compelling evidence that something fundamental had changed over the course of the Younger Dryas was a more ambitious and skilful construction than even the largest of these granaries. And this took the form of what for now is thought to be the oldest example of monumental architecture in the ancient world: a complex of buildings, chambers, megaliths and passageways discovered at Göbekli Tepe in the hills near Orencik in south-eastern Turkey in 1994. With construction at Göbekli Tepe having begun during the tenth millennium BC, it is also by far the oldest evidence of large groups of people anywhere coming together to work on a very big project that had nothing obvious to do with the food quest.

The ruins at Göbekli Tepe were once described by their discoverer, the German archaeologist Klaus Schmidt, as a 'Stone Age zoo'.[18] It is a fair description of what is arguably the most enigmatic of all prehistoric monuments. But it was not only because of the near-countless animal bones, from some twenty-one different mammal and sixty bird species, which have been recovered from the site and which are thought to be the leftovers from sumptuous feasts, that persuaded Schmidt to describe it as a zoo. It was also because carved into each of the estimated 240 limestone monoliths organised into series of imposing dry-stone-walled enclosures is a veritable ark of ancient animal life. Included among the images are scorpions, adders, spiders, lizards, snakes, foxes, bears, boars, ibis, vultures, hyenas and wild asses. Most pose in low relief and take the form of engravings. But some of the most impressive among them are carved in high relief or take the form of free-standing statues and statuettes.

Schmidt's zoo analogy didn't end with the animals alone. For presiding over this lithic menagerie and standing at the centre of each enclosure is a procession of giant limestone zookeepers in the form of matched pairs of T-shaped monoliths. Each of these stands five to seven metres tall and the largest weigh up to eight tonnes. The most impressive among these formidable slabs of precisely worked limestone are very obviously anthropomorphic. They have human arms and hands carved into them as well as ornamental belts, patterned garments and loincloths.

There is nothing modest about this monument. Göbekli Tepe's builders were obviously not restrained in their ambitions by the jealousy-fuelled mockery that sustained the fierce egalitarianism of small-scale hunter-gatherers like the Ju/'hoansi. They also clearly did not consider time away from the food quest as time for private pleasures. Constructing this complex of winding passageways linking rectangular chambers and imposing ovulate enclosures, the largest of which has a similar diameter to the dome in St Paul's Cathedral in London, took a considerable amount of time, energy, organisation and, above all, work.

Only a small proportion of the site has been excavated, but at over nine hectares in size it is many orders of magnitude larger than Stonehenge and three times larger than Athens' Parthenon. So far, seven enclosures have been excavated, and geophysical surveys suggest that there are at least thirteen more buried in the hill.

Unlike many later monuments, this complex was built piecemeal. New enclosures were added periodically over the course of a thousand years, with some older structures being back-filled and new ones built on top of them.

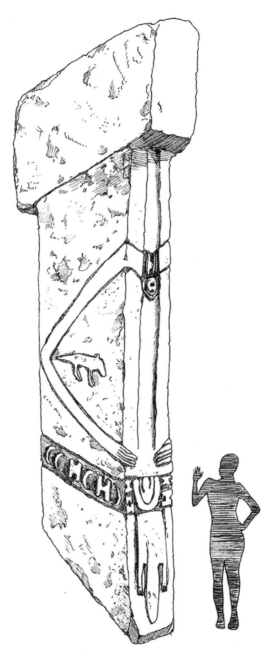

A monolithic 'zookeeper' at Göbekli Tepe

Construction was also almost certainly seasonal and done in the winter months. And, given that people back then were lucky to live beyond forty years, it is unlikely that anyone who participated in the start of the construction on any one of the bigger enclosures would have still been alive to witness its completion.

Up until the discovery of Göbekli Tepe, the established narrative of how early farming societies were able to build some monuments was simple. Buildings this big were as much monuments to the surpluses generated by intensive agriculture as they were to the ingenuity and vanity of their makers, and the might of the gods or kings they were built to honour. This is because the building of structures like these required not only leaders with the ambition and power to organise their construction, but also plenty of skilled and unskilled manpower to do the hard work.

But ever since Klaus Schmidt and his team started burrowing into the hill at Göbekli Tepe in 1994, it has become clear that this narrative was much too simple. And the deeper Schmidt and his growing battalion of archaeologists dug, and the more samples they dated, the more it revealed that the historical dynamic between agriculture, culture and work was far more complex, and far more interesting, than anyone had ever imagined. Göbekli Tepe, they revealed, was not a monument made by well-established farming peoples. Instead construction of it began around 11,600 years ago, more than a millennium earlier than the appearance of domesticated cereals or animal bones in the archaeological record.[19]

Enigmatic sites like Göbekli Tepe are easily forced into serving as props for all sorts of fantasies. It has been variously declared to be the remains of the biblical Tower of Babel, an oversized catalogue of the creatures that were herded into Noah's Ark, and a temple complex constructed under the supervision of an ancient race of guardian angels assigned by God to watch over Eden.

Based on the prevalence of hyenas, vultures and other scavengers engraved in the pillars, as well as the recent recovery of some human skull parts that show signs of manipulation and decoration, some have speculated that Göbekli Tepe may, for a while at least, have housed an ancient 'skull cult'.[20] Other possible interpretations of the site by archaeologists have veered between the sacred, in the form of a temple complex, and the profane, in the form of an ancient nightclub that hosted great feasts.

Göbekli Tepe will always cling to its deepest secrets. But at least its importance in the history of our species' relationship with work is clear. For beyond being a monument to the first experiments with agriculture, it is the first evidence anywhere of people securing sufficient surplus energy to work over many consecutive generations to achieve a grand vision unrelated to the immediate challenge of securing more energy, and one that was intended to endure long beyond the lives of its builders.

Göbekli Tepe may not be anything near the scale and complexity of the Pyramids or Mayan temples built by more recent agricultural societies. But its construction must have demanded a similarly complex division of labour and skilled masons, artists, carvers, designers and carpenters, who depended on others to feed them. It is, in other words, the first unambiguous evidence of a society in which many people had something resembling full-time, highly specialised jobs.

8

Feasts and Famines

Some 2,000 years after the first monoliths at Göbekli Tepe were erected, something persuaded dozens if not hundreds of ancient Anatolians to assemble there and then spend months – perhaps even years – systematically filling in each of its deep passageways, chambers and enclosures with rubble and sand until the site was transformed into a nondescript hill that within a few short years would become overgrown and dissolve into an already undulating landscape.

For at least a thousand years after the construction of Göbekli Tepe, foraging still played an important role in ancient Anatolian life. The archaeological record indicates that, initially at least, there were many communities in the Levant who turned their noses up at the idea of engaging in even low-level food production. But over time, as communities across the Middle East grew more dependent on farmed grains, their fields and farms displaced wild animal and plant populations, making it increasingly hard for even the most determined foragers to sustain themselves by hunting and gathering alone.

As a result, by the time of Göbekli Tepe's inhumation, 9,600 years ago, much of the Middle East had been transformed into a network of small agricultural settlements and at least one town-size settlement, Çatalhöyük, in south central Turkey, which at its peak is thought to have been home to more than 6,000 people. These settlements stretched from the Sinai Peninsula through to eastern Turkey and inland along the banks of the Euphrates and Tigris Rivers. Domesticated variants of wheat and other crops, as well as the tools used to harvest, process and store them, litter many regional archaeological sites from this period, as do the bones of the sheep, goats, cattle and pigs – even if some of the highly distinctive physical features we associate with fully domesticated cattle and pigs - like the humps on some cattle breeds - only appear widely in the archaeological record.[1] There is also evidence to suggest that some Levantines had even taken to the seas and settled in Crete and Cyprus, which would in time serve as a launch pad for the expansion of farming people into southern Europe and beyond.

There is no doubt the mass burial of Göbekli Tepe's giant zookeepers alongside their silent stone menageries was a very well-organised act of vandalism, one that required similar levels of commitment to that which its makers brought to the job of building it in the first place. Humans, like masked weavers, often seem to take as much pleasure in destroying things as they do in making them, and history is punctuated by many other similarly monumental acts of architectural erasure. The clumsy dynamiting of the temples and tombs in the ancient Semitic city of Palmyra a few short hours' drive from Göbekli Tepe by the angry young men of Daesh is just one of many recent examples.

We will never know what motivated the Anatolians to bury Göbekli Tepe under rubble. But if its construction was a celebration of the abundance its builders enjoyed as a result of learning to intensively manage wild crops and accrue and store surpluses at the end of the Younger Dryas, it is tempting to imagine that two millennia later their descendants destroyed it convinced that the serpents carved into Göbekli Tepe's monoliths had banished them into a life of eternal toil. For, by any measure, early agricultural populations lived tougher lives than the builders of Göbekli Tepe did. Indeed, it would take several thousand years before any farming populations anywhere had the energy, resources or inclination to devote much time to building grand monuments to either themselves or their gods.

As farming societies grew more productive and captured more energy from their environments, energy appeared to be scarcer and people had to work harder to meet their basic needs. This was because, up until the Industrial Revolution, any gains in productivity farming peoples generated as a result of working harder, adopting new technologies, techniques or crops, or acquiring new land were always soon gobbled up by populations that quickly grew to numbers that could not be sustained. As a result, while agricultural societies continued to expand, prosperity was usually only ever fleeting, and scarcity evolved from an occasional inconvenience that foragers stoically endured every once in a while to a near perennial problem. In many respects, the hundreds of generations of farmers who lived before the fossil-fuel revolution paid for our extended lifespans and expanded waistlines now by enduring lives that were mostly shorter, bleaker and harder than ours, and almost certainly tougher than those of their foraging ancestors.

It is hard to argue that a long and miserable life is any better than an abbreviated and joyful one. Even so, life expectancy is still a rough proxy for material and physical well-being. Demographers typically use two measures of life expectancy: life expectancy at birth and life expectancy after reaching the age of fifteen. These numbers tend to be wildly different in all pre-industrial societies because the high numbers of deaths during childbirth, infancy and early childhood send the total average plummeting. Thus while foraging Ju/'hoansi and Hadzabe had a life expectancy at birth of thirty-six and thirty-four years respectively, those who reached puberty would be considered very unlucky if they did not live well beyond sixty.[2]

Comprehensive demographic data documenting births, deaths and age at death only ever began to be systematically collected anywhere in the eighteenth century. The first places to do so were Sweden, Finland and Denmark, and it is for this reason that their data appear in so many studies looking at changes in life expectancy around the time of the European Enlightenment and the Industrial Revolution. Life-expectancy data on earlier farming populations is more incomplete. It comes mainly from the osteological analysis of bones retrieved from ancient cemeteries. But this is hardly a reliable resource, not least because we have no idea as to whether the same funerary rights were afforded to everyone and hence how representative bones recovered from cemeteries are. Some later farming populations have the benefit of funerary inscriptions on gravestones and sometimes even partial census data, as in the case of Roman Egypt, but again this data is usually too incomplete to serve as anything more than a rough guide. Even if demographers are cautious when making pronouncements regarding life expectancy in early agricultural societies, there is broad consensus that before the Industrial Revolution kicked into gear and significant advances in medicine began to make an impact, the agricultural revolution did nothing at all to extend the lifespan of the average person, and indeed in many instances shortened it relative to the lifespans of remote foragers like the Ju/'hoansi. A comprehensive study of human remains from Imperial Rome, arguably the wealthiest agricultural society in history, for instance, shows that most men there were lucky to live much past the age of thirty,[3] and analysis of the earliest well-documented mortality figures, which come from Sweden between 1751 and 1759, suggests that the Ju/'hoansi and the Hadzabe expected to live slightly longer lives than Europeans on the cusp of the Industrial Revolution.[4]

Osteological studies of ancient bones and teeth also offer some insights into the quality of ancient people's lives. These show not only that early farmers had to work a whole lot harder than foragers did, but also that the rewards they gained from all this additional backbreaking effort were often marginal at best. Thus, when the remains of the small pampered elites are excluded from the equation, graveyards from all the world's great agricultural civilisations through to the Industrial Revolution tell an enduring tale of systematic nutritional deficiencies, anaemia, episodic famines and bone deformations as a result of repetitive, arduous labour, in addition to an alarming array of horrendous and sometimes fatal work-induced injuries. The biggest trove of very early farmers' bones comes from Çatalhöyük. These reveal a bleak picture of 'elevated exposure to disease and labour demands in response to community dependence on and production of domesticated plant carbohydrates, growing population size and density fuelled by elevated fertility, and increasing stresses due to heightened workload . . . over the nearly 12 centuries of settlement occupation'.[5]

Both ancient farmers and foragers suffered seasonal food shortages. During these periods children and adults alike would go to bed hungry some days and everyone would lose fat and muscle. But over longer periods of time farming societies were far more likely to suffer severe, existentially threatening famines than foragers.[6] Foraging may be much less productive and generate far lower energy yields than farming but it is also much less risky. This is firstly because foragers tended to live well within the natural limits imposed by their environments rather than skate perpetually on its dangerous verges, and secondly because where subsistence farmers typically relied on one or two staple crops, foragers in even the bleakest environments relied on dozens of different food sources and so were usually able to adjust their diets to align with an ecosystem's own dynamic responses to changing conditions. Typically, in complex ecosystems when weather one year proves unsuitable for one set of plant species, it almost inevitably suits others. But in farming societies when harvests fail as a result of, for example, a sustained drought, then catastrophe looms.

For early farming communities, droughts, floods and untimely frosts were by no means the only existential environmental risks. A whole host of pests and pathogens could also lay waste to their crops and herds. Those who focused their energy on rearing livestock learned quickly that one of the costs of selecting in favour of traits like docility was that it made their livestock easy pickings for predators, with the result that they required near constant supervision. It also meant that they had to build enclosures for their safety. But in penning their livestock into cramped enclosures at night, they inadvertently hastened the evolution and spread of a whole host of new viral bacterial and fungal pathogens. Still now few things evoke panic in livestock farming communities as easily as an outbreak of foot-and-mouth disease or bovine pleuropneumonia.

For cultivators, the list of potential threats was even longer. Like herders, they also had to cope with wild animals, but in their case the set of potentially problematic species was more than a few sharp-toothed apex predators in search of an easy meal. As remains the case for cultivators, in places like Kavango in northern Namibia, the range of pests extends well beyond the aphids, birds, rabbits, fungi, slugs and blowflies that frustrate urban horticulturalists. It includes several species that individually weigh more than a tonne, most notorious among them being elephants and hippos, and others, like monkeys and baboons, with the speed, agility and intelligence to find their way past any protective measures a diligent farmer might put in place, as well as a whole host of hungry insect species.

209

In domesticating some crops, early farmers also played a vital role in speeding the evolution of a whole series of pathogens, parasites and pests. Natural selection helped them to adapt to and piggyback on nearly every intervention the farmers made in their environments, and unsurprisingly followed closely behind farmers wherever they went. Foremost among these were weeds. While the concept of a weed remains simply a plant in the wrong place, there are a number of species of plants that, despite being considered undesirable from a human perspective and actively eradicated by farmers, owe their now extraordinary resilience to their adaptation to survive, despite the efforts of farmers who over the years have worked countless hours variously poisoning them or ripping them from the soil. Most notable among these are the extended family of Middle Eastern arable weeds that have since spread across the world and have adapted very quickly to every imaginable agricultural niche, and which have developed dormancy cycles closely aligned to those of wheat and barley.

Early farmers' livestock and crops were not the only victims of these new pathogens. The farmers were too. Their livestock in particular were fifth columnists who quietly introduced a whole new suite of lethal pathogens to humanity. Currently, zoonotic pathogens (those passed on by animals) account for nearly 60 per cent of all human diseases and three-quarters of all emerging diseases. This translates to roughly 2.5 billion cases of human sickness and 2.7 million deaths every year.[7] Some of these come from the rats, fleas and bedbugs that flourish in the dark corners of human settlements, but most come from the domestic animals we depend on for meat, milk, leather, eggs, transport, hunting and, ironically in the case of cats, pest control. Included among them are a bucketload of gastrointestinal diseases, bacterial pathogens like anthrax and tuberculosis, parasites like toxoplasmosis, and viral pathogens like measles and influenza. And our history of consuming wild animals from pangolins to bats has introduced numerous pathogens to our species, including SARS and SARS-CoV-2 coronavirus. The difference is that in the deep past when human populations were considerably smaller and widely dispersed, these outbreaks usually died off as soon as they killed their hosts or their hosts developed an immunity to the pathogens.

These microscopic pathogens are less mysterious now than they were in the past. We also have a measure of control over some of them, even if evolution will always ensure that this control is only ever temporary. But in pre-industrial farming societies, these accomplished and invisible murderers were angels of death visited upon them by angry gods. And, as if to add insult to injury, because diets in pre-industrial farming societies tended to be erratic and dominated by only one or two crops, people also often suffered from systemic nutritional deficiencies that left them ill equipped to resist or recover from diseases that most well-nourished people would have shrugged off.

Another critical environmental challenge ancient farmers faced was the fact that the same patch of soil could not keep producing reliable harvests year after year. For those who were lucky enough to farm in alluvial floodplains where periodic floods conveniently refreshed topsoils, this was not an eternal problem. But for others it was a harsh lesson in the challenges of sustainability, which they solved mainly by moving to new, under-exploited turf, so speeding the expansion of agriculture across Europe, India and South East Asia. Rudimentary crop-cycling systems based on switching grains with legumes, or leaving a field fallow once in a while, were adopted in many early agricultural societies but it would take until the eighteenth century before the benefits of long-cycle sequential crop rotation were properly established anywhere, with the result that early farmers everywhere must have experienced the same sense of frustration, followed by impending doom, when despite the weather being just right, the seed stock plentiful and the pests under control, they ended up producing anaemic harvests inadequate to sustain them for the year ahead.

There are plenty of written records documenting the many catastrophes that have befallen agricultural societies since the classical era. But there are no such records for the first 6,000 years of farming or among non-literate agricultural societies. Up until recently archaeologists based their belief that similar catastrophes also afflicted early farming societies on evidence indicating the spontaneous collapse of populations or abandonment of towns, settlements and villages in the ancient world. Now, clear evidence of these collapses has been found in our genomes. Comparisons of ancient and modern genomes in Europe, for example, point to sequences of catastrophes that wiped out between 40 and 60 per cent of established populations, so dramatically reducing the genetic diversity of their descendants. These genetic bottleneck events clearly coincided with the expansion of farming societies through central Europe around 7,500 years ago, and then later into north-western Europe about 6,000 years ago.[8]

Depleted soils, diseases, famines and later conflicts were recurrent causes of catastrophe in farming societies. But these only ever briefly stalled the rise of agriculture. Even despite these challenges, farming was ultimately much more productive than foraging, and populations almost always recovered within a few generations, so sowing the seeds for a future collapses, amplifying their anxieties about scarcity and encouraging their expansion into new space.

Entropy's eternal diktat that the more complex a structure, the more work must be done to build and maintain it applies as much to our societies as it does to our bodies. It takes work to transform clay into bricks and bricks into buildings in the same way it takes energy to transform fields of grain into loaves of bread. Accordingly, the complexity of any particular society at any particular time is often a useful measure for the quantities of energy that they capture, and also the amount of work (in the raw, physical sense of the word) that is needed to build and then maintain this complexity.

The problem is that inferring the quantities of energy captured and then put to work by different societies at different times over the course of human history is hard, not least because it depends on where and how the energy was sourced and how efficiently it was used. Unsurprisingly, researchers only rarely agree on the detail. There is thus lots of debate as to whether energy-capture rates by Romans during the height of their empire were broadly equivalent to those of peasants in Europe on the cusp of the Industrial

Revolution, or more akin to those that characterised the earlier agricultural states.[9] But there is broad agreement that human history is marked by a sequence of surges in the amount of energy captured as new energy sources were added to those already in use. Nor do they disagree that on a per capita basis, those of us living in the world's more industrialised countries have an energy footprint in the region of fifty times that of people in small-scale foraging societies and close to tenfold greater than that in most pre-industrial societies. There is also a broad consensus that after the initial mastering of fire, two processes have dramatically amplified energy-capture rates. The more recent was the intensive exploitation of fossil fuels associated with the Industrial Revolution. But in terms of work, the most important energy revolution was farming.

Adults in the United States consume on average around 3,600 kilocalories of food per day,[10] mainly in the form of refined starches, proteins, fats and sugar. This is a good deal more than the recommended 2,000–2,500kcal per day necessary to stay healthy. Despite the tendency to eat more food than is actually good for us, energy from food now accounts for a tiny proportion of the total energy we capture and put to work. But the energy footprint of food production is another matter.

Because plants need carbon dioxide to grow and soils have the capacity to sequester carbon, agriculture could theoretically be climate neutral, or potentially even sequester more carbon dioxide than it emits. Instead, the process of growing food to eat has a massive energy footprint. If you include the systematic clearing of forests and the conversion of grassland into arable land in the calculation, then

214

agriculture now accounts for up to a third of all greenhouse gas emissions. Much of the remainder comes from the manufacture and decomposition of fertilisers, the power required to manufacture and run farm machinery, the infrastructure necessary to process, store and transport food products, and the megatons of methane that escape the bloated guts of livestock.

In modern industrialised societies, where most of our energy is sourced from burning fossil fuels, carbon footprints offer a rough proxy for energy capture. It is only a rough proxy because a minor but nevertheless growing proportion of the energy we use is now sourced from 'renewables' like wind, and we are getting far better at using energy more efficiently and incurring lower net losses to heat. This means that in most instances a pound of coal does much more useful work than it used to.

Over the course of the half-million years or so between their mastering of fire and the first tentative experiments with agriculture, the quantities of energy captured and used by our foraging ancestors did not change a great deal. There was little difference between the energy-capture rates of the Ju/'hoansi foragers Richard Lee worked with in 1963 and the archaic humans who warmed themselves by their fires in Wonderwerk Cave. This is not to say that all foragers had precisely the same rates of energy capture or that all did the same amount of work. The proportion of meat in their diets made a difference, as did where they lived. The total energy captured over the course of a year by the ivory-carving foragers in Sunghir in present-day Russia 35,000 years ago, for example, was larger than any of the foragers living in warm climates at any time in the last 100,000 years. They had

215

to build sturdier shelters to withstand winter storms, make heavy-duty clothing and footwear, burn more fuel on their fires, and eat more energy-rich food simply to maintain their body temperature. This means that if foragers in southern and eastern Africa captured perhaps 2,000 kilocalories per day in food energy and maybe a thousand more in non-food energy (in the form of fuel or resources to make tools like their spears or ostrich-eggshell ornaments), then it's likely that foragers in the icy north may have needed to capture around double that to survive during the coldest months.

While the volume of food produced for human consumption today is staggering, the number of distinct plant and animal species we routinely consume is not. Despite the fact that in most of the world's cities, one can now eat cuisine from countries from every continent, only the most cosmopolitan have a diet approaching the diversity of hunter-gatherers living in territories not much larger than a suburb in a modern city. The majority of land under cultivation across the globe is used for the purposes of growing a limited number of high-energy-yielding crops. Nearly two-thirds of it is now used for growing cereals (mainly wheat, maize, rice and barley). The next largest crop category, accounting for roughly one-tenth of all land under cultivation, is devoted to producing oil-based crops like canola and palm oil for cooking, cosmetics and other applications. The remaining 30 per cent or so of land under cultivation forms a patchwork of pulses, sugar crops, roots and tubers, fruits, vegetables, herbs, spices, teas, coffees, non-food crops like cotton, and also narcotics like coca leaves and tobacco. Part of the reason for the huge tracts of land used for cultivating high-yielding cereals, other than the fact that it provides us with low-cost carbohydrate-rich calories, is that it is needed to fatten domestic animals, which are farmed on roughly 75 per cent of all agricultural land, to slaughter-weight as quickly as possible, or assist them to produce prodigious quantities of milk, meat and eggs.

Every single one of the many thousands of different plant species that humans have historically harvested for food is theoretically domesticable, given enough time and energy or access to the technologies to manipulate its genome. In herbariums and botanic gardens across the world, botanists frequently mimic the conditions necessary to successfully cultivate even the most temperamental and sensitive plants, and quickly develop new cultivars that are robust enough for amateur gardeners in many different environments to shovel them into their shrubberies without worrying too much. But some plant species are far easier to domesticate, because there are fewer steps to develop strains that can be reliably grown and harvested at scale. Some are also far more economic to domesticate, because they generate more energy for consumption than is needed to grow them successfully in the first place. The economics of domestication is now shaped as much by anticipated necessity as it is by the vagaries of food faddism and the existence of elites prepared to pay a great deal of money for exotic products like truffles, which are hugely expensive to propagate. Historically, the economics of domestication hinged almost entirely on energy returns alone.

217

To biologists, domestication is just one among many examples of mutualism, the form of symbiosis which occurs when the interactions between organisms from different species benefit them both. Intersecting networks of mutualistic relationships sustain all complex ecosystems and occur at every imaginable level, from the smallest bacteria to the largest organisms like trees or big mammals. And while not all mutualistic relationships are essential to the survival of one or other of the species, many are based on mutual dependency. Some of the most obvious include the relationship between plants and the bees, flies and other creatures that pollinate them; animals like buffalo and the egrets and oxpeckers that remove parasites like ticks; or the thousands of species of trees which depend on animals to consume their fruit and then disperse their seeds in their scat. Other less immediately obvious ones include our relationships with some of the many species of bacteria that inhabit our guts and aid us, for instance, in the digestion of cellulose.

The relationship between a farmer and their wheat is of course different in many important ways from most other mutualistic relationships. For domesticated wheat to reproduce, it needs first to be threshed by farmers to release its seeds from the rachis – the fibrous packaging – it is enclosed in. There are only a handful of species like wheat that depend on specific interventions or attention from a different genetically unrelated species to nudge them through a significant milestone in their life cycle. But as rare as it is, cultivation is usually a particularly successful form of mutualism, as evidenced by the success of the few other species that cultivate food, like fungus-farming termites.

Some plant species, like the wild wheat and barley of Anatolia and the indigenous millet in East Asia, almost invited domestication. A characteristic of pretty much all the founder crops, like these that form the basis of our diet today and were domesticated thousands of years ago, is that because they were already high-yielding and self-pollinating it took relatively few generations before they achieved the mutations characteristic of domesticity. In the case of wheat, for example, the mutation for its brittle rachis was controlled by a single gene that was already a frequent mutation in most stands of wild wheat, along with the mutations that produced larger seeds.

Just as importantly, some ancient environments were better incubators of plant domestication than others. It is no coincidence that a significant majority of the plants that we now think of as staples originated between 20 and 35 degrees north in the Old World, and 15 degrees south and 20 degrees north in the Americas, all of which were temperate, had seasonally distinct rainfall patterns, and were as well suited to growing annuals as they were perennials. It is also no coincidence that when agriculture spread, it did so, initially at least, within these broad latitudes.

In several centres of domestication where there were no indigenous high-yielding, energy-rich cereals, it was hard for populations to achieve the energy surpluses necessary to build and sustain big cities or centralised states. This is one of the reasons why among many of the 'horticultur-alist' cultures in Oceania, South and North America and East Asia, who domesticated relatively low-yielding crops, and whose energy-capture rates rarely much exceeded those achieved by foragers, agriculture never really got out of first

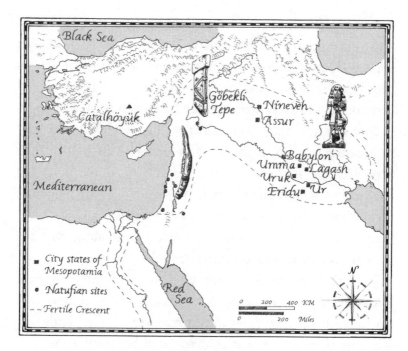

Neolithic Middle East

gear and populations remained relatively small, dispersed and mobile. They also typically enjoyed much more free time than people living in societies where they depended primarily or exclusively on agriculture. This is why to European sailors like the crews on Captain Cook's grand voyages, the Melanesian islands seemed like paradises in which the locals rarely had to do more than pluck fruit from trees or fish from the abundant seas.

In some instances, it took thousands of generations of painfully slow artificial selection before domesticated cultivars generated yields comparable to those of grain producers in the Middle East or rice and millet farmers in

East Asia. This is why even though the basal form of maize arose as a result of five relatively common mutations that occurred in the genome of its ancestor plant, teosinte, perhaps some 9,000 years ago, it took close to 8,000 years before anyone produced maize crops of sufficient scale to support populations and cities of a similar size to those that flourished in the Mediterranean from around seven millennia earlier.

But if the trajectory of human history was shaped by those farming societies with the highest-yielding, most productive, energy-rich crops, why was life in these societies so much more laborious than it was for foragers? This was a question that preoccupied the Reverend Thomas Robert Malthus, one of the most influential of the Enlightenment's cohort of pioneering economists who, like Adam Smith and David Ricardo, were trying to understand why in seventeenth-century England poverty had endured despite advances in food production.

Thomas Robert Malthus suffered from syndactyly. This genetic condition often manifests, among other things, in an individual's fingers and toes being fused together, which persuaded his students at the East India Company College, where he was Professor of History and Political Economy from 1805, to grant him the nickname 'web-toe'. But worse was yet to come. Within a few decades of his death in 1834, *An Essay on the Principle of Population*, by far his most important work, in which he argued that overpopulation would lead to societal collapse, would be ridiculed again and again as a piece of apocalyptic hysteria and his name become a synonym for unfounded pessimism.

History has been unkind to Malthus. He was not perpetually pessimistic as he is often portrayed. Even if much of the detail of his most famous argument was wrong, the simple principle behind it was right. More than this, his arguments about the relationship between productivity and population growth offer a compelling insight into how the transition to agriculture reshaped our species' relationship with scarcity, so giving rise to the 'economic problem'.

The main problem that Malthus set out to solve was simple. Why, he wondered, after centuries of incremental progress that raised agricultural productivity, did most people still work so hard and yet live in poverty? He proposed two answers. The first was theological: Malthus believed that evil 'exists in the world not to create despair, but activity', by which he meant that it was always part of God's plan to ensure that His earthly flock would never prosper to the point that they could afford to be idle. The second was demographic.

Malthus observed that agricultural output only ever grew 'arithmetically', whereas population, which he calculated (erroneously) tended to double naturally every twenty-five years, grew 'geometrically' or exponentially. He believed that, as a result of this imbalance, whenever improvements in agricultural productivity increased total food supply, peasants would inevitably set about creating more mouths to feed, with the result that any per capita surplus was soon lost. He viewed land as an ultimate constraint on the amount of food that could be grown, noting that the marginal utility of additional labour in agriculture diminished rapidly, because having ten people work a small field of wheat that was once easily managed by one would not result in ten times the wheat, but instead result in a diminishing share of its yield for each of those who worked it. Malthus was of the view that the relationship between population and productivity was ultimately self-regulating, and that whenever population growth overtook productivity, a famine or some other form of collapse would soon reduce the population down to a more manageable level. On the basis of his calculations, Malthus insisted that Britain, which was going through a huge population spurt at the time courtesy of the Industrial Revolution, was due an imminent and severe correction.

Malthus's bruised reputation now is not only a result of the fact that the collapse he insisted was imminent didn't occur. Neither is it because his warnings were enthusiastically embraced by fascists to justify their enthusiasm for genocide and eugenics. It is also because when viewed through a contemporary lens his argument does a remarkable job of upsetting people across the political spectrum. Malthus's insistence that there are clear limits to growth upsets those who support unbridled free markets and perpetual growth, and chimes favourably with those who are concerned about sustainability. But his insistence that the majority of people will always be poor because inequality and suffering are part of God's divine plan pleases some religious conservatives, yet gravely offends many on the secular left.

No one disputes that Malthus radically underestimated the extent to which food production in the fossil-fuel era would keep pace with a surging global population, nor that he failed to anticipate the trend in industrialised societies towards steadily declining birth rates that began almost as soon as his essay was published. Yet despite this, his observation that, historically, population growth gobbled up any benefits yielded by improvements in productivity was accurate for the period of human history beginning when people started producing food and generating surpluses, through to the Industrial Revolution. It also helped explain why those societies that were the most economically productive tended to expand at the expense of those that were not.

———

Two parts of Malthus's legacy endure. First, whenever an improvement in a society's agricultural or economic output is diluted as a result of population growth, it is now convention to describe this as a 'Malthusian trap'. Economic historians who like to reduce global history to the dull metric of 'real incomes' have found no shortage of good evidence of Malthusian traps catching out unsuspecting societies all over the world before the Industrial Revolution. And in every instance, they note, where a surge in agricultural productivity as a result of a clever new technology made one or two lucky generations thrive, population growth quickly restored everything back to a more miserly baseline. They have also noted the opposite effect when populations declined suddenly as a result of disease or war. Thus, for instance, once the initial shock caused by the huge numbers of deaths from the bubonic plague in Europe in the mid-fourteenth century died down, average material living standards and real wages improved considerably for a couple of generations, before populations recovered and living standards declined to their historical average.

Second, he put his finger on one of the main reasons that people in agricultural societies had to work so hard. Malthus believed that the reason peasants bred so enthusiastically is because of raw uncontrolled lust. But there is another, more important reason too. Farmers were all too aware of the correspondence between how hard they worked and how well they might eat over the course of a year. There were many variables that they couldn't control when it came to making sure they took in an adequate harvest and the health of their livestock – like droughts, floods and disease – but there were many variables that they could manage. There were also things they could do to limit the impact of big, near-existential risks, and all of these involved work. The problem was that there was rarely labour to spare, and for most farmers the only obvious solution to this problem was to procreate. But in doing so they stumbled into one of Malthus's snares. For each new labourer they gave birth to was not only an additional mouth to feed, but after a point resulted in a noticeable decline in food yields per person.

This left farmers with few options: go hungry, take land from a neighbour or expand into virgin territory. The history of agriculture's rapid spread through Asia, Europe and Africa shows that in many instances they chose the last.

When Vere Gordon Childe was still teaching in Edinburgh and London, most archaeologists were convinced that agriculture spread because it was enthusiastically adopted by foragers who admired their well-fed farming neighbours. There was, after all, plenty of evidence to show that our evolutionary ancestors were just as excited by novelty as we are now, and that good (and sometimes bad) ideas spread with surprising speed from one relatively isolated population to the next. This kind of diffusion is almost certainly why, for example, new techniques for flaking rocks into blades and points often occur almost simultaneously in the architectural record in many different places at once. Agriculture had also clearly spread this way in some parts of the Americas.

Up until recently, the only reason to doubt that agriculture may not have been transmitted in this way was the fact that a handful of minor hunter-gatherer populations, such as the BaMbuti in the Congo and the Hadzabe in Tanzania, had continued to hunt and gather despite having been in contact with farming societies for thousands of years. As with so many other mysteries about the deep past, it is the busy algorithms set loose by the palaeogeneticists that have offered new insights into agriculture's expansion. And taken in conjunction with archaeological data and oral histories, the story they tell in most cases is one of the displacement, replacement and even genocide of established hunter-gatherer populations by rapidly growing populations of agriculturalists on the run from Malthusian traps.

Comparison of DNA extracted from the bones of Europe's early farmers[11] with that of DNA extracted from the bones of Europe's ancient hunting and gathering populations, shows that agriculture in Europe spread courtesy of populations of farmers expanding into new lands, and in the process displacing and eventually replacing

226

established hunter-gatherer populations[12] rather than assimilating them. It also suggests that from around 8,000 years ago the growing community of farmers expanded beyond the Middle East into mainland Europe by way of Cyprus and the Aegean Islands. A similar process occurred in South East Asia, where from around 5,000 years ago rice-farming populations expanded inexorably from the Yangtze River Basin, eventually colonising much of South East Asia and reaching the Malaysian Peninsula 3,000 years later.[13] And in Africa, there is now unambiguous genomic evidence of the sequential replacement of nearly every indigenous forager population from East Africa to central and southern Africa over the course of the last 2,000 years. This followed Africa's own agricultural revolution and the expansion of farming peoples who established sequences of civilisations, kingdoms and empires across much of Africa.

When the Natufians started experimenting with agriculture, the global human population was probably something in the region of 4 million people. Twelve thousand years later, when the foundation stones of the Industrial Revolution's first fossil-fuel-powered factory were laid, the population had grown to 782 million. Twelve thousand years ago nobody farmed, but by the eighteenth century, only a barely significant percentage of the global population still depended on foraging.

For all but a lucky few who lived in the handful of grand cities that emerged to siphon energy from the countryside or who lorded it over hard-working serfs, life was often a struggle. The rapid population growth occurred in spite of declining life expectancies.

For subsistence farming societies in other words, the 'economic problem' and scarcity was often a matter of life and death. And the only obvious solution to it involved working harder and expanding into new territory.

It is perhaps unsurprising, then, despite the fact that hardly any of us now produce our own food, that the sanctification of scarcity and the economic institutions and norms that emerged during this period still underwrite how we organise our economic life today.

9

Time is Money

Benjamin Franklin – founding father of the United States, intrepid flyer of kites in thunderstorms, inventor of bifocals, the Franklin Stove and the urinary catheter – had a conflicted relationship with work. On the one hand, he lamented that he was 'the laziest person in the world' and quipped that his inventions were nothing more than labour-saving devices intended to spare him from future effort. Like John Maynard Keynes 150 years later, he also believed that human ingenuity might spare future generations from a life of hard labour.

'If every Man and Woman would work four Hours each Day on something useful,' he enthused, 'that Labour would produce sufficient to procure all the Necessaries and Comforts of Life.'[1]

Yet on the other hand, courtesy of his fiercely Puritan upbringing, Franklin was also of the view that idleness was a 'Dead Sea that swallows all virtues',[2] that all humans were born sinners, and that salvation was only on offer to those who, through God's grace, were both hard-working and frugal. As a result, he took the view that it was incumbent on anyone fortunate enough not to have to spend every waking hour procuring the 'necessaries and comforts of life' to find other useful, productive and purposeful things to do with their time.

To help him stick to the path of righteousness, Franklin always carried on his person a list of thirteen 'virtues' against which he logged his conduct every day. Among the most hallowed of these was 'industry', which he explained meant to 'lose no time; be always employ'd in something useful'.[3] He also stuck to a strict daily routine that began every morning at 5 a.m. with the making of 'a resolution' for the day, followed by blocks of time allocated variously to work, meals, chores and, towards the end of the day, some form of enjoyable 'distraction'. At 10 p.m. every night, he took a few moments to reflect on the day's achievements and give thanks to God before putting himself to bed.

By 1848 Franklin, only aged forty-two, was well off enough to devote the bulk of his time and energy to the kinds of work that satisfied his soul rather than fattening his wallet: politics, making gadgets, scientific research and offering unsolicited advice to his friends. This was possible courtesy of the steady income he earned through subscriptions to the *Pennsylvania Gazette*, the newspaper he'd purchased two decades earlier, and the day-to-day running of which was managed by his two slaves (who Franklin eventually freed when in later life he finally and enthusiastically embraced the abolitionist cause). During the course of that year, he took a little time out to write a letter in which he offered some advice to a young 'tradesman' starting out in business.

'Remember that time is money,' Franklin said, before reminding the young tradesman of money's apparently organic powers to grow over time, in the form of either interest on loans or assets accruing value. 'Money can beget

Money', he warned, 'and its Offspring can beget more [but] whoever kills a breeding sow destroys all her Offspring to the thousandth Generation.'

Authorship of the phrase 'time is money' is now often attributed to Franklin, whose face stares from every hundred-dollar bill minted by the United States Treasury. But it has a far more venerable provenance than Franklin's famous letter. The oldest recorded use of the phrase is in the book *Della Mercatura et del Mercante Perfetto* (*Commerce and the Perfect Merchant*), a tome published in 1573 by a Croatian trader, Benedetto Cotrugli, who was also the first person anywhere to challenge readers with a detailed description of the principles of double-entry bookkeeping. But the sentiment behind this apparently self-evident idea is far older still, and like our contemporary attitudes to work, also had its origins in farming.

The basic correspondence between time, effort and reward is as intuitive to a hunter-gatherer as it is to a packer in a warehouse sealing boxes on minimum wage. Gathering firewood and wild fruits or hunting a porcupine takes time and effort. And while hunters often found joy in the chase, gatherers often viewed their work as no more spiritually rewarding than most of us regard moving down the aisles of a supermarket. But there are two critical differences between the immediate rewards accrued by a hunter-gatherer for their work and that of a short-order chef flipping burgers, or a stockbroker making a trade. The first is that where hunter-gatherers enjoy the rewards of their labour immediately in the form of a meal and the pleasure of feeding others, the warehouse packer only ever secures the promise of future reward in the form of a token that can later be exchanged for something useful or to pay off a debt. The second is that while food was not always plentiful for foragers, time always was and so its value was never accounted for in the granular vernacular of scarcity. To foragers, in other words, time could not be 'spent', 'budgeted', 'accrued' or 'saved', and while it was possible to squander an opportunity or waste energy, time itself could not be 'wasted'.

Much about the enigmatic circles of standing stones at Stonehenge, Britain's most iconic Neolithic monument, remains a puzzle for archaeologists. They still argue with one another about how and why over a period spanning a millennium and beginning roughly 5,100 years ago, ancient Britons decided it was a good idea to drag up to ninety colossal slabs of rock weighing as much as thirty tonnes from quarries as far away as Wales's Preseli Hills to what is now commuter-belt Wiltshire (about 250 kilometres). They also remain unsure how these ancient builders positioned the heavy horizontal plinths atop the standing stones.

What is certain, though, is that the people who constructed this and several other grand monuments that appeared over the course of the fourth millennium BC in France, Corsica, Ireland and Malta were the beneficiaries of thousands of years of slowly improving agricultural productivity, and so were among the first farmers to reliably generate sufficiently splendid surpluses to abandon their fields for months at a time and expend a lot of time and energy dragging huge rocks over mountains and valleys and then assembling them into monumental structures.

What is also certain is that Stonehenge is a massive – albeit low resolution – calendar that was designed specifically to chart the ebb and flow of the seasons and to mark the summer and winter solstices. Stonehenge has this in common with many other examples of Neolithic monumental architecture. But it is no surprise that the passage of the seasons is such a common leitmotif in monuments built by farming societies. Farming is above all about timing, and until the advent of climate-controlled polytunnel agriculture all farmers lived at the mercy of the seasons, and were hostage to a calendar determined by their crops and livestock, and the regular passage of the earth round the sun. Most still are. For cultivators who depend on annual crops, there are specific, often brief windows of time to prepare the soil, to fertilise, to plant, to water, to weed, to get rid of pests, to prune and to harvest. Then there are specific windows in which to bring in and process harvests and then store them, preserve them or get the produce to market before it spoils. The industrialisation of meat production means it is no longer always the case, but up until the second half of the last century the seasons were also a similarly inflexible master for most livestock farmers too. They have to align their working lives to the reproductive and growth cycles of their livestock, which in turn are aligned to those of the environments that feed them.

In all traditional farming societies, there were predictable periods in the annual calendar where urgent work tailed off, even if, as was the case with the work-obsessed followers of the Abrahamic religions, these holidays sometimes had to be imposed by divine edict. In most farming societies, regular work was either frowned upon or forbidden over the course of long seasonal festivals. These periods were reserved for religious observance, for making sacrifices, for finding love, for eating and drinking and for squabbling. In good years, they were an opportunity for people to celebrate their industry and the generosity of their gods. In bad years, they were moments of respite during which people drank to forget their troubles and uttered muted thanks to their gods through gritted teeth.

In places like northern Europe and inland China, where the summers were hot and winters bitterly cold, there were also seasons when the urgent workload tailed off. But these were not time off from all work, just several weeks of reprieve from urgent, time-sensitive tasks, and an opportunity to do the equally necessary but less time-sensitive jobs like rebuilding a dilapidated granary. In some places and in some years, these periods were long enough for farmers to abandon their fields and pastures and come together to drag massive boulders across the landscape and eventually build grand monuments. In others, the time was needed to prepare for another year of working the land. But outside of these windows, whenever work urgently needed to be done, the consequences of not doing so were almost always considerably greater for farmers than they were for foragers. The Ju/'hoansi, for example, were often content to spontaneously take a day off from foraging simply because they didn't feel like it. Even if they were hungry, they knew that putting off the food quest for a day would not have any serious ramifications. For farmers, by contrast, taking a day off just because they need a rest is rarely an option. Not doing an urgent job in a timely fashion almost always incurs significant costs and creates additional work. Failing to mend a broken fence could translate into days blundering through the countryside in pursuit of lost sheep as well as time needed to source materials and then mend the fence. Failing to irrigate a thirsty crop, deal with pests or remove weeds at the earliest possible opportunity might be the difference between a good harvest, a poor harvest and no harvest at all. And failing to milk a cow whose udders were swollen with milk would leave it uncomfortable at first, result in a possible infection, and, if left long enough, would mean the cow would cease to produce milk again until it is with calf.

But there was more to the relationship between time and work in early agricultural societies than the tedious reality of being tied to an inflexible seasonal cycle. One of the most profound legacies of the transition to farming was to transform the way people experienced and understood time.

Foragers focused almost all of their attention on the present or immediate future. They went foraging and hunting when they were hungry, and moved camps when water points dried up or when food resources within easy walking distance needed time to recover. They only thought of the distant future when trying to imagine how a child might be when they were an adult, what aches they might expect when they were old, or who among a group of peers would live the longest. By having just a few wants that were easily satisfied and living within societies where status-seekers were scorned, they were not hostage to outsized ambitions. They also saw no substantive difference between their lives and those of their ancestors, and typically considered their world to be more or less as it had always been. To foragers, change was immanent in the environment – it happened all the time, when the wind blew, the rain fell or an elephant cleared a new path. But change was always constrained by a deeper sense of confidence in the continuity and predictability of the world around them. Every season was different from those that preceded it, yet these differences always fell within a range of predictable changes. Thus for the Ju/'hoansi, when they were still free to forage as their ancestors had, carrying the weight of history was as inconvenient as carrying a house around, and abandoning the deep past freed them to engage with the world around them unencumbered by ancient precedents or future ambitions. For this reason, the Ju/'hoansi also didn't care about or spend time calculating genealogical lineages, invoke the names and achievements of their ancestors, or relive past catastrophes, droughts or heroic deeds. Indeed, once mourned, the dead were forgotten within a generation or two and their burial sites left abandoned and unvisited.

To produce food requires that you live at once in the past, present and future. Almost every task on a farm is focused on achieving a future goal or managing a future risk based on past experience. A cultivator will clear land, prepare soils, plough, dig irrigation ditches, sow seeds, weed, prune and nurture their crop so that, all being well, when the seasons change they will at the very least bring in a harvest adequate to support them through the next seasonal cycle, and provide sufficient seed stock for them to plant the following year. Some jobs are, of course, taken with an even longer view on the future. The early farmers in Britain who built

236

Stonehenge did so with a view to it lasting for years if not generations. And when a farmer took a cow to stud, he did so in the hope that in forty weeks or so it would bear a calf that, if looked after well, would not only produce milk but also more calves and so form part of an ever-expanding herd before finally ending its life on the butcher's block.

But to focus most of your effort working for future rewards is also to dwell in a universe of endless possibilities – some good, some hard to call and many bad. So when farmers imagined overflowing granaries, fresh-baked bread, meat curing in the shed, new-laid eggs on the table, and punnets of fresh fruit and vegetables ready to be eaten or preserved, these same cheerful visions simultaneously invoked images of droughts and floods, rats and weevils battling it out over the mouldy remains of anaemic harvests, disease-ridden livestock being hounded by predators, weed-infested vegetable gardens and orchards producing rotten fruit.

Where foragers stoically accepted occasional hardships, farmers persuaded themselves that things could always be better if they worked a little harder. Farmers who put in the extra hours would, over time, usually do better than lazier ones who only ever made contingency for the one or two risks they considered to be the most likely. Thus among the Ju/'hoansi's farming neighbours along the Kavango River the wealthiest ones were usually the most risk-averse – those who worked hardest to build good enclosures to protect their cattle and goats from predators at night; who spent long summer days diligently chasing birds, monkeys and others drawn to their fields; who planted their seeds a little deeper; who went to the trouble of dragging bucketloads of water from the river to irrigate their crops just in case, as occasionally happened, the rains arrived late.

———

In much the same way that cooks use fire to transform raw ingredients into food or blacksmiths use their forges to work iron into tools, farmers use their labour to transform wild forests into pastures and barren land into productive fields, gardens and orchards. In other words, farmers work to transform wild natural spaces into domestic cultural ones.

Foragers, by contrast, did not distinguish between nature and culture, or between the wild and the tame. At least not in the same straightforward way that farming peoples and those of us who live in cities do now. In Ju/'hoan, for instance, there are no words that one can translate straight-forwardly as either 'nature' or 'culture'. As far as they were concerned they were as much part of the landscape – 'the earth's face', as they called it – as all the other creatures, and it was the responsibility of the gods to render it productive.

To farm you have to set yourself apart from your envir-onment and assume some of the responsibilities once exclusively performed by the gods, because to a farmer an environment is only ever potentially productive and has to be worked to be rendered productive. Thus farming societies routinely divided the landscape around them into cultural and natural spaces. Spaces that they successfully rendered productive through their labour, such as farmhouses, yards, granaries, barns, villages, gardens, pastures and fields, were domesticated, cultural spaces, whereas those outside of their immediate control they considered wild, natural spaces. And, critically, the boundaries between these spaces were often demarcated by fences, gates, walls, ditches and hedgerows. Similarly, animals that lived under their control were domesticated, whereas those that roamed free were 'wild'. Importantly, though, farmers were always acutely aware that for any space to remain domesticated constant work was required. Fields that were left untended were soon reclaimed by weeds; structures that were not properly maintained soon fell into disrepair; and animals that were left unsupervised either went feral or perished, often as a result of predation by wild creatures. And while farmers recognised that their livelihoods depended on their ability to harness natural forces and operate within natural cycles, they also took the view that wherever nature intruded unbidden into domesticated spaces it became a pest. Unwanted plants growing in a ploughed field were declared weeds and unwanted animals were declared vermin.

By investing labour into their land to produce the 'necessaries of life', farmers saw their relationships with their environments in far more transactional terms than foragers ever did. Where foragers' provident environments shared unconditionally with them and they, in turn, shared with others, farmers saw themselves as exchanging their labour with the environment for the promise of future food. In a sense, they considered the work they did to make land productive to mean that the land *owed* them a harvest and in effect was in their debt.

Unsurprisingly, farmers tended to extend the labour/debt relationship they had with their land to their relationships with each other. They shared with one another, but beyond the immediate household or a core group of kin, sharing was framed as an exchange, even if an uneven one. In farming societies, there was no such thing as a free lunch. Everyone was expected to work.

———

Adam Smith wasn't sure whether the urge we have 'to truck, barter, and exchange' stuff with one another was a result of our acquisitive nature or whether it was a by-product of our intelligence – what he called the 'necessary consequence of the faculties of reason and speech'. But he was sure that our appreciation for the art of the deal was one of the things that distinguished us most clearly from other species.

'Nobody ever saw a dog make a fair and deliberate exchange of one bone for another with another dog,' he explained.[4]

He was also convinced that money's primary function was to facilitate trade and that money was invented to replace primitive systems of barter. While he was the most thorough in making the case that money evolved from primitive barter, he was by no means the first. Plato, Aristotle, Thomas Aquinas and many others had already offered similar arguments to account for the origins of money.

It is no surprise that Adam Smith believed that the origins of money lay in trade and that its primary function was to aid people's efforts to exchange things with one another. The windswept town of Kirkcaldy on Scotland's Fife coast, where Adam Smith grew up with his widowed mother, is now a monument to the decline in Scotland's manufacturing industries. But for the duration of Smith's childhood it was a bustling port town filled with merchants and mongers. It had a busy market and a thriving textile industry, and Smith spent his early life watching a near-ceaseless procession of three-masted merchantmen cutting across the black-green waters of the North Sea, coming to deposit cargoes of flax, wheat, continental beer and hemp at the harbour, before disembarking again with holds stuffed with coal and salt, or decks piled with bales of linen.

An ageing Adam Smith returned to his childhood home, after several decades studying and teaching in Cambridge, Glasgow and Europe, to write his most celebrated work, *An Inquiry into the Nature and Causes of the Wealth of Nations*, which he published in 1776. Influenced by the 'physiocrats'– a French intellectual movement that, among other things, lobbied for idle aristocrats to shoulder a greater proportion of the king's extravagant tax demands, and who believed that neither governments nor nobles should meddle in the natural order of the markets – Smith was convinced that reason could reveal the fundamental laws of human economic behaviour in the same way that Isaac Newton had used reason to reveal some of the fundamental laws that governed the movement of celestial bodies.

The *Wealth of Nations* has a biblical quality to it, not least because Smith had a particular genius for presenting complex ideas in the form of neat parables similar in structure to those that were issued from church pulpits across the land every Sunday.

His most often quoted parable deals with the 'division of labour'. It tells the story of a tribe of 'savage' hunters – for which he drew inspiration from stories of Native Americans – each of whom fends only for themselves and their immediate dependants. But then one of the hunters discovers that he has a particular talent for making bows and arrows and so starts making them for others in exchange for venison. Before long he realises that by staying home and making bows he ends up with more venison to eat than he could ever acquire as a hunter. Not being a fan of the chase, he gives up hunting altogether and specialises as an 'armourer', a line of work that keeps him well fed and satisfied. Inspired by his example, other 'savages' decide that specialisation is the way of the future. Soon one hangs up his bow to become a carpenter, another a blacksmith and another a tanner, with the result that this once inefficient village of hunters, in which everyone was a jack of all trades and duplicated the work done by others, is transformed into a highly efficient community of skilled professionals all of whom cheerfully barter the products of their labour for the products of others'.

'Every man thus lives by exchanging, or becomes in some measure a merchant,' Smith concludes, 'and the society itself grows to be what is properly a commercial society.'[5]

But as Smith noted, barter economies are struck by a single simple problem. What happens when the hunter wants the carpenter to make him a new bow and the carpenter is sick and tired of eating meat but is really desperate for a new chisel from the blacksmith? The solution, Smith argued, lay in their agreeing on a 'common instrument of commerce' – what economic historians now often call 'primitive currency' – in the form of 'one commodity or the other', whether it be cattle, salt, nails, sugar or, as would ultimately become the case, gold, silver and coinage.

For much of the nineteenth and early twentieth centuries, it was believed that Benjamin Franklin and Adam Smith had been friends, and that Franklin had offered Smith the benefit of his thoughts on an early draft of *An Inquiry into the Nature and Causes of the Wealth of Nations.* The appeal of this tale of Enlightenment collaboration stemmed principally from the fact that the publication of *Wealth of Nations* in 1776 not only coincided with the United States wresting its independence from the British Crown, but also because it could be read as a velvet-gloved critique of the tariffs, taxes and customs duties that inspired North American colonists to cast off the shackles of British imperial rule in the first place. But even more than this, the *Wealth of Nations* articulated the entrepreneurial spirit of free enterprise that America later co-opted as the central narrative of its success.

It turns out that the transatlantic friendship between these two titans of the Enlightenment was fake news. Franklin and Smith shared some mutual friends and had read many of the same books. They may also have met one another socially during the period when Franklin served as the representative for Massachusetts and Pennsylvania to the British Crown in London during the 1770s. But there is nothing to suggest that their intellectual exchanges extended beyond Adam Smith purchasing a copy of the book in which Franklin described his experiments with electricity.[6]

Had the tale of their friendship not been a fantasy, then it is possible that the parable may have taken a different form. Because even though Franklin also believed that money must have been invented to overcome the inconveniences of barter, his experiences negotiating treaties with the 'Indians' from Iroquois Confederacy[7] suggested to him that 'savages' like them were not interested in trading to accumulate wealth. He believed that they had other priorities, which gave him cause to question some of his own.

'Our laborious manner of life . . . they esteem slavish and base,' Franklin observed of his Indian neighbours, and noted that while he and his fellow colonists were hostage to 'infinite Artificial wants, no less craving than those of Nature' that were often 'difficult to satisfy', the Indians had only 'few . . . wants', all of which were easily met by 'the spontaneous productions of nature with the addition of very little labour, if hunting and fishing may indeed be called labour when Game is so plenty'. As a result, compared to the colonists, Franklin noted somewhat enviously, the Indians enjoyed an 'abundance of leisure',[8] which, in happy accordance with his views that idleness was a vice, they used for debate, reflection and refining their oratorical skills.

As the anthropologist David Graeber has pointed out, Adam Smith's parable of the entrepreneurial savages has become 'the founding myth of our system of economic relations'[9] and is retold uncritically in pretty much every introductory academic textbook. The problem is that it has no basis in fact. When Caroline Humphrey, a Professor of Anthropology at Cambridge, conducted an exhaustive review of the ethnographic and historical literature looking for societies that had barter systems like that described by

Smith, she eventually gave up and concluded 'no example of a barter economy, pure and simple, has ever been described, let alone the emergence from it of money', and that 'all available ethnography suggests that there never has been such a thing'.[10]

The Six Nations of the Iroquois Confederacy Franklin wrote about (and whom it is thought Smith had in mind when imagining his 'savage' entrepreneurs) had a clear division of labour based on gender, age and inclination. Individuals specialised in tasks like growing, harvesting and processing maize, beans and squash; hunting and trapping; weaving; house building; and the manufacture of tools. But they didn't barter or trade the products of their efforts among one another. Instead they held most resources communally in grand 'longhouses' and afforded responsibility for their distribution to councils of women. They did, however, make elaborate ritual exchanges with their neighbours. But these exchanges resembled neither the free-wheeling barter of Smith's imagination nor the primitive currency-based transactions that Smith insisted logically followed the division of labour. More than anything, they involved trade in symbolic objects and served the principal goal of purchasing peace by satisfying moral debts, like those that arose when young men from one tribe encountered and killed a young man from another.

Economists often develop tin ears when people in other fields raise awkward questions about the fundamental assumptions of their discipline. Even so, it is increasingly hard for them to ignore the now-overwhelming evidence that while money may be used principally as 'store of value' and a medium of exchange, its origins do not lie in barter, but rather in the credit and debt arrangements that arose between farmers – who were, in effect, waiting for their land to pay them for the labour they invested in it and the people who depended on their surpluses.

Around the same time that ancient Britons were busy dragging massive boulders from Wales to Wiltshire, the first agricultural states with kings, bureaucrats, priests and armies began to emerge in the Middle East and in North Africa. These states had their roots in the rich alluvial soils of the Euphrates, Tigris and later Nile River valleys.

The earliest Mesopotamian city-states, like Uruk, were almost certainly the first societies in which farmers were productive enough to sustain significant urban populations who didn't want or need to muddy their feet digging in the fields. These were also the first places for which there is solid evidence for money in the form of inscribed clay ledgers. And while this currency was enumerated in silver and grain, it rarely changed hands in physical form. Many transactions took the form of IOUs that were logged by temple accountants, so enabling value to exchange hands virtually, in much the same way that occurs now in the near-cashless cities of the digital world.

People in these city-states made exchanges based on credit for the same reasons that ancient farming societies liked to build monumental timepieces. Farmers' lives were subject to the agricultural calendar, and operated on the basis of the expectation of predictable harvests in late summer that would sustain them through the course of the year. Thus over the course of the year when farmers took credit from beer-brewers, merchants and temple officials, they were in effect simply transferring onwards the debts owed them by their land. And because economic activity was almost all based on delayed returns, this meant that everybody else operated on the basis of credit, with debts only ever being temporarily settled up when harvests were brought in.

In other words, foragers with immediate-return economies saw their relationships with one another as an extension of the relationship they had with the environments that shared food with them, and farmers with their delayed-return economies saw their relationships with one another as an extension of their relationship with the land that demanded work from them.

Benjamin Franklin's view that 'time is money' also reflected his belief that diligent effort always merited some reward. Trade is 'nothing else but the exchange of labour for labour', he explained, and as a result 'the value of all things is . . . most justly measured by labour'.[11]

The message that hard work creates value is drip-fed or beaten into children almost everywhere in the hope of instilling a good work ethic in them. Even so, there is little obvious correspondence today between time worked and monetary reward in the world's largest economies, beyond the now almost quaint convention that the very highest earners tend to take the majority of their income annually in the form of dividends and bonuses, medium and high earners take theirs monthly, and lower earners tend to be paid hourly. After all, economists insist that value is ultimately apportioned by markets and that 'supply and demand' only sometimes corresponds neatly with labour effort.

The correspondence between labour effort and monetary reward wasn't always so out of kilter. Before the fossil-fuel energy revolution, almost everyone apart from a handful of aristocrats, wealthy merchants, generals and priests believed that there was a clear, organic correspondence between labour effort and reward. Unsurprisingly, the broad principle that work creates value features prominently in classical European, Middle Eastern, Indian, medieval Christian and Confucian philosophy and theology. Ancient Greek philosophers, for instance, may have been contemptuous of hard manual labour but they still acknowledged its fundamental importance, even if they had slaves to do it for them. The same principle is also discussed in the writings of fourteenth-century scholars like Thomas Aquinas – who insisted that any commodity's value should 'increase in relation to the amount of labour which has been expended in the improvement' of it.[12]

When Adam Smith returned to Kirkcaldy to write the *Wealth of Nations*, this idea still retained a kind of primal currency across Western Europe, where more than half of the population still made a living as small-scale farmers and so saw an obvious correspondence between how hard they worked and how well they ate.

Smith was well aware that most people felt there was an organic link between labour and value. But he also noted that when it came to the buying and selling of things, value was established by what price people were prepared to pay rather than the value the manufacturer placed on his wares.

Thus in his view the labour value of a bow or anything else was established not by the amount of work that went into making it but by the amount of work the purchaser was prepared to do in order to acquire it.

The two best known of the many other versions of the labour theory of value come from Adam Smith's near contemporary, the economist David Ricardo, and, most famously of all, Karl Marx. Ricardo's version was an elaborate riff on Franklin's. He argued that the labour value of any object needed to incorporate the total effort required to make it. This meant it had to take into account the effort put in to source the materials and the effort involved in the manufacture of the item, as well as the labour that went into acquiring the skills and making the tools necessary to manufacture the good. Thus, he argued, the labour value of a good made by a highly accomplished and expensively tooled artisan in an hour might be equivalent in value to the work of an unskilled labourer digging a ditch over the course of a week.

Perhaps surprisingly, given the extent to which Marxism would later be viewed as the embodiment of everything un-American, Karl Marx was a great admirer of the United States' Founding Fathers, none more so than Benjamin Franklin, whose name is invoked approvingly in many sections of *Das Kapital.* He also credits 'the celebrated Franklin' for setting him on the course to developing his own version of the labour theory of value, which he called 'the law of value' and which is a considerably more convoluted and complex creature than the versions proposed by Adam Smith or David Ricardo. It also served a different purpose. Beyond the fact that Marx wanted to re-establish labour as a just arbiter of value, he developed his law of value specifically to demonstrate how capitalists were able to generate profit by forcing their workers to create more value in the workplace than the wages they were paid, and so expose what he believed was one of the fundamental contradictions that would, in time, lead to the inevitable collapse of capitalism. And he did this with a view to exposing how under capitalism the 'exchange value' of any good had become untethered from its 'use-value' – the fundamental human need a product, like a pair of shoes, actually fulfils.

The idea that 'money might beget money' in the form of interest, or that money might be 'put to work' through being invested so that it can generate returns, is now so familiar to most of us that it feels almost as intuitive as the relationship between time, effort and reward. To foragers like the Ju/'hoansi and others still trying to get to figure out the basics of the monetised economy, this idea is anything but intuitive. To them it seems ridiculous. As ridiculous as their insistence that the death of an elephant or the birth of a child can change the weather sounds to the state officials and others charged with bringing economic development to them.

Where foragers like the Ju/'hoansi find the idea that money might beget money bizarre, their cattle-herding neighbours living on the better-watered fringes of the Kalahari do not. They are descended from the sophisticated agricultural societies who spread across southern, central and eastern Africa in the second millennium, but who did not historically use money, aggregate in large cities or care a great deal about trucking and trading and bartering one thing or another. They did care about wealth, influence and power, though, and measured status according to the numbers and quality of the cattle they owned, and the number of wives they had.

Unlike gold or silver, wealth in the form of a well-managed herd will always grow. While most cattle are now herded into abattoirs before they reach two years of age, the full natural lifespan of the lucky few cattle offered a natural retirement these days is typically between eighteen and twenty-two years. And for a good proportion of this time they remain reproductive. Thus over a full lifespan an average cow might be expected to produce between six and eight calves and a prize bull might sire hundreds. In other words, like any investment-grade asset, as long as farmers don't do anything to destroy their capital and have space to run their herds, they can expect to see their capital beget capital because their cattle beget cattle. Unsurprisingly, in almost every pastoralist society, the loan of livestock usually incurs some form of interest, and the expectation that not only will the animal loaned be returned, or one similar to it, but also a proportion of the offspring it produces under the other person's care.

While they typically were not as obsessed with cattle as the highly mobile African civilisations were, European, Middle Eastern and South East Asian farming societies were similarly influenced by the reproductive capacities of livestock when it came to thinking about how wealth might spontaneously reproduce. It is no coincidence then that the roots of much of the financial lexicon in European languages – words like capital and stock – have their roots in livestock farming. The word 'capital', for instance, stems from the Latin root of *capitalis*, which in turn comes from the Proto-Indo-European word *kaput*, meaning head, which to this day remains the principal term used when denominating live-stock. The word 'fee' likewise is an elaboration on the old Proto-Germanic and Gothic word for cattle – *feoh* – just as the word pecuniary and currencies like the peso have their roots in the Latin term *pecu*, meaning cattle or flock, which itself is thought to share similar origins to the Sanskrit term *pasu*, which also refers to cattle.

But in these societies, most of which were more dependent on large-scale cultivation than the consumption of animal products, the value of cattle especially lay not in their meat or even their milk. Instead it lay in the physical work they did, pulling ploughs and other heavy loads for people. And because they were valuable in this way, they begot value not only by making calves but also through the work they did. And in this respect at least they were not so different from the machines we depend on now.

10

The First Machines

When the eighteen-year-old Mary Shelley first imagined Dr Victor Frankenstein fleeing the monster that he had designed and brought to life, her ambition was to come up with a 'ghost story' to frighten her husband, the poet Percy Bysshe Shelley, and clever enough to impress the controversy-courting ego-in-chief of the Romantic movement, Lord Byron, with whom they were holidaying in Switzerland in the rainy summer of 1816. But in creating the story of Dr Frankenstein's 'unnatural' ambitions made flesh, she created a parable of the dangers of progress and a larger-than-life symbol of disruptive technologies, like artificial intelligence, poised to punish their creators for their hubris.[1]

It was no coincidence that Dr Frankenstein's artificially intelligent monster was the child of 'godlike science', 'mechanics' and the 'working of some powerful engine'. Four years previously, other powerful engines, this time in the north of England, had sparked an 'insurrectional state' that the *Leeds Mercury* declared had 'no parallel in history since the troubled days of King Charles I'. The insurrectionists were the 'Luddites', a group whose name would become as enduring as Mary Shelley's fable and who counted her travelling companion Lord Byron among their few celebrity supporters. The objects of the Luddites' rage were the stationary steam engines, the automated spinning and weaving machines they powered, and the men who owned them who collectively were strangling the life out of the north of England's once thriving cottage-based textile industry.

The Luddites named their movement after Ned Ludd, a troublesome young apprentice in a cotton mill who, one day in 1779, according to legend, grabbed a mallet and pounded two stocking frames into matchsticks in a fit of anger. After this incident, it became customary for anyone who accidentally damaged any machinery in a mill or factory in the course of their work to proclaim their innocence and deadpan that 'Ned Ludd did it'.

At first the Luddites were content to channel the ghost of their namesake. They would smash up some cotton frames with mallets and return home content that a strong message had been sent. But, frustrated by mill owners who knew all too well that their engines bestowed upon them both economic and political influence that surpassed even that held by all but the most established hereditary nobles, the Luddites eventually resorted to systematic sabotage, arson and assassination. This escalation marked the beginning of the end of the movement. In 1817, Parliament promptly declared machine-smashing a capital crime and dispatched 12,000 troops to the troubled regions. With those Luddites caught and convicted of their crimes either sent to penal colonies or sentenced to the gallows, the rebellion came to an abrupt end.

Luddism is now a shorthand for technophobia, but the Luddites didn't think of themselves that way. Their movement's aim was twofold. Firstly, they wanted to protect the livelihoods and lifestyles of the skilled artisans who could no longer compete with clever machines, and secondly, they wanted to alleviate the dismal conditions under which the ever-expanding numbers of people who had no option but to work in the mills laboured. In the first they were singularly unsuccessful, but in the second they made a lasting impact. It would not take long before Luddism would morph into the labour movements that so dramatically shaped political life in Western Europe and beyond over the course of the next two centuries.

Ever since its publication in 1818, Mary Shelley's fable has resonated with new generations of readers who have had to adjust their lives to accommodate successive waves of ever-more transformative, wondrous and occasionally terrifying technologies. If nearly two centuries after it first emerged from Mary Shelley's imagination, Frankenstein's monster now appears to have finally come of age, it is because it embodies our fears about robotics and artificial intelligence. But when viewed from the perspective of a deep history of work, our anxieties about artificially intelligent machines turning on their owners are not without precedent. For as contemporary as Shelley's fable is, it is one that would also have resonated in some ways with Roman senators and plebeians alike during the reigns of the Caesars, sugar and cotton plantation owners in the Caribbean and southern states of the USA, nobles in Shang Dynasty China, ancient Sumerians, Mayans and Aztecs. Indeed, it would have resonated with any and all societies who rationalised slavery by dehumanising those they enslaved.

Were Dr Frankenstein to build a similar monster today, its cognitive circuits would be designed to emulate the plasticity, creativity and lateral-thinking capabilities characteristic of human thought. And even though reanimating dead human flesh is not yet on the cards, its robotic body would almost certainly resemble that of a human or other animal. In the restless world of robotics, engineers building the most versatile and dextrous autonomous systems are looking ever more to the natural world for inspiration. New drone technologies mimic the flight mechanisms of wasps, hummingbirds and bees; new submersibles mimic sharks, dolphins, squid and rays; and among the most dextrous, agile and superficially least threatening robots are those that mimic dogs.

For now, the only mass-marketed home robot capable of doing anything more interesting than vacuuming floors is Sony's Aibo puppy. The 2018 version of Sony's $3,000 (£2,400) digital pet shimmers with life compared to its well-publicised, clunky ancestor, who was first manufactured in 1999. But its arthritic movements mean that even the newest version is quickly abandoned whenever a real puppy shows up.

Its shortcomings notwithstanding, there is a symmetry to the fact that Sony's puppy may in time prove to be the first widely used domestic robot, because the story of our species' reliance on autonomously intelligent beings harks back beyond 20,000 years ago to the first tentative relationships forged between people and flesh-and-bone puppies.

In 1914, labourers digging ditches in Oberkassel, a suburb on the outskirts of Bonn in Germany, unearthed an ancient grave in which they found the decomposed remains of a man and woman lying buried among a modest collection of antler and bone ornaments. These have since been dated to around 14,700 years ago. They also found what were later revealed to be the bones of a twenty-eight-week-old puppy. Osteological analysis of its bones and teeth shows that a couple of months before its death the puppy had contracted canine distemper virus, a disease still fatal to nearly half the domestic dogs that contract it.[2]

Apart from the fact that this puppy is the oldest irrefutable evidence of domestication anywhere,[3] what was most remarkable about this grave is the fact that the dog would not have lived as long as it did after contracting canine distemper without being cared for by humans. In other words, this particular puppy was not much good for work, but its owners nevertheless spent energy caring for it when it was ill.

The busy genomic algorithms have added layers of detail and confusion to the story of our species' long relationship with dogs. In 2016, researchers at the University of Oxford announced that their analyses of both ancient and modern dog bones, and genomic material, supported the idea that dogs were domesticated independently twice.[4] The following year another team announced that their data, based this time on the detailed analysis of the genomes of a larger set of dog bones from Germany suggest that domestication probably only happened once and that it occurred sometime between 20,000 and 30,000 years ago.[5] And while some ancient mitochondrial DNA indicates dog domestication occurred first in Europe, analyses of mitochondrial and genomic data from modern dogs have indicated East Asia, the Middle East and central Asia as centres for domestication too.

The Oberkassel Puppy meets Aibo

The fact that dogs were domesticated long before any other creatures and still share the closest partnership with humans is a reminder that while most domestic animals are now food, for much of the history of domestication the primary job of most domestic animals was to do work, and through the intimacy of that work the relationship was sometimes transformed into one of mutual loyalty and even love.

Fifteen millennia ago, when the partnership between humans and dogs began to evolve into something more special than neighbourliness, humans and domesticated animals comprised a barely measurable fraction of a per cent of the total mammalian biomass on earth. Since then, however, humans and their domesticated animals have increased the total volume of mammalian biomass on earth by a factor of roughly four, courtesy of agriculture's ability to transform other forms of biomass into living flesh. As a result of this and the appropriation of other mammalian habitats for agriculture and human settlement, people and their domestic animals now comprise a remarkable 96 per cent of all mammalian biomass on the planet. Humans account for 36 per cent of that total, and the livestock that we nurture, nourish and then send to the slaughterhouse – mainly in the form of cattle, pigs, sheep and goats – account for 60 per cent. The remaining 4 per cent are the ever-diminishing populations of wild animals who now cower in our hedgerows, pose for tourists and dodge poachers in our nature reserves, national parks and a dwindling number of wild refuges. Wild avifauna have not fared that much better. With around 66 billion chickens being produced and destroyed for human consumption every year, the total living biomass of domesticated fowl at any one time is estimated to now be triple that of wild birds.[6]

Domestic animals also played a vital role in determining which agricultural societies captured the most energy, grew the fastest and supported the largest human populations. They did this firstly through consuming plants that were not palatable to people and converting that energy into fertiliser (and meat), and secondly by using their muscle power to pull ploughs, drag tree trunks, carry people and distribute surpluses. While the value of a living steer is now less than the sum of its parts in the form of meat, leather and other animal products once it has reached optimum slaughter weight, up until the Industrial Revolution cattle almost everywhere were worth more alive than dead, as long as they could drag a plough.

———

Over the course of the 12,000 years since the Natufians first started to experiment with managing wild strands of wheat, there were remarkably few technological innovations that dramatically expanded the quantities of energy individuals were able to capture and put to work. Wheels, pulleys and levers all made a big difference. So did technologies associated with metalwork that helped people produce stronger, more precisely made and enduring tools. But up until the invention of waterwheels in the third century BC and windmills in Roman Egypt in the first century AD, by far the most important new sources of non-food energy were the animals, like llamas, camels, donkeys, oxen, Asiatic elephants and horses, who were forced into human service, and who until the invention of the steam and later internal combustion engine were our primary non-human source of motive power.

It is not clear how each of the individual species that are now thoroughly domesticated were brought into the human fold. It is generally accepted that a variety of pathways were followed, some of which did not, at first, involve either bribery or beatings. Pigs, like domestic cats and dogs, may have gradually infiltrated their way into the human world by loitering around their settlements in search of food scraps. or as a result of being captured by hunters to fatten them up.

Besides dogs, the oldest animal domesticates were probably sheep and goats. These appear in the archaeological

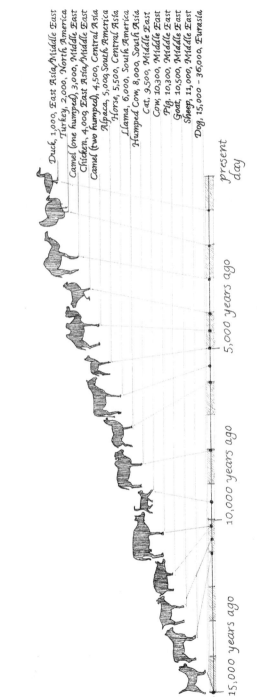

Duck, 1,000, East Asia/Middle East
Turkey, 2,000, North America
Camel (one humped), 3,000, Middle East
Chicken, 4,000, East Asia/Middle East
Camel (two humped), 4,500, Central Asia
Horse, 5,000, South America
Alpaca, 5,500, Central Asia
Llama, 6,000, South America
Humped Cow, 8,000, South Asia
Cat, 9,500, Middle East
Cow, 10,300, Middle East
Pig, 10,300, Middle East
Goat, 10,500, Middle East
Sheep, 11,000, Middle East
Dog, 15,000 – 36,000, Eurasia

present day

5,000 years ago

10,000 years ago

15,000 years ago

Timeline indicating estimated dates and location of major animal domestications record in the Middle East from around the same period that domesticated wheat does. It may well be that this first domestication of herbivores was achieved with the assistance of dogs, because the same genes that made wild goats and sheep sociable and inclined to assemble in herds also made these animals responsive to being herded by dogs snapping at their fetlocks.

Sheep and goats are tasty and have rich fat. They also produce milk and in some cases wool, but they are not much use when it comes to doing actual work. The most transformative of all animal domestications were almost certainly the five species of cattle beginning 10,500 years ago. Most domestic cattle are descended from aurochs, the long-legged, big-horned mega-cattle that roamed in vast herds across Europe, North Africa and central Asia. They were domesticated first in the Middle East around 10,500 years ago, then again independently in India 6,000 years ago, and possibly yet again a couple of thousand years later in Africa. Among the other domestications of cattle species, like the yak and the banteng, the most important was the swamp buffalo. This was domesticated around 4,000 years ago. It is thought to be one of the few species that was subject to a targeted domestication specifically to do work, because the old evidence for its domestication coincides broadly with the intensification of rice production in South East Asia, as laborious hoeing was replaced by deep furrow ploughing.

If the eastern, central and southern African 'cattle cultures' saw their cattle as symbols of wealth and power, in the first agricultural states cattle were thought of more as pathways to wealth and power, because when it came to heavy-duty tasks like ploughing, a single good ox could do the work of

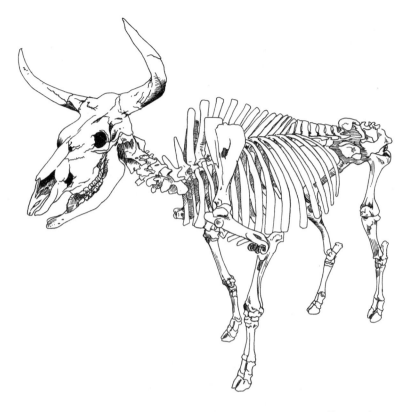

*10,000-year-old skeleton of a 1,000kg, two-metre-tall auroch
recovered from Vig in Denmark in 1905*

five burly men. In other words, the domestication of cattle
was important not because it provided people with protein, but rather because it enabled the greater intensification
of grain farming and a means to transport these surpluses
from the country to the city. And what's more, they did so
mainly by capturing and converting energy from plants that
humans couldn't eat, and through their labour, manure and
in the final instance their flesh, converting those into forms
that humans could eat.

The eventual demotion of cattle from hallowed and respected work-partner to food in many places was accelerated by the domestication of another big, docile and easily trainable herbivore: the horse. Horses were not only far more amenable to carrying people over long distances much more speedily than cattle could, but a big carthorse could do twice the work of a big ox and had the added benefit of working 30–50 per cent faster.[7] The only places where cattle were safe from demotion by horses were the tropics, where humpback cattle coped better with heat than horses and where water buffalo were especially well adapted to wading through muddy paddy fields and resisting tropical pathogens.

In 1618, at the age of twenty-two, René Descartes signed up to fight for the Protestant Prince of Nassau's army during the exploratory skirmishes of what would later be remembered as the Thirty Years War. More of a boffin than a bully boy, he was assigned to work with the military engineers, focusing his energies on solving mathematical problems, like calculating the trajectories of cannonballs and the number of horses the army required. Light and heavy cavalry often played a decisive role in battles, but they were no more important than the herds of carthorses that dragged cannons, tents, food wagons, gunpowder, smiths' forges, ammunition, siege engines and other material from place to place, or the ponies that carried spies and messengers. It was during one of these manoeuvres in 1619 near Neuberg in Germany that Descartes had his famous 'night of visions' – a sequence of dreams that persuaded him that his ability to reason was sufficient proof of his own existence, giving rise to the now famous dictum, *cogito, ergo sum* – I think, therefore I am. It also persuaded him that the human body was no more than 'a statue or machine made of earth', and animals, like the warhorses that sustained his army, lacked the faculty for reason and so were nothing more than elaborate barley- and oat-fuelled automata.[8]

Of course Descartes was not the first philosopher to imagine the animal world as a vast collection of Sony Aibos packed into different, organic, robot bodies. The idea that animals are biological automata echoed prior theological and philosophical arguments that suggested that human bodies alone were animated by souls, whereas animals merely existed.

Almost all societies that depended on hunting for meat considered animals to have souls of a sort, even if they weren't always exactly the same as human souls. Many also considered the fact that hunters were in effect harvesters of souls to be morally troubling and came up with a different way to rationalise the killing. This is why for instance Inuit and Siberian foragers like the Yukhagir insisted that the animals they hunted often gifted them-selves to humans for food and other animal products, while hunters like the Ju/'hoansi took the view that most of the animals they pursued were complex thinking creatures and so also afforded them the dignity of a soul or at least, as the Ju/'hoansi put it, a kind of life force.

For farmers involved in meat production or butchers, there is little room for the intimacy that comes from hunting an animal on foot with a spear or bow. The emotional weight of animals' souls would be too great a burden to bear. Humans, though, have evolved the ability to be selective in deploying the empathy that underwrites our social natures. Fortunately for workers in large abattoirs, denying empathy is relatively easy to do because, unlike hunters who often saw their prey at their magnificent best, butchers often see livestock at their diminished worst, inhaling the smells of death while standing in pens outside the slaughterhouse.

Even so, farming societies adopted a variety of different approaches to dealing with the ethical problem of killing animals. Some simply chose to hide the messy business. This is the approach we take in many cities now, where living animals are transformed into chops, kebabs and burgers by butchers who work far from the public gaze. This out-of-sight-out-of-mind approach was the one often taken in places where theological and philosophical traditions did not dispose of the idea of animals having souls. Thus, for example, in the Hindu tradition, in which animals are thought to have diminished versions of human souls, the slaughter and preparation of meat and animal products was delegated to members of lower castes like the Chamar, the leather workers, and Khatiks, the butchers, whose neighbourhoods and workplaces were studiously avoided by members of higher, purer castes who did not wish to soil themselves with the blood of animals.

Another option was regulation. This too is a characteristic of many modern industrial societies where a host of rules and directives on animal welfare govern the rearing and eventual slaughter of animals. This is the approach taken by followers of Abrahamic religions. Thus traditional Judaism holds that it is an offence against God to sever a limb from a live animal and then eat it (Genesis 9:4); that slaughter must always involve the swift cutting of the throat to spare the animal suffering; that cows and their calves should never be killed on the same day; that the meat of a kid should never be served in its mother's milk (Leviticus 22:28 and Deuteronomy 14:21); that working cattle (like people) are entitled to a day of rest on the Sabbath (Exodus 20:10, 23:12); and that people must always ensure that their animals are well fed.

The final option was to take Descartes' approach and think of animals as little more than machines and so assume that they were already dead even while they still lived. This meant that farmers and soldiers need not worry about the morality of working an animal to death.

Outside of philosophy, Descartes' most important contributions to shaping the modern world were in the field of analytical geometry. It was, for example, using the approach he devised to map coordinates on graphs with horizontal 'x' and vertical 'y' axes that Pythagoras' theorem for calculating the length of a triangle's hypotenuse came to be routinely represented by the simple notation $x^2+y^2=z^2$. But while Descartes saw himself as something of an heir to Pythagoras when it came to geometry, he would not have approved of the avowedly vegetarian Pythagoras' habit of purchasing live animals from local markets solely to spare them the indignity of the butcher's knife.

Pythagoras' sentimentality towards animals was unusual in ancient Greece, where the likes of Aristotle's views better reflected the norm. Even if Aristotle believed animals to possess diminished souls, like Descartes, he insisted that animals lacked reason and because of this it was fine to kill and consume them without qualm. To his mind, this was all part of the natural order. 'Plants are for the sake of animals, and . . . other animals are for the sake of human beings.'[9]

When he argued that animals are for the sake of man, Aristotle wasn't only talking about food but also the work done by creatures like oxen, horses and hunting dogs. This too was part of the natural order of things. Perhaps unsurprisingly he rationalised slavery in a similar way. He believed that slavery was a natural condition and that while some men and women were enslaved legally as a result of ill fortune, others, especially those who did manual work, were 'slaves by nature'.

'The usefulness of slaves doesn't differ much from that of animals,' he explained, since they both provided 'bodily service for the necessities of life'. And because Aristotle considered slavery to be both natural and moral, the only circumstances he imagined slavery no longer being an institution would be if there was no work for slaves to do. And the only circumstances in which he believed that could happen were if somehow people might invent machines that could work autonomously, 'obeying and anticipating the will of others', in which case 'chief workmen would not want servants, nor masters, slaves'.[10] To him, though, that was something that might only happen in the world of fantasy and the false stories religious people told one another, like that of the blacksmith of the gods, Hephaistos, who cast fire-breathing bulls from bronze and constructed singing maidens from gold.

Aristotle may have built his reputation by using reason to interrogate the nature of uncertainty, but he had no doubt that slaves existed precisely so that people like him could spend their days solving maths problems and having clever arguments rather than producing and preparing food. His defence of slavery is a reminder of how people in all societies have insisted that their often wildly different economic and social norms and institutions reflect nature.

In the ancient Greek city-states, like Athens, Thebes, Sparta and Corinth, slavery and serfdom sustained economies that depended first and foremost on agricultural production. But while the majority of their slaves toiled in the fields, it was considered appropriate, even desirable, for slaves to do more cerebral work too. Indeed, in ancient Greece the only jobs that were the sole preserve of freemen were those in politics. And while slaves were not entitled to claim any rewards for their labours because they could not, by definition, own any property themselves, those who worked as lawyers, bureaucrats, merchants and craftsmen often enjoyed influence that far exceeded their official status.

The likes of Aristotle may have sneered at manual labourers, but there were long periods in the history of ancient Greece where hard work was considered to be a virtuous duty. Thus in *Work and Days*, the poet Hesiod's description of peasant life in Greece in 700 BC, a Grecian version of the story of the fall is recounted, in which an angry Zeus punishes humankind by concealing from them the knowledge of how to sustain themselves for a year on the basis of only a day's labour. He also insists that the gods are angered by 'the man who lives in idleness' and moreover that it was only through hard work that 'men become rich in flocks and wealthy'.[11]

In 1982, the Jamaican-born historical sociologist Orlando Patterson published a monumental comparative study of sixty-six slaveholding societies, ranging from ancient Greece and Rome to medieval Europe, pre-colonial Africa and Asia. It was the result of several years' work to establish a sociological rather than a legal or property-based definition of slavery.[12] In it he concluded that being enslaved was above all a form of 'social death', and noted that in every instance, regardless of the duties they performed, slaves were distinguished from other marginalised or exploited social classes because they could not appeal to the social rules that governed behaviour between freemen; could not get married; could not owe debts or be owed debts; had no right of appeal to judicial institutions; an injury to them was an injury to their master; and they could not own anything, because all that they had in their possession belonged legally to their masters. This meant that even if they could reason, unlike Descartes' robotic animals, they were often treated as if they were soulless automata who like Frankenstein's monster could only ever dream of being accepted as whole persons. Therefore when a Roman legionnaire was taken as captive in war, his family was expected to perform the same ritual duties as if he had died in battle.

For some slaves, physical death was often preferable to the social death they endured. In Rome, slaves sometimes attacked their master knowing full well that the only possible outcome for such an act was execution. Others, however, gritted their teeth, made the best of their circumstances and often found community, rough kinship and solidarity among other slaves, and sometimes even with those they served. Deprived of so much else, many found purpose, pride and meaning in their work as well, especially if they were among the luckier few who had more to offer than just muscle power.

Well-to-do Romans were more likely than Greeks to kill and torture their slaves for trivial indiscretions. But otherwise they expressed similar attitudes to slavery and work as the ancient Greeks and, like Victorian Britons nearly two millennia later, considered themselves to be the inheritors of the ancient Greeks' civilisation. They too considered manual work demeaning, and working for a living to be vulgar. It was only appropriate for citizens to engage in big business, politics, law, the arts or military pursuits.

In Imperial Rome, slaves were the muscle used to transform the grand ambitions of senators, consuls and Caesars into a sprawling empire; the mortar that held the magnificence of Rome together and the means for some to achieve the plebeian dream of retiring as a wealthy landowner. But during the early years of the Republic, Romans kept relatively few slaves compared to later. It was only following the influx of slaves captured during military campaigns as Rome extended its empire that the agricultural model that fed Rome changed from being one where small-scale freeman farmers provided the bulk of grain to one where large farming estates called *latifundia* dominated agricultural production. Each of these estates depended almost entirely on slaves, who were enumerated alongside live-stock in farm inventories.

For the four centuries between 200 BC and AD 200, it is thought that between a quarter and a third of the popula-tion of Rome and greater Italy were slaves. The majority worked as labourers on farms or in quarries whose surplus produce was hoovered up into the cities. But in the city of Rome, like ancient Greece, there were few skilled jobs that were not also performed by slaves. Besides gladiators and prostitutes, and the eighty-nine recorded different roles that slaves performed in grand and not-so-grand households,[13] slaves worked in almost every imaginable occupation. In fact, the only profession they were barred from was mili-tary service. And while not as widespread a phenomenon as in ancient Greece, Roman slaves did occasionally occupy important bureaucratic and secretarial roles, with a number, the *servus publicus*, being owned not by individuals but by the city of Rome itself.

The fact that the Roman economy was sustained by what were, from the point of view of most citizens, intelligent working machines posed some similar economic challenges to those posed by large-scale automation. One of these was wealth inequality.

Early Rome was fed by a network of smallholder farmers across Italy and as a result there was a relatively close cor-respondence between household labour effort and reward. But when much of the work started to be done by slaves, this economic correspondence proved difficult to sustain.

Those with lots of capital and lots of slaves were able to amass wealth many orders of magnitude larger than poorer Roman citizens, who had to work for a living in a labour marketplace in which competent slaves would always be the economic choice.[14] It also made it difficult for small-scale farmers to compete with larger ones. As a result many sold their farms to large landowners and set off to the city in the hope of making a living there. Indeed, by some calculations, during the final century of the Roman Empire, three families 'may have been the richest private landowners of all time'.[15]

Romans competing with slaves for jobs were not helpless. In much the same way that train drivers on London's Underground now rely on their unions to protect their jobs from self-driving or remotely operated trains, ordinary Romans organised trade guilds to ensure that slaves would not undermine their interests. Called 'artisan colleges' – *collegia* – these hybrid religious, social and commercial organisations often functioned like mobster-infiltrated members' clubs, and were the antecedents of the trade guilds that later wielded considerable power in medieval Europe. In addition to leveraging their people power to secure lucrative public contracts for members, many also operated as crime syndicates and ensured that some wealth at least trickled downwards. With separate guilds established for weavers, fullers, dyers, shoemakers, smiths, doctors, teachers, painters, fishermen, salt merchants, olive-oil traders, poets, actors, cart drivers, sculptors, cattle dealers, goldsmiths and stonemasons among other professions, there was little that happened in the Roman capital without the involvement of one guild or another.

As powerful as the artisan *collegia* were, though, they were rarely able to do more than fight over the scraps falling from the tables of the wealthy patricians on whose patronage they depended. Rome's eventual collapse was ultimately hastened by the corrosive inequality at its heart.

Many city-states had acquired large empires by conquest before the Romans dispatched their legions to impose their *Pax Romana* – Roman Peace – across most of Europe and the Mediterranean; they were just not very good at holding them together. There was the Akkadian Empire under Sargon the Great that blossomed briefly in Mesopotamia around 2,250 years ago; the Egyptian Empire that extended down the Nile as far as modern Sudan; there were the Persian empires of Cyrus, Xerxes and Darius that were later dwarfed by and briefly incorporated into Alexander of Macedon's vast but short-lived empire. Then there were those like the Muaryan Empire, which after defeating Alexander ruled over much of the Indian subcontinent between 322 BC and 187 BC; and those of the Qin and Han dynasties in what is now modern China. But where these ancient empires fragmented almost as quickly as they were spliced together, the Roman Empire endured for 500 years.

Classicists still argue about what it was that accounted for the Roman Empire's exceptionalism, but few dispute that one of the many things that sustained it was the fact that all roads led to Rome. Because of resources procured through slave labour in greater Italy and its empire, Rome at its peak hosted a million citizens and was able to maintain its legions, armies of bureaucrats, senators, slaves, guilds and circuses by sucking in energy surpluses generated by farmers across the empire.

Much as is the case today in the world's booming metropolises, the energy footprint of individuals living in large Roman cities vastly exceeded that of individuals working the land, and much of that came as a result of slaves. This energy went into building aqueducts, roads, circuses and thoroughfares; keeping goods flowing through Roman markets; and maintaining the gilded lifestyles of some very wealthy people. And while the plebeians scraping a living on Rome's grimier streets were constantly reminded of their poverty relative to the patricians, because they lived in a centre to which energy resources flowed they were nevertheless very well off compared with the peasant farmers working the fields in the provinces. As a result, some classical scholars have argued that even the lower classes in the Roman Empire's provincial towns 'enjoyed a high standard of living not equalled again in Western Europe until the 19th century'.[16]

Rome translated its military conquests into colonies garrisoned and administered by Romans living in Roman-style towns, and estates which, while siphoning off wealth, also dispatched shiploads of plunder, taxes and tributes to Rome. Some of this wealth took the form of gold, silver, minerals, textiles and luxury items. But mostly it took the form of the agricultural surpluses and other food. As a result, the million or so people living in the capital, as well as the major provincial towns, happily consumed olives from Portugal, garum from Spain, oysters from Brittany, fish from the Mediterranean and Black Sea, figs from Carthage, wine from Greece, and honey, spices, cheeses, dried fruits and aromatics from across the empire. But most importantly of all, they consumed bread and porridge made from wheat or barley. These were regularly distributed as rations to as many as 200,000 poorer Romans every month at the expense of the Roman treasury by consuls and emperors alike, who recognised that curbing civil dissent in their swollen city required making sure the plebeians were well fed and occasionally distracted by lavish triumphs, circuses and other public entertainments.

The trouble Rome's leaders went to in order to keep their citizens distracted, and the efforts taken by Roman *collegia* to protect their trades from slaves, are a reminder of the next great transformation in the history of work after the initial embrace of agriculture: the congregation of ever more people in big cities and towns, places where for the first time in human history a majority of people's work did not focus on the procurement of the energy resources they needed to survive.

PART FOUR

CREATURES OF THE CITY

11

The Bright Lights

In August 2007, Thadeus Gurirab packed his clothes and a laminated copy of his school-leaving certificate into a flimsy carry-all, and made his way from the small family farm in eastern Namibia to the capital city, Windhoek. Thadeus's parents always knew that their small farm could never support more than one family. They insisted that he, the second of four siblings, attend school so he might eventually get a 'city job'.

On arrival, Thadeus moved in with his paternal uncle, his aunt, her mother and their three children. They lived in a corrugated-iron shack on a rocky 'plot' in Havana, a sprawling informal settlement on the hilly outskirts of the city.

Over a decade later, Thadeus still lives on the same plot in Havana. His uncle and aunt moved away in 2012, leaving the plot to him. He now has a 'double-job' as a security guard and janitor at one of the many evangelical churches where urban migrants congregate every Sunday to pray for good fortune. And he generates a little extra cash by renting out an additional corrugated-iron shack he built on the plot, which has enough space for a single mattress. It is home to two young men, both recent arrivals from the east, who also work as security guards. One sleeps in the shack during the day and works night shifts, while the other works day shifts and sleeps there at night.

Thadeus is pleased with this arrangement. It means that someone is always on the plot to keep an eye on things. Since 2012 Havana has nearly doubled in size and is not as safe as it used to be. He points out that the hills his shack overlooks, which were deserted when he arrived, are now just as crowded with structures as the side of the valley he lives on. And because hardly any of the new arrivals can find jobs, they have no choice but to beg or steal.

With a population of just half a million people, greater Windhoek is a fraction of the size of many of the world's larger cities. Yet what has happened there is much the same as what has happened in many other parts of the developing world, albeit on a smaller scale.

Back in 1991, close to three-quarters of all Namibians still lived in the countryside. In the little over a quarter of a century since, Namibia's total population has almost doubled. But while the rural population has increased by only one-fifth, Namibia's urban population has quadrupled in size, mainly because of people like Thadeus making their way to the cities because the countryside was full. As a result, there are now nearly as many Namibians living in cities as there were people in the whole country in 1991. And with a government insufficiently solvent to take on a mass housing programme and unemployment rates hovering around 46 per cent among young adults, most of these new arrivals have to make do in informal settlements like Havana.

In 2007, Thadeus was one of an estimated 75 million[1] new urban dwellers across the globe, many of whom, like him, left their countryside homes to make their fortunes in cities and towns. Each of them played a small role in pushing our species across an important historical threshold. By the beginning of 2008, more people lived in cities than in the countryside for the first time in our species' history.[2]

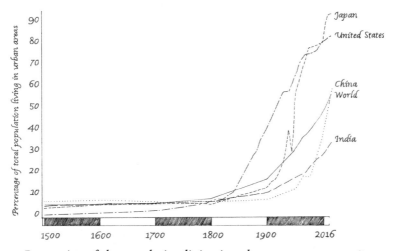

Proportion of the population living in urban areas 1500–2016[3]

The speed of our transition from a species who didn't much care to modify their environments to one that dwells in vast, complex, manufactured colonies is unique in evolutionary history. Where the urbanisation of termites, ants and bees occurred over millions of years, among humans it occurred in the blink of an evolutionary eye.

Humans may have only recently become what the Ju/'hoansi used to describe as 'creatures of the city'. Even so, ever since the first small ancient cities started to coalesce in the Middle East, China, India, Mesoamerica and South America, they have been crucibles of creativity, innovation, power and diversity. They have also exercised an outsized influence over human affairs relative to their populations. It was not until the Industrial Revolution that cities anywhere routinely accounted for more than a fifth of the total population of any region, yet by then what happened in cities had already been dictating the trajectory of human history for upwards of 5,000 years.

———

Many of the most recent chapters in the story of *Homo sapiens'* transformation into an urban species are written in the improvised, often chaotic freehand of crowded shanty towns which, like Havana, bloom on the fringes of the developing world's cities and towns. Up to 1.6 billion people now live in slums and shanty towns. The largest – like Kibera in Kenya, Ciudad Neza outside Mexico City, Orangi Town in Pakistan and Mumbai's Dharavi – have populations counted in millions and are in some ways cities-within-cities. Their spidery thoroughfares stretch for mile after unplanned mile and have grown so fast that the best local municipal authorities have been able to do is scurry frantically behind them, clipboards in hand, trying to calculate how much it would cost and whether it is possible to retrofit basic services like water, sewerage and electricity.

Other recent chapters in the story of our drift into cities are written in altogether more orderly scripts. Most impressive is the oversized calligraphy of modern China's urban planners and architects. Forty years ago, four in five Chinese lived in the countryside; now three in five live in homes and workplaces made of glass, cement and steel.

Many of these are organised around wide, ruler-straight tar roads, and served by a well-integrated water, energy, waste and communications infrastructure. The movement of 250 million rural Chinese into cities to take up jobs in its rapidly growing manufacturing sector between 1979 and 2010 was the single largest migration event in human history. It resulted not only in the almost overnight appearance of brand-new, still under-occupied 'ghost-cities' but also saw established cities swallowing up sequences of quiet rural hamlets, villages, farms and towns, as they expanded into the countryside.

For Vere Gordon Childe, the 'urban revolution' was the crucial second phase of the agricultural revolution. The first phase involved the painfully slow process of gradually domesticating livestock, grains and other plant crops over many generations. It was also characterised by gradual development and refinement of simple technologies like artificial irrigation, the plough, draught animals, brick-making and metallurgy, which 'demonstrably furthered the biological welfare of our species by facilitating its multiplication'.[4]

By contrast, the urban phase, he argued, only ever came about once a critical threshold in agricultural productivity was crossed and farmers were able to generate consistently large enough surpluses to support bureaucrats, artists, politicians and others that they were generous enough not to think of as 'freeloaders'. It was characterised by the appearance of cities that were provisioned by merchants, governed by monarchs and administered by priests, soldiers and bureaucrats.

Childe was almost certainly right, at the very least in terms of the history of work. Ancient cities only ever appeared once local farmers were able to produce sufficiently grand energy surpluses to reliably sustain large populations that did not need to work in the fields. And where energy was abundant, people, like masked weavers, first used it to build great monolithic monuments like Göbekli Tepe or Stonehenge, and later proper towns and cities.

The first cities in Asia, the Middle East and the Americas were as much accidents of geography as they were testaments to the ingenuity of local people. People in both Papua New Guinea and China, for instance, started to experiment with agriculture sometime between 10,000 and 11,000 years ago. But by 4,000 years ago, when Chinese farmers, who lucked out by domesticating high-yielding rice and millet, were consistently generating surpluses large enough to establish and then sustain the first line of urban-based imperial dynasties, Papua New Guinean farmers were never able to develop much more than largish villages based on the humbler energy yields they generated from cultivating taro and yam and husbanding pigs. Indeed, it was only during the colonial era after high-yielding cereals like rice were imported into New Guinea that anything like a proper city could be sustained there. Mesoamericans were similarly hamstrung by the lack of high-yielding food plants. They only generated surpluses big enough to sustain cities less than a thousand years ago when, after thousands of generations of artificial selection, maize eventually came to resemble something like the high-yielding crop we know today.

Besides getting lucky with indigenous cultivars, the other two important variables in the geographical equation were climate and topography. It is no coincidence that the first cities in the Middle East, South East Asia and the Indian sub-continent all developed in climates particularly well suited to cereal production, and in the floodplains of magnificent river systems that were subject to seasonal flooding. Before anyone worked out the value of fertiliser or established the principles of well-organised crop rotation, populations in these areas relied on floods dispatched by their river gods to refresh their topsoils with rich alluviums and organic matter gathered from further upstream.

In much the same way that some scientists speculate that entropy meant that the appearance of life on earth was almost inevitable, so history suggests that the creation of cities and towns wherever people became sufficiently pro-ductive food producers was inevitable too.

Like living organisms, cities are born, sustained and grown by capturing energy and putting it to work. And when for one reason or another cities cease to be able to secure the energy they need, like organisms deprived of air, food and water, they surrender to entropy, decay and die. In the early years of our species' urban history, this was more common than one might think. Sometimes cities and towns were throttled by rivals who laid siege to them. On other occasions they perished because of droughts, plagues and other acts of God. This is thought to have been the fate of the many ancient cities, towns and settlements that appear to archaeologists to have been abandoned for no obvious reason almost overnight.

Up until the Industrial Revolution, even in the most sophisticated and productive agricultural civilisations, like ancient Rome, four out of five people still lived in the countryside and worked the land. But the one in five people who lived in cities in the most productive ancient agricultural economies were pioneers of a whole new way of working.

As the first large assemblies of people who did not spend any time or effort producing food, they were led by a cocktail of circumstances, curiosity and boredom to find other creative things to do with their energy. And like well-fed weaver birds heeding entropy's demand to do work, the more energy cities captured from surrounding farmland, the bigger they grew and the busier their citizens got. Much of that energy went into sourcing the materials for building, maintaining and renewing basic infrastructure. This resulted in the emergence of many new specialist trades, like carpentry, stonemasonry and architecture, engineering, hydrology and sewerage. Lots of energy also went into building temples and sustaining holy orders, to flatter and appease demanding deities with sacrifices and tributes, as well as meeting the entirely novel challenge of maintaining order among large assemblies of people whose ancestors for 300,000 years had lived in small mobile bands. This required bureaucrats, judges, soldiers and those who specialised in keeping order and binding people together into urban communities with common values, beliefs and goals.

Legends telling of the origins of ancient cities, like the tale of the abandoned twins Romulus and Remus who were suckled by wolves before Romulus murdered his brother and established Rome, fill a vacuum in our collective history. In most instances, we can only speculate how and why small villages mushroomed into towns or cities, beyond the expansions being made possible by energy surpluses from agriculture. Doubtless there were as many paths that led to the foundation of ancient metropolises like Athens, Rome, Chengzhou (now Luoyang), Memphis in Egypt, Great Zimbabwe and Mapungubwe in southern Africa, and Tenochtitlán whose ruins lie beneath Mexico City, as there were roads that would later lead into and out of them. Some cities almost certainly began life as ceremonial centres or as geographically well-positioned meeting places, where people congregated seasonally to socialise, worship and exchange gifts, ideas, fears, dreams and spouses. Others almost certainly coalesced during times of conflict in places that were easy to defend; where the strong might offer patronage or protection to the weak, and where people fell under the spell of charismatic leaders with grand ambitions and inflated egos.

Cities lived or died on the basis of common rules of behaviour and the ability of their citizens to bind themselves together with shared experiences, beliefs and values, and then to extend these into the countryside that fed them.

As farming populations grew courtesy of additional energy, so territory and access to resources like good soils and water assumed ever greater value. On top of this, during periods after harvests when food was plentiful and there were no great monolithic monuments to build, men were left with time to think about impressing women, impressing one another and following up on grudges, enmities and insults that had festered while they were too busy working. Thus as often as people came together to expend seasonal surpluses on building monuments like Stonehenge, they also came together to fight. It is because of this that archaeologists interested in digging up sites from early Neolithic Europe will expect to spend a good deal of their time excavating the buried remains of fortified villages and mass graves showing evidence of torture, ritual murder and sometimes cannibalism.[5]

Even if the prospect of being butchered by villagers on the other side of the valley left many early Neolithic people constantly on guard, few would have ever thought of themselves as soldiers, or the episodic assemblies of angry, warpainted farmers from one or two villages as an army. Most armed conflict during the early Neolithic must have been similar to that which occurred in many pre-colonial African farming societies like the Nuer and Dinka, as well as among forest horticulturists in South America like the Yanomamo, or rival villages in Papua New Guinea. In other words, gruesome massacres were far rarer than ritualised battles that involved more dressing-up, strutting, posturing and insult-hurling than actual bloodshed.

With the emergence of cities and states all that changed. City dwellers' work was determined by the demands of expending energy, and one of the first things it was used for was the development of professional standing armies capable of keeping peace within the city walls and protecting energy resources or expanding access to them.

With urbanites no longer hostage to the challenges of food production, the first cities gave rise to an efflorescence of new professions. And in cities, some of these professions assumed a level of social importance that would have been unimaginable to mobile foragers or even farmers living in small villages.

Working life for most people in the oldest proper city we know of, Uruk in Mesopotamia, was probably not very different from working life in cities like Paris, London, Mumbai or Shanghai on the cusp of the Industrial Revolution. The ruins of Uruk lie on a fertile bend on the Euphrates River some thirty kilometres east of modern Samawah in Iraq. The city was founded around 6,000 years ago and was only finally abandoned after the Islamic conquest of Mesopotamia in the seventh century AD. At its prime, 5,000 years ago, it is thought to have been home to up to 80,000 citizens. And like most other big cities that emerged later, people involved in similar trades in Uruk tended to live and work together in the same districts.

Many neighbourhoods in modern London, for instance, retain close historical associations with specific trades. While some of these trades have since disappeared and many old neighbourhoods have lost their distinctive associations with specific trades courtesy of the arrival of shopping malls, online retail, superstores and gentrification, some still remain. London's Harley Street, Hatton Garden, Savile

Row, Soho and the Square Mile all retain close associations with trades that have been going on for centuries. Others, like Camden for offbeat urban fashion or Tottenham Court Road for electronics, are associated with relatively new ones.

The historical association of specific neighbourhoods with particular trades was not a quirk of zoning regulations or the result of careful urban planning. Nor was it the consequence of the fact that it makes good commercial sense for consumers looking for particular items to be able to go to one part of town to compare different wares on offer. It was because in the pulsing, plural hearts of big cities, people found companionship and comfort among others who did similar work and so shared similar experiences, with the result that in cities people's individual social identities often merged with the trades they performed.

Inscriptions on tombstones and written records from Imperial Rome describe 268 different career paths that ancient Romans pursued. Besides bureaucratic, construction, engineering, artisanal, mercantile and soldiering jobs, many other jobs Romans did were the antecedents of some of the service-sector jobs that now account for most employment in modern, mainly urban states like the United Kingdom. And among the ranks of Roman service-sector personnel were lawyers, scribes, secretaries, accountants, chefs, administrators, advisers, teachers, prostitutes, poets, musicians, sculptors, painters, entertainers and courtesans who – assuming they could secure the right patronage or were independently wealthy – could dedicate all their working lives to achieving mastery of their particular arts.

In both early Neolithic and forager communities, most individuals' sense of belonging, community and identity was shaped by sharing geography, language, beliefs and kinship, and underwritten by the fact that people did similar kinds of work, often together.

People in ancient cities didn't have the security of being part of a single geographically distinct community cross-cut with ties of kinship. They also didn't have the luxury of knowing everybody they encountered. Like urban dwellers today, they spent much of their time rubbing shoulders with complete strangers, many of whom led very different lives despite perhaps sharing loyalty to a common leader, having a common language, living under the same laws and in the same geography. And many of the regular day-to-day interactions between people in different professions in cities only ever took place in the context of performing those roles. Thus, for example, a chef in ancient Rome would have interacted regularly, if only ever briefly, with the toga-wearing patricians who feasted on the herb-stuffed dormice he prepared, the dormouse catcher who slept rough and the merchants who provided his other ingredients. He would have had very little to do with any of them outside of the context of work, and possibly even found encountering them at social gatherings awkward. But he would have spent a great deal of time with his colleagues and co-workers in the kitchen, probably more than he did with his family at home, or the acquaintances he sometimes played knucklebones with in the forum when he had time off. He would have also spent time with fellow chefs whose perspective on the world had been shaped and moulded by the skills they learned in the kitchen and symbolised in the burn scars on their arms. In short, they had a great deal more in common with one another than they did with soldiers, senators, cup-bearers and full-time dormouse trappers. The same held true for anybody in any other skilled profession.

Just as is the case now, to be a chef or a poet or a bricklayer in ancient Rome was to join a community of practice built on shared experiences and shared skills often mastered over the course of long apprenticeships. And in Rome, as with many other cities, over time people involved in similar trades often coalesced into multi-generational micro-communities whose children played together and married one another, and who shared religious practices, values and social status. Indeed, as urban societies grew more established, so professions merged ever more with social, political and even religious identity. Nowhere was this process more obvious than in India, where individual trades came to be inseparable from the rigid castes that prescribed where and among whom individuals lived, how they worshipped, how they were treated by others and what the professions of their offspring would be.

In Rome, these communities of practice formed the basis of the artisan *collegia*, which in addition to helping to protect workers in key trades from being marginalised by slaves gave individuals a sense of community, civic identity and belonging. As a result, contrary to the current narrative that the marketplace is a hotbed of kill-or-be-killed competition, for much of history people in similar trades usually cooperated, collaborated and supported one another.

These tightly bound communities evolved because people who shared skills and experiences unique to their crafts tended to make sense of the world in similar ways, and also because their social status was often also defined by their trade. Unsurprisingly, this remains the case now. Many of us not only spend our working lives in the company of colleagues, but also a fair portion of our lives outside of the workplace in their company too.

Of these myriad new professions that emerged when people congregated in cities, two entirely new classes of work were especially important. The first was a by-product of the invention of writing, and the second of the emergence and increasing power of the merchants who controlled the allocation and distribution of energy and other resources procured from the countryside.

All foraging and early Neolithic societies had rich visual cultures and communicated with one another by means of a host of symbols pregnant with meaning. But it was not until the emergence of cities that anyone developed any visual representation system as versatile as writing.

Like agriculture, writing systems were developed independently by unrelated populations in different parts of the world within a relatively short period of time. At least three entirely self-contained writing systems, from which most of the contemporary scripts we are familiar with today developed, came out of the Middle East, South East Asia and Mesoamerica. The origins and meanings of the voluptuous glyphs and symbols used by the Olmecs in the Gulf of Mexico sometime around 600 to 500 BC that were adopted into the Mayan writing system a thousand years later are uncertain. As are the origins of the already sophisticated standardised signs and symbols inscribed onto the oldest examples of writing from China, which take the form of inscribed animal bones and turtle shells from the Shang Dynasty three and a half millennia ago.

But it has been easier to chart the origins of the oldest system of writing we know of, that of the Sumerians in Uruk. Their distinctive cuneiform script's evolution has been tracked through three stages. In the oldest phase, spanning 4,500 years and beginning possibly 10,000 years ago, transactions were accounted for using clay tokens representing units of goods. The next phase involved transforming these three-dimensional tokens into pictographs on clay tablets, again used for accounting. And the final phase, the precursor to alphabetic writing, began around 5,000 years ago and involved using pictographs to systematically represent spoken language.

The specific cognitive implications of literacy continue to be debated. Like any other complex skills acquired and mastered when young and cognitively plastic, it clearly has some impact on shaping how our brains are organised and how we think and perceive the world. The debate focuses not on whether this happens but how profound the consequences are. Some insist that the cognitive and psychological changes brought about by literacy are fundamental. They argue that it resulted in the privileging of sight over other senses and encouraged the development of a more scientific, visually ordered and 'rational' way of looking at the world. Others, though, are much more sceptical and take the view that the fundamental intellectual architecture required to read and write is no different from that needed to translate the sounds we use to make meaningful vocal speech, or to interpret animal tracks in the sand, and other meaningful visual signs.

There is, however, no debate about the fact that even if the ability to faithfully represent spoken words and

complex ideas in the form of written symbols did not radically change the way people perceived the world around
them, without it we would be deprived not only of much
history, philosophy and poetry, but also of the tools
necessary to develop complex abstract models that made
most important discoveries in mathematics, the sciences
and engineering possible. There is also no debate that the
invention of writing led to a whole universe of new, previously unimaginable desk jobs and professions, from
scribes to architects, many of which were high status not
least because of the energy and effort that was invested
in mastering literacy. 'Put writing in your heart that you
may protect yourself from hard labour of any kind,' an
Egyptian father famously said to his son as he dispatched
him to school in the third millennium BC, adding that 'the
scribe is released from manual tasks' and that it is 'he who
commands'.[6]

It is clear that literacy fundamentally transformed the
nature and exercise of power as well. It did this by providing
the means for early states to establish functioning bureaucracies and formalised legal systems, by means of which
they could organise and manage far larger populations and
implement far more ambitious projects. It also provided
those who had mastered reading and writing with the ability
to claim privileged access to the words and will of gods.

There is no doubt that literacy transformed the world
of commerce, by enabling the establishment of formalised
currencies, the keeping of complex accounts, the creation of
financial and banking institutions, and also the possibility
of accumulating wealth that often existed only in the form
of ledgers.

Archaeologists have recovered more than 100,000 samples of Sumerian cuneiform writing, among them letters, recipes, legal documents, histories, poetry and maps, as well as many documents relating to commerce. These include a 5,000-year-old payslip showing that the thirsty citizens of Uruk, like the labourers who built Egypt's Pyramids, were content to be remunerated for their work in beer; 4,000-year-old receipts documenting the exchange of goods ranging from animal fodder to textiles; and the oldest known complaint letter which was written by an irate customer to a merchant complaining of the delivery of substandard goods sometime around 1750 BC.

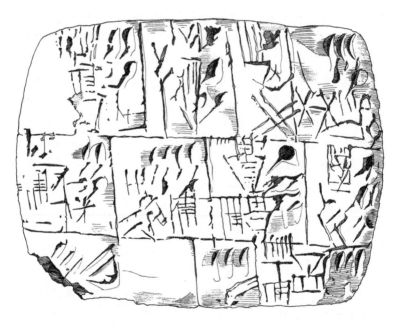

The world's oldest payrecord: a cuneiform tablet documenting payment of workers in beer c.3000 BC, on display at the British Museum

In cities, material security was not based on producing food energy or other raw materials but on controlling its distribution and use. All ancient cities had marketplaces, from Athens's sprawling *agora* to Rome's somewhat more orderly forum with its boutique-like shops.

The development of markets in ancient cities like Uruk was partially a consequence of the fact that the kind of exchange relationships typical between people in small agricultural settlements was simply not possible in cities. Where people in rural communities tended to exchange and share things mainly with people they knew or were related to, in cities most exchanges occurred between strangers. This meant that the traditional norms and customs dealing with reciprocity and mutual obligation couldn't apply.

Liberated from these obligations, city merchants quickly learned that trade was a possible route to wealth and power. And this was important because while among farming communities people were preoccupied with meeting their basic needs, in towns and cities other, different needs and desires shaped people's ambitions, and correspondingly how and why they worked.

12

The Malady of Infinite Aspiration

It takes roughly twenty-five minutes to drive from Thadeus's shack in Havana to Windhoek's city centre, if you avoid the chaos of battered taxis that clog the roads during the morning and evening rush hours. The journey takes you first through two old townships, where black and 'mixed race' people were required to live during apartheid, then into Windhoek's middle-class north-western suburbs, before you finally reach the well-manicured heart of the city, where from the roof terrace of the Hilton Hotel you can see grand shopping malls, restaurants, air-conditioned multi-storey offices and, in the distance, smoke from cooking fires in Havana are visible. As you progress from Havana to the city centre, increasing wealth is signified by the fancier vehicles parked in driveways and the escalating grandeur of the houses, shops and office buildings. It is also signified by the elaborateness of the security systems. In Havana, security consists mainly of the eyes and ears of trusted neighbours; in the township it takes the form of low walls surrounding simple cement brick houses with barred windows and firmly padlocked doors. But as you enter the city proper you progress from smaller houses surrounded by low walls topped with razor wire or broken glass to grand houses with towering walls crowned with ominously buzzing electric fencing, infrared motion detectors, mounted cameras and uniformed security guards armed with sticks, whips and sometimes guns. Many of the security personnel, like Thadeus, come from Havana. And they are there to guard homes, shops and businesses from other people from Havana.

No one in Windhoek considers their security arrangements to be overkill. It is rare for robberies there to be accompanied by the callous brutality that so often characterises similar crimes in neighbouring South African cities, but even so, there are few people, rich and poor, in Windhoek who have not been victims of a robbery or mugging. And while richer Windhoekers complain incessantly about crime being out of control and attribute it to race, immorality and the incompetence of the police, they all know that it is not going to change any time soon.

Some robberies in Windhoek are perpetrated by people who are simply hungry. If the intruders manage to circumvent the security in your house, the first place they ransack is the kitchen. But many others are motivated by a different kind of scarcity. One shaped by the fact that in the city people are constantly confronted by others who have much more (and better) stuff than they do.

In this sense, Windhoek is the same as every other city in the world. For as long as people have congregated in cities, their ambitions have been moulded by a different kind of scarcity from that which shapes those of subsistence farmers, a form of scarcity articulated in the language of aspiration, jealousy and desire rather than of absolute need. And for most, this kind of relative scarcity is the spur to work long hours, to climb the social ladder and to keep up with the Joneses.

Most economists are wary of interrogating the specific needs or desires that might make things seem scarce in the first place. They dispose of questions such as why non-essential things like diamonds are more valuable than essential things like water as the 'paradox of value', and for the most part are content to say that it doesn't much bother them why or what motivates different needs, as the relative value of those needs will be adjudicated by markets.

John Maynard Keynes broke ranks with many of his colleagues in this respect when he made the case that automation would solve the economic problem. He argued that the economic problem had two distinct components and that automation could only ever solve the first of these: those that dealt with what he called the urge to meet our 'absolute needs'. These needs, like food, water, warmth, comfort, companionship and safety, were universal, absolute and experienced equally by everyone, from a prisoner in chains to a monarch in a palace. And while these needs were critical, Keynes believed they were not infinite. After all, when you are warm enough, putting another log on the fire might make you too hot, or when you have eaten enough, eating more will make you feel ill. The second component of the economic problem was our desire to meet what Keynes called our 'relative needs'. These needs, he believed, truly were infinite, because as soon as we met any of them they would be quickly replaced by another probably more ambitious one. These needs were those that reflected people's ambitions to 'keep up with the Joneses', to secure a promotion at work, to purchase a grander house, to drive a better car, to eat fancier food and to achieve greater power. These needs, he also believed, were what motivated us to work harder still, even after our absolute needs were met.

Keynes was not clear about whether he considered his absolute needs to include having wines appropriately matched to the food he was eating, a country house for weekends or decent Turkish tobacco for his pipe. But in distinguishing between absolute and relative needs, he recognised the importance of social context and status in shaping people's desires. In this respect, he was thinking more like social anthropologists who unlike economists are interested in understanding why in some contexts, such as cities, diamonds are more valuable than water, whereas in others, such as traditional foraging communities in the Kalahari Desert – which now hosts the two richest diamond mines ever discovered – diamonds were worthless but water was priceless.

———

The idea that inequality is natural and inevitable is invoked as often in the teachings of Vedic, Confucian, Islamic and European classical philosophy as it is in the rhetoric of many politicians. For almost as long as people have lived in cities and recorded their thoughts in writing, there have been those who, like Aristotle, have insisted that inequality is an inescapable fact of life. There have, of course, been many dissenting voices too; those whose message of equality has chimed with those at the bottom of the economic, social or political pile, and which has periodically been screamed from behind makeshift barricades across roads during periods of upheaval, rebellion and revolution.

Foragers like the Ju/'hoansi remind us that we are as capable of ordering ourselves into fiercely egalitarian societies as we are of ordering ourselves into rigid hierarchies. As a result, many historians have argued that even if inequality is not a brute fact of human nature, then along with zoonotic diseases, despotism and war, it was probably a direct and immediate consequence of our embrace of agriculture. They reason that as soon as people had big surpluses to hoard, exchange or distribute, the more miserable angels of our nature took over.

But extreme inequality was not an immediate and organic consequence of our ancestors' transition to farming. Many early agricultural societies were far more egalitarian than modern urban ones, and in ancient rural villages and hamlets people often worked cooperatively, shared the product of their labours evenly, and only hoarded surpluses for collective benefit. There is also plenty of evidence to suggest this archaic form of 'kibbutz' egalitarianism endured because it was an effective way to manage the recurrent episodes of material scarcity that fast-growing farming populations routinely suffered. Thus, for instance, the small-scale farmers who established themselves across much of what is now Spain and Portugal over the course of the first millennium BC are thought by some archaeologists to have been 'assertively egalitarian'– until the Roman legions appeared on the horizon in the first century BC.[1]

Interestingly, the oldest almost-urban settlement discovered so far, Çatalhöyük in Turkey, was probably similarly materially egalitarian too. But it was not like any of the other ancient towns and cities that followed. Its ruins are made up of hundreds of similar-sized domestic dwellings clustered tightly together, almost like cells in a beehive, suggesting no one was measurably richer than anyone else. There were also no obvious public spaces like markets, squares, temples or plazas and no public thoroughfares, paths or roads, leaving archaeologists to conclude that people got from one place to the next by scrambling across rooftops and entering their and others' homes through the ceilings.

The absence of evidence for extreme material inequality based on the layout and size of individual dwellings does not imply the existence of anything resembling the fierce egalitarianism that was characteristic of small-scale forager societies like the Ju/'hoansi. Based purely on the layout of domestic dwellings, for example, the great Bantu civilisations that expanded through much of central, eastern and southern Africa over the course of the last 1,500 years might at first appear highly egalitarian. But this was not remotely the case. For centuries, these societies were animated by grand ambitions, political intrigue and power plays, and were structured around ranked age-group sets, gender hierarchies and huge differentials in wealth measured in the form of cattle that often grazed far beyond the village perimeters under the stewardship of herd boys. Indeed, in many agricultural societies, dwelling size, which to those of us who live in the world's heavily commoditised property markets is an unambiguous indicator of wealth, was considered unimportant. Likewise, in many hierarchical societies, chiefs, nobles, commoners and slaves often lived in the same buildings. Just as importantly, wealth was often measured in highly abstract ways. In many Native American civilisations, for instance, the right to use specific crests or perform specific songs and rites was an arbiter of status and power, just as access to ritual knowledge was an arbiter of power in many African societies. Whether or not some small-scale Neolithic farming settlements were highly egalitarian, life in the world's big cities has historically been anything but, despite the episodic attempts by revolutionary-minded populations to remedy this.

The oldest written history of a city takes the form of an epic poem and describes the achievements of Gilgamesh, an early king of Uruk, famed for building the city's walls, and who was later determined to have been a god. Drafted in cuneiform, the oldest of many versions of *Gilgamesh* found so far was written some 4,100 years ago, and was almost certainly an inscription of an oral narrative passed down and judiciously embroidered over the generations. The *Epic of Gilgamesh* is of course more myth than history; more gilded flattery than fact. But when read alongside other cuneiform documents from the same time, detailing the rights and requirements of ordinary citizens under the reforms implemented by the Sumerian King Urukagima 4,500 years ago, they offer a surprisingly nuanced insight into life in this, the most ancient of all urban centres.

These indicate not just the many different professions that people in Uruk and other early Mesopotamian city-states pursued, but also the fact that Uruk, like New York, London or Shanghai today, was anything but egalitarian and that, also like New York, London or Shanghai, merchants and moneymen were able to leverage their control over the supply and distribution of surpluses to achieve a status comparable to that of nobles and clergy.

Citizens of Uruk 4,500 years ago fell into five distinct social classes. At the top of the pile were royalty and nobility. They claimed their privileged status by descent from ancient kings like Gilgamesh and kinship with gods. Immediately below them were the holy orders: the priests and priestesses. They claimed their power from proximity to kings and their role as intermediaries between men and gods, as the custodians of holy places and objects, and their more mundane role as bureaucrats in charge of the most important urban spaces. Besides slaves, who were not counted as proper persons, those at the bottom of the pile were what might be referred to now as the 'working classes'. These included the farmers who mainly lived outside the city walls and, within the city, tradesmen and women, among them the butchers, fishermen, cup-bearers, brick-makers, brewers, tavern owners, masons, carpenters, perfume-makers, potters, goldsmiths and cart drivers, who either worked for others or ran small businesses of their own. Squeezed between them and the holy orders were soldiers, accountants, architects, astrologers, teachers, high-end prostitutes and wealthy merchants.

In places like Uruk, becoming a wealthy merchant was almost certainly the only path, short of fomenting revolution, that ordinary people could follow to bridge the chasm that separated them from nobility. Accumulating wealth in other words offered the opportunity of upward mobility for those who worked the hardest, were luckiest, and were the most cunning.

The archaeology of ancient Sumerian cities suggests, perhaps unsurprisingly, that among the most promising trades to take up for those with ambitions of climbing the social ladder was brewing and selling beer. In part this was because beer, like wheat and silver, was a form of currency. It was also because beer houses provided loans to skint farmers who probably agreed to interest rates and default penalties that they would never have dreamed of accepting when sober. While it is not certain how significant the opportunities for upward mobility for barkeeps were, it is telling that the only woman who appears on the list of ancient Sumerian monarchs, Queen Kubaba, started life as a lowly tavern owner before assuming power over the city of Kish, which she is recorded as having ruled for a hundred years.

The proportion of people employed in agriculture in any country is usually a pretty good measure of that country's wealth. Those with the highest proportion in farming-related jobs are typically among the poorest, have the lowest levels of agricultural productivity and the lowest levels of industrialisation. All of the ten countries where over three-quarters of the workforce still describe themselves as farmers are in sub-Saharan Africa. By contrast, in the United States, less than 2 per cent of the working population are now employed in a hi-tech agricultural industry that routinely produces such huge surpluses that close to 300 kilograms of food per person is wasted in the pipeline between field and plate every year.[2] This is the norm in most industrialised countries where agriculture has been transformed over the last three centuries from a labour-intensive enterprise to a capital-intensive one, by a series of new technologies and practices that have dramatically increased productivity while simultaneously vastly reducing the dependency on human labour.

The rapid expansion of the northern towns and cities that were to become the epicentre of Britain's Industrial Revolution in the eighteenth century was not solely to meet the labour demands of new mills, foundries, mines and factories. Nor was it the result of hordes of optimistic country folk moving into the cities with ambitions of either making or marrying into a fortune. Rather it was catalysed by substantial and rapid improvements in agricultural productivity that were made possible by technological advances. Coupled with the consolidation of agricultural landholdings by wealthier farmers, this meant that there was simply no useful work for many among the fast-growing rural population to do in the countryside.

Life for farmers in the earliest agricultural states was not very different from that of farmers in Renaissance Europe. The basic technologies they used for ploughing, planting, harvesting, weeding, irrigating and processing their crops may have been refined over time, and sometimes very cleverly adapted for use in different environments, but they were in many respects fundamentally unchanged up until the late sixteenth century, when the near-simultaneous development and widespread adoption of a sequence of new techniques and technologies dramatically improved energy yields on European farms. Most important among these were the adoption of the highly efficient Dutch plough, which turned the sod better than its predecessors could, and could be pulled by a single draught animal; the intensive use of both natural and artificial fertilisers; a greater focus on selective breeding; and more sophisticated crop rotation systems. Between 1550 and 1850, net yields in wheat and oats per acre farmed in Britain nearly quadrupled, yields in rye and barley tripled, and yields in peas and beans doubled.[3] This increase in productivity catalysed a surge in population growth. In 1750, the population of Great Britain was around 5.7 million people. But thanks to the surge in agricultural productivity it tripled to 16.6 million by 1850, and by 1871, double that again. And where roughly half of Britain's workforce were farmers in 1650, by 1850 that had dropped to one in five.

The process was further accelerated by slavery, colonialism and trade with the New World. Apart from the fact that profits from the slave trade helped finance the construction of Britain's textile mills, by 1860 roughly 4 million enslaved Africans in the United States also provided nearly 90 per cent of the raw material for industrial Britain's first large-scale industry: cotton.

In the century preceding the Industrial Revolution, Mughal India, which by then was under the effective control of Britain's East India Company, was the largest manufacturer and exporter of goods anywhere in the world. Its relatively cheap chintz, cotton and calico textiles fed a consumer revolution among the well-to-do in urban Europe, as a result of which Britain's by then well-established cottage industry producing mainly woollen garments began to struggle. In 1700, with irate shepherds, weavers, dyers and spinners hounding local politicians and anyone else who would listen, Parliament enacted the first of its Calico Acts, under which the importation and sale of finished cotton products into Britain was at first restricted and then banned. What at first sounded like good news for the shepherds, weavers and dyers proved to be the worst possible result for them. Raw cotton flooded in from plantations in North America to fill the gap, giving just the boost the textile mills needed to completely undermine the cottage textile industry.

Just as important were the millions of Caribbean slaves. Where the slaves in North America's southern states shredded their hands picking cotton, Caribbean slaves spent their days hacking through fields of sugar cane and stoking the fires needed to transform the raw cane into molasses, sugar and rum. Sugar products soon became by far the most important of all of colonial Britain's food imports from the New World. Before the Caribbean colonies started producing and exporting sugar in huge quantities, it was a fashionable luxury consumed only in the grandest houses in Europe's cities. If ordinary folk had a hankering for something sweet they had to make do with ripe fruit or, if they were lucky, a spoonful of honey.

But in lateeighteenth- and nineteenth-century Britain, as sugar became more affordable, it was wolfed down in ever more prodigious quantities by people who quickly learned that a warm cup of very sweet tea accompanied by a slice of bread smeared with cheap, very sweet jam was a cost-effective way to sustain them over a twelve-hour shift. Thus,

310

by 1792, it was widely accepted even by abolitionists like the attorney William Fox, who campaigned for an end to plantation slavery in the Caribbean, that sugar was no longer a 'luxury, but has become by constant use a necessary of life'. By the dawn of the twentieth century, per capita sugar consumption in the United Kingdom was a tooth-rotting quarter of a pound every day,[4] a level of consumption that Britons maintianed through to the twenty-first century.

Sugar fuelled the bodies of many workers during Britain's Industrial Revolution. But its factories, barges, railways and ships were powered by coal.

Some foragers had worked out that coal could be burned as fuel as long as 75,000 years ago, and bronze-casters in ancient China made routine use of it from around 4,600 years ago.[5] But outside of East Asia few saw much use for it until the invention of energy-hungry machines and engines. Coal after all was not always easy to find. It was also hard, often dangerous, work to mine, a challenge to transport and, when burned, produced foul, sulphurous smoke and a sticky black soot. More importantly, in most places there was still more than enough wood around with which to make domestic fires. The only places where coal ever rivalled wood as a domestic fuel source were those where shallow deposits were easily accessed and dense populations had already burned their way through most of the local forests.[6] Elsewhere it was only after steam engines came into widespread use that coal and other fossil fuels became an important energy source. This was not only because demand for combustible fuel sky-rocketed as people became aware of its potential, but also because the first widespread use of steam engines was to pump water from sodden coal pits, so making it possible for miners to dig out more coal than they ever could before.

The first rudimentary steam engines were built long before any Enlightenment scientists began to worry about how to measure how much work these machines were capable of doing. Hero of Alexandria, an engineer in Roman Egypt, built a simple spinning steam engine he called an *aelopile* in the first century AD. But like the wind-powered music-making organ he also built, he couldn't think of a use for it other than making it spin and whistle to entertain dignitaries at parties. Versions of this simple pressurised steam turbine are still reproduced every year in thousands of school classrooms.

Engineers in Ottoman Turkey and later in Renaissance France also experimented with building rudimentary engines over a thousand years later, but it was only when the English military engineer Thomas Savery filed a patent in 1698 for 'a new invention for raising of water and occasioning motion to all sorts of mill work by the impellent force of fire' that anyone put steam to serious use. His engines, nicknamed 'miners' friends', were simple condensers with no moving parts. They drew water upwards by creating partial vacuums when hot steam cooled in sealed chambers. They also had an annoying tendency to explode and shower their operators with searing hot shrapnel. But they were powerful enough to pump water from mine pits and so aid miners to retrieve more coal than the tonnes they needed to burn to keep these desperately inefficient machines running in the first place.

An aelopile – the first steam engine as described by Hero of Alexander in AD 50

Savery's big, immobile engines earned him a hallowed place in the history books. But perhaps because he persuaded the British Parliament to extend his exclusive patent, it didn't take long before others came up with new more effective engines based on different designs.

The most important new design was unveiled in 1712 by Thomas Newcomen, an ironmonger who specialised in making equipment for coal and tin miners. His engine powered a separate piston and as a result was far more efficient and powerful than Savery's. Even so, Newcomen's engines were also used mainly to pump water from coal mines and for providing reusable water to drive waterwheels.

Versions of Newcomen's engine remained in widespread use until 1776, when James Watt, who had spent two decades experimenting with new engine designs, realised that by keeping the condenser and the piston separate he could build an even more efficient and versatile engine. Over the course of the eighteenth century, fortunately for those who had to stoke the fires of these engines, the widespread use of coal in foundries increased the scale and quality of their iron output, so enabling the manufacture of ever more precisely engineered and robust engines capable of operating at higher pressures without exploding. As a result, the following century was marked by the appearance and rapid adoption of successive new, increasingly efficient and versatile variants of Watt's engine. From 1780, stationary ones were installed in factories across Europe and used to drive the sometimes bewilderingly complex systems of pulleys, levers, gears and winches that lined factory floors, while mobile ones powered an ever speedier transportation infrastructure capable of moving big cargoes at what a century earlier would have seemed like breakneck speeds.

The construction of at first dozens and then hundreds of large steam-powered textile mills and factories between 1760 and 1840 created thousands of new jobs for migrants to Britain's cities and towns. But it did not – at first – create very many new professions or trades. If anything, the early years of the Industrial Revolution were marked by the mass culling of a whole range of well-established and sometimes even ancient professions, from weavers to farriers, while creating a handful of opportunities for a new class of workers comprised of aspirant engineers, scientists, designers, inventors, architects and entrepreneurs, almost all of whom came from the private school- and Oxbridge-educated urban classes. For those destined to work on the factory floors, actual skills were not on the list of qualities that their employers wanted. What they required were bodies that could be trained to operate their spinning jennys, water frames and power looms.

Life was hard even for those working for the most enlightened employers – by the grim standards of the time – like Richard Arkwright. The inventor of the spinning frame – a machine for binding thread – he established a series of mills across the north of England between 1771 and 1792, was one of the principal targets of the Luddite Rebellion, and is now often thought of as 'the inventor of the factory system'. Those who worked in his factories were expected to perform six thirteen-hour shifts over the course of a week, and any who showed up late were docked two days' pay. He did allow employees a week of annual vacation (unpaid) on the condition that they did not leave town while taking it.

For the first few decades of the Industrial Revolution, and possibly for the first time since ancient cities began to coalesce in the valley of the Euphrates River, farmers had cause to feel better off than many city folk. Where they breathed fresh air and drank mostly clean water, those in the cities laboured longer hours, ate poorly, breathed air fouled with smog, drank dodgy water, and endured diseases like tuberculosis – which accounted for up to one-third of all recorded deaths in the UK between 1800 and 1850 – that raced through their crowded, perpetually coughing tenements. And even though real wages for factory workers slowly crept up over the course of the first half of the nine-teenth century, the average height of both men and women declined, along with their life expectancy.

But perhaps even more importantly, where farmers found at least some immediate satisfaction from applying the skills they accumulated over a lifetime to creatively solve problems on the farm each day, most factory workers had to endure endless hours of mind-numbing, repetitive labour.

Fortunately for the factory owners, former farmers migrating to the cities from the countryside were no strangers to hard work, and where they couldn't find adults to fill empty roles, or needed small bodies to work in cramped spaces or nimble fingers to fix fiddly parts on big machines, there were plenty of children who could be drafted in, as often as not from local orphanages. Children were such compliant and versatile labourers that by the turn of the nineteenth century, close to half of all Britain's factory workers were under the age of fourteen. But the routine exploitation of children in factories was not universally approved of. As a result, the Factory Act passed by His Majesty's Government in 1820 prohibited factories from employing children under the age of nine on a full-time basis. It was subsequently amended in 1833 to require that all children between the ages of nine and thirteen had to receive at least two hours of schooling every day, and that children aged between thirteen and eighteen should not be required to work daily shifts longer than twelve hours at a time.

The early decades of the Industrial Revolution may have been miserable for those who found themselves in the mills and factories, but it did not take long before this steam-powered wealth was translated into some measurable benefits for them too.

At first, the immense new wealth created by industrialisation accrued mainly to those at the top and middle of the economic pile, further entrenching inequality in an already class-obsessed society. But by the 1850s a proportion of it began to trickle down to those working on the factory floors in the form of improved wages and better housing.

In the absence of any meaningful government interventions beyond legislation like the Factory Act, this process was led by several very wealthy factory owners in an early incarnation of what now would be labelled 'corporate social responsibility'. Some of them felt it was their

Christian duty to better support their workers, but most of them had realised that in order for workers to be productive they also needed somewhere adequate to live, enough food to eat and sufficient income to afford an occasional luxury. As new Lords of Commerce, they set out to emulate the feudal aristocrats who came before them by spending a proportion of the often eye-wateringly large fortunes they accrued on building mass housing and public facilities for their workers within easy walking distance of their factories and mills.

Economic data from eighteenth- and nineteenth-century Britain is patchy and researchers don't all agree about how and when this began, but using real wages – wages adjusted to take inflation into account – as a measure, some economists have argued that in the seventy years after 1780, British labourers saw their household incomes double. Others have insisted that the data doesn't support this.[7] They argue that up until the 1840s, the only thing factory workers would have noted growing were the deprivations and miseries that were heaped upon them.[8] Even so, there is no doubt that from the middle of the nineteenth century, most factory and mill workers began to notice a determined upward trend in the quality of their material lives, and for the first time ever they had a little money to spend on the luxuries that until recently had been the exclusive preserve of the middle and upper classes.

It also marked the beginning of many people viewing the work they did exclusively as a means to purchase more stuff, so closing the loop of production and consumption that now sustains so much of our contemporary economy. Indeed, for much of the following 200 years, labour movements and later trade unions would focus almost all of their resources on securing better pay for their members and more free time to spend it in, rather than trying to make their jobs interesting or fulfilling.

———

Over the course of the seventeenth and eighteenth centuries, increasing agricultural productivity, a corresponding increase in artisanal manufacturing, and the import of exotic novelties like linens, porcelain, ivory, ostrich feathers, spices and sugar from the colonies sparked the stirrings of a 'consumer revolution' in the more prosperous parts of Europe.

The embrace of conspicuous consumption was at first confined to the aristocratic and well-to-do merchant classes, but as more and more people became dependent on cash wages rather than the product of their own labours, consumption became more influential in shaping both the fortunes and the aspirations of what would later be referred to as the working classes.

Of course, many of the new luxury items that fuelled Europe's consumer revolution were things that were useful regardless of the status they bestowed on their owner. Light cotton shirts were far more comfortable than scratchy woollen vests, especially in the muggy summer months; a tot of good-quality rum was far easier on the gut than a shot of backstreet gin in a brothel; and ceramic crockery was far easier to clean and store than plates rough-hewn from wood and pewter mugs, even if it was much more delicate and so needed to be replaced more often. But many other luxury items appealed exclusively to the pursuit of status. People

wanted items for no reason but because they wished to emulate others who had them. Thus while aristocrats sought to
emulate royalty, aspirant merchants and members of the
educated professional classes sought to emulate aristocrats,
tradesmen sought to emulate merchants and those at the
base of the pile sought to emulate those in the middle.

It was no coincidence that clothing and textiles were
the first mass-produced items during Britain's Industrial
Revolution. Farmers historically tended to think only
about practicalities when they dressed up for a day's work,
but urban dwellers, even in ancient cities, often dressed
to impress. After all, among the crowds in a busy urban
plaza it is impossible to tell a noble from a commoner if
they both happen to be wearing identical outfits. The tendency among lower classes and castes in cities the world
over to emulate those of higher social standing historically
caused much fretting and tutting among elites determined
to maintain the optics of rank. Some urban elites, like
the extravagantly bewigged and sequinned courtiers who
strutted about the gardens in the Palace of Versailles
during the reign of the Sun King, Louis XIV, achieved this
by adopting insanely elaborate and expensive fashions
that the poor could never hope to copy. Others, like the
Romans, did so by enacting laws that imposed restrictions
on the kinds of clothing that people from different classes
might wear.

This was also the approach adopted across much of
medieval Europe, and was embraced with particular enthusiasm in status-obsessed England, which from the reign of
Edward III (1327–77) through to the Industrial Revolution
enacted a whole host of laws designed to prevent peasants

and merchants from acting as if they were nobility. These sumptuary laws were often packaged in the populist language of economic nationalism. Thus a 1571 Act of Parliament, apparently enacted to support local wool producers, weavers and dyers in England, demanded that, with the exception of hereditary nobles, all men and boys over six years of age had to wear distinctive woollen caps every Sunday and all other holy days, thus introducing the distinctive flat cap as an essential marker of class identity in Britain, which endured all the way through to the twenty-first century when it was cheerfully re-appropriated as a symbol of prosperity by hipsters.

The problem with sumptuary laws was that they were nearly impossible to police, and often made aspirational folk even more determined to dress like their 'betters'. In late seventeenth-century Britain, this inspired a thriving market for second-hand clothes abandoned by the upper classes. It also persuaded some anguished aristocrats to dress down to distinguish themselves from the rabble who were dressing up, much to the horror of some continental visitors like the French *abbé* Jean le Blanc, who noted caustically that in England 'masters dress like their valets and duchesses copy after their chambermaids'.[9]

Clothing may have been the most obvious and immediate signifier of status outside of the home, but as Britain's cities began to swell over the course of the seventeenth and eighteenth centuries, aspirant families sought to emulate the wealthier classes within the home too. Homewares in particular emerged as important signifiers of status, especially among people living in the rows and rows of undifferentiated houses that were built to accommodate urban migrants. Unsurprisingly, it did not take long for ambitious entrepreneurs to begin to explore opportunities to mass-produce things like affordable porcelain and ceramic homewares, mirrors, combs, books, clocks, carpets and all sorts of different kinds of furniture.

Over the course of the seventeenth and eighteenth centuries, the desire of poorer people in cities across Europe to consume what were once luxuries enjoyed only by the very rich was just as influential in shaping the history of work as the invention of technologies to exploit the energy in fossil fuels. Without it, there would have been no markets for mass-produced items, and without markets the factories would never have been built. It also rewrote the rules by which much of the economy operated. The growth of Britain's economy increasingly came to depend on people employed in manufacturing and other industries reinvesting their wages in the very same products they and their factory workers manufactured.

———

When he was appointed the first ever lecturer in sociology at the University of Bordeaux in 1887, Emile Durkheim was in no doubt that new fashions were often quickly embraced by the poorer and more marginal hoping to emulate the rich and powerful. He was also in no doubt that fashions were, by their nature, ephemeral. 'Once a fashion has been adopted by everyone,' he noted, 'it loses all its value.'[10]

Durkheim had good reason to be worried about the transience of fashions, especially in the fickle world of academia where new voguish theories came and went with the seasons.

It was after all only five years previously that as a freshly graduated student in his mid-twenties he had set out to convince the grandees of French and German intelligentsia that not only was the study of society more than just an intellectual novelty, it also merited being recognised as a science in its own right. As sociology's self-appointed architect, he saw in his own ambitions an echo of when, a century earlier, Adam Smith had established economics. Coincidentally, like Smith, many of Durkheim's ambitions were also shaped by an abiding interest in the 'division of labour'. But unlike Smith, Durkheim was not especially interested in trucking, trading and bartering. Nor was he particularly concerned with the economic efficiencies that might be achieved by reorganising production processes in factories. When he contemplated the division of labour, he had a much broader vision of the role 'work' played in shaping both individual lives and society as a whole. And as far as he was concerned, many of the challenges faced by people living in complex urban societies had to do with the fact that in modern cities people did all sorts of different kinds of work.

Durkheim believed that a crucial difference between 'primitive' societies and complex modern ones was that where simple societies operated like rudimentary machines with lots of easily interchangeable parts, complex societies functioned more like living bodies and were made up of lots of very different, highly specialised organs that, like livers, kidneys and brains, could not be substituted for one another. Thus chiefs and shamans in simple societies could simultaneously be foragers, hunters, farmers and builders, but in complex societies lawyers could not moonlight as surgeons any more than admirals could moonlight as architects. Durkheim also believed that people in primitive societies typically had a far stronger sense of community and belonging than people in more complex urban ones, and to this extent were happier and more sure of themselves. If everyone in a primitive society performed interchangeable roles, he reasoned, then they would be bound into a kind of 'mechanical solidarity' that was easily reinforced by shared customs, norms and religious beliefs. He contrasted this with life in modern urban societies, where people performed many, often very different roles and so developed very different perspectives of the world, and insisted that this not only made it harder to bind people together but also induced a potentially fatal and always debilitating social disease that he dubbed 'anomie'.

Durkheim introduced the idea of anomie in his first book, *The Division of Labour in Society*, but developed it much further in his second monograph *Suicide: A Study in Sociology*, in which he aimed to show that suicide, which at the time was widely thought to be a reflection of profound individual failings, often had social causes and so presumably could also have social solutions. He used the term to describe the feelings of intense dislocation, anxiety and even anger that drove people to behave antisocially and, when desperate, perhaps take their own lives. When Durkheim described anomie in this way he was trying to make sense of how the rapid changes brought about by industrialisation affected individual well-being. He was particularly intrigued by the fact that, almost paradoxically, the increase in prosperity that accompanied industrialisation in France had resulted in more suicides and greater social stress. This led him to conclude that it was the changes associated with urbanisation and industrial development that were a major driver of anomie. An example he offered was of traditional craftsmen whose skills were suddenly rendered redundant by technological advances and who, as a result, lost their status as valuable, contributing members of society, and were forced to endure lives robbed of the purposefulness that their work once provided them. Durkheim not only credited anomie with suicide, but also with a whole host of other social problems that up to then were commonly attributed to bad character, like crime, truancy and anti-social behaviour.

Durkheim believed that there was more to anomie than the sense of profound individual dislocation arising out of the changes associated with the Industrial Revolution. He insisted that anomie was characterised by what he called the 'malady of infinite aspiration', a condition arising when there are 'no limits to men's aspirations' because they 'no longer know what is possible and what is not, what is just and what is unjust, which claims and expectations are legitimate and which are immoderate'.[11]

It was not his explicit intention, but in invoking the 'malady of infinite aspiration' he offered a strikingly original take on the problem of scarcity, different from that used by economists. Where Adam Smith and generations of economists after him were convinced that we would always be hostage to infinite desires, Durkheim took the view that being burdened by unattainable expectations was not normal but rather a social aberration that arose only in times of crisis and change, when a society lost its bearings as a result of external factors like industrialisation. Times like those he was living in.

As grim as his subject matter often was, a vein of undiluted optimism runs through much of Durkheim's writing. He believed that having diagnosed the causes of anomie, it was just a matter of time before a social medicine was devised strong enough to treat the malady of infinite aspirations. He also believed that he was living through a unique period of transition, and that in time people would adjust to life in the industrial age. In the intervening period, he thought that the adoption of a benign form of nationalism, like the gentlemanly loyalty he felt towards France, and possibly also the establishment of trade guilds like ancient Roman *collegia* that would provide harried urbanites with a sense of belonging and community, might ease the malady of infinite aspiration.

In hindsight, it is clear that Durkheim was wrong to think that the malady could be so easily cured. Anomie continues to be invoked time and time again in analyses of social alienation arising from change, but few share Durkheim's optimism about a cure. There is good reason to think that by the time of his death in 1917 Durkheim was no longer so certain of it either. By 1914, the nationalism that he believed might cure people of anomie had morphed into something altogether uglier, which in combination with the boundless ambitions of Europe's leaders, and courtesy of the new-found capacity to mass-produce ever more destructive weapons, had plunged the continent into the first war of the industrial age. The war soon claimed the lives of many of Durkheim's favourite students, and in 1915 the life of his only son, André. Durkheim was shattered by the loss and died soon after suffering a stroke in 1917.

Since then, the kind of stability that Durkheim imagined would eventually settle in following industrialisation has come to resemble just another infinite aspiration that slips frustratingly further away whenever it seems to be nearly in reach. Instead, as energy-capture rates have surged, new technologies have come online and our cities have continued to swell, constant and unpredictable change has become the new normal everywhere, and anomie looks increasingly like the permanent condition of the modern age.

13

Top Talent

'Hardly a competent workman can be found . . . who does not devote a considerable amount of time to studying just how slowly he can work and still convince his employer he's going at a good pace,' Frederick Winslow Taylor explained to a meeting of the American Society of Mechanical Engineers in June 1903.[1] He was lecturing them about the perils of the 'natural tendency of men to take it easy' or to 'loaf' in the workplace, a phenomenon he called 'soldiering' because it reminded him of the half-hearted efforts of military conscripts, who only ever showed ambition when dodging unpleasant duties. He also explained how, through the rigorous application of his 'scientific method of management', factory owners could not only eliminate soldiering but also shave considerable time and costs from their manufacturing processes. Costs that could be transformed into profits.

Taylor, who was so highly strung that he had to strap himself into a straitjacket to help him fall asleep at night,[2] was anything but a loafer. When he was not welding sheet metal, designing machine tools, preparing reports, recommendations and manuscripts, or conducting meticulous time-and-motion studies, stopwatch in hand, he could be found playing tennis or golf. He approached his leisure with the same frantic intensity he brought to his work. He won the US National Championship in tennis in 1881 and then, nineteen years later, played golf for team USA in the 1900 Summer Olympics. The son of well-to-do Quakers who traced their family back to the *Mayflower* Pilgrims, Taylor eschewed the career path he was expected to follow on leaving school. After declining the place he was offered at Harvard, he showed up at the gates of the Enterprise Hydraulic Works in Philadelphia to begin a four-year apprenticeship as a machinist.

Born in 1856, Taylor was part of the first generation of Americans to grow up inhaling the sulphurous fumes emitted by big American factories. By the time of his death in 1915, he was eulogised by the glassy-eyed titans of industry like Henry Ford as the 'father of the efficiency movement', and declared by management consultants to be the 'Newton [or] Archimedes of the science of work'.[3]

His legacy was viewed with mixed feelings by factory workers. Despite the fact that he lobbied for workers to be paid a proper wage, to work reasonable hours and take time off, his methods robbed them of what little initiative they were free to exercise when performing their jobs. They also gave far greater licence to managers to meddle with what workers were doing. A factory organised according to Taylor's scientific method was a workspace where patience, obedience and the ability to lose oneself in the metallic beat of the mechanical hammers in a forge were far better qualifications than imagination, ambition and creativity.

Like Benjamin Franklin before him, Taylor swore by the adage that 'time is money'. But where Franklin believed that time spent on any earnest endeavour nourished the soul, Taylor saw no point in working inefficiently. And where Franklin was content to be disciplined about time, Taylor was determined to translate every second into profit, courtesy of the decimal stopwatch he carried everywhere in his pocket.

Taylor was not greatly impressed by his colleagues during his apprenticeship at Enterprise Hydraulic. Many 'soldiered', most cut corners and, to Taylor's mind, even the most diligent among them were irritatingly inefficient. When his apprenticeship came to an end, he was nevertheless determined to remain on the factory floor and soon accepted the offer of a job as a labourer in the machine shop at the Midvale Steel Works, a manufacturer of high-spec alloy parts for military and engineering applications. He liked it there, and the management liked him. He was quickly promoted from a lathe operator to gang boss and eventually chief engineer. It was there that he also began to conduct experiments with his stopwatch, carefully observing and timing different tasks to see whether he could shave a few seconds off various critical processes, and redesign job roles to ensure that labourers would find it difficult to waste effort.

The same freedom that Taylor was granted to conduct his efficiency experiments at Midvale would be denied to other similarly innovative and ambitious individuals in workplaces that adopted his scientific management technique. Instead, they'd be shackled to rigid, target-driven, repetitive work regimes where innovation was prohibited and the most important role of managers was to ensure that workers performed as they were instructed to.

Taylor's scientific method was based on breaking down any production process into its smallest component elements, timing each of them, evaluating their importance and complexity, and then reassembling the process from top to bottom with a focus on maximising efficiency. Some of the solutions he proposed were as simple as changing where tools and equipment were stored on a workbench to eliminate small but unnecessary movements. Others were much more comprehensive and involved totally reorganising a production process or redesigning a factory. 'It is only through *enforced* standardization of methods, *enforced* adoption of the best implements and working conditions, and *enforced* cooperation that this faster work can be assured,' he explained in *Scientific Management*.

'Taylorism', as it came to be called, was adopted in many workplaces, but never more famously than at the Ford Motor Company. In 1903, Henry Ford hired Taylor to assist him in developing a new production process for the now iconic Model T Ford. The result of Ford and Taylor's collaboration was the transformation of the private motor vehicle from an ostentatious luxury into an accessible, and very practical, symbol of success and good hard work. Instead of having teams of skilled mechanics assemble vehicles from start to finish, the vehicle's chassis was shunted down a production line, alongside which were stationed teams of workers who only ever performed one relatively straightforward task. This meant that Ford did not need to hire skilled mechanics. All he needed was anyone capable of learning a few simple techniques and diligently following instructions. It also meant he could produce more cars, faster and more cheaply than before. He cut down the production time of a single Model T Ford from twelve hours to ninety-three minutes, and with that cut the price of them from $825 to $575 (about £670 to £470).

The stockholders and senior executives in the companies that adopted Taylorism considered it a tremendous success. After all, it almost instantly yielded greater productivity and glorious dividends. From the perspective of workers on the factory floor, though, Taylorism was a mixed blessing. On the positive side, as much as loafers set Taylor's teeth on edge, he believed that 'first class workers' should be rewarded for their productivity. Taylor thought that the reason that most people took jobs and went to work was, fundamentally, for the financial rewards and the products they might purchase with them. He thus insisted that workers should be incentivised by taking some of the profits his efficiencies generated, and transforming them into bigger wage packets and more time off to spend them.

Taylor, whose scientific management approach also helped lay the foundation for 'human resources management' as a corporate function, firmly believed that you needed to find the right person for the right job. One problem was that the right person for most of the non-managerial jobs Taylor designed was someone with limited imagination, boundless patience and a willingness to obediently do the same repetitive tasks day in and day out.

Taylor had many critics. Among the most outspoken was Samuel Gompers, the charismatic president and founder of the American Federation of Labor, an organisation that lobbied on behalf of the many skilled-craft unions in the United States, including cobblers, hat-makers, barbers, glass-blowers and cigar-makers. As a young immigrant to the tough streets of New York, he learned how to roll cigars and had found great satisfaction in the performance of what he considered to be a highly skilled and satisfying craft. The problem with Taylorism as he saw it was not the profits it generated for factory owners, but the fact that it robbed workers of the right to find meaning and satisfaction in the work they did, by transforming them into nothing more than 'high speed automatic machines' that were installed in factories as if they were 'a cog or a nut or a pin in a big machine'.[4]

Taylorism may have inspired much criticism from the likes of Gompers, but just like the Luddites, Taylor's critics were paddling against the profitable tides of history. Thus in 2001, ninety years after it was first published, Taylor's *Scientific Management* was voted the most influential management book of the twentieth century by members of the Institute of Management. But had Taylor taken up the place he was offered at Harvard and gone into law as he was expected to, instead of taking up his apprenticeship at Enterprise Hydraulic, someone else would have assumed the mantle of the high priest of the 'efficiency movement'. Efficiency had been in the air ever since the very first stirrings of the Industrial Revolution – Adam Smith had already outlined the basic principles of the efficiency movement in his *Wealth of Nations* – and by the nineteenth century factory owners everywhere understood the correspondence between productivity, efficiency and profit, even if they hadn't yet worked out the best means to achieve it. Working hours for manual labourers in particular were declining rapidly as productivity went up. Taylor's genius was simply that he was the first to approach the problem as methodically as a scientist might approach an experiment in a laboratory. He was also the first to realise that in the modern era most people went to work to make money rather than products, and that it was the factories themselves that made actual things'.

———

Charles Darwin's friend and neighbour, Sir John Lubbock, 1st Baron Avebury, was the very model of a modern Victorian gentleman. And like his near contemporary, Frederick Winslow Taylor, he was also a very busy man.

Lubbock, who died in 1913 at the age of seventy-nine, is now remembered by anthropologists and archaeologists as the man who coined the terms 'Palaeolithic' to describe Stone Age foragers and 'Neolithic' to describe the oldest farming cultures. But he ought to be remembered by many others too, at least in the United Kingdom and its former colonies, where one of his achievements is still celebrated on eight or more occasions every year. As the Member of Parliament for Maidstone in Kent, John Lubbock was the driving force behind Parliament's adoption of the Bank Holiday Act of 1871, as a result of which most Britons and citizens of Commonwealth countries still enjoy public 'bank holidays' every year.

'Saint Lubbock', as he was affectionately known in the 1870s, was an early and enthusiastic advocate of maintaining a good work–life balance. 'Work is a necessity of existence,' he explained, but 'Rest is not idleness', because 'to lie sometimes on the grass under trees on a summer's day, listening to the murmur of the water, or watching the clouds float across the sky, is by no means a waste of time'.[5]

It is hard to imagine that someone as busy as Lubbock ever found the time to surrender himself to the clouds.

As well as being a Member of Parliament, he won county colours for Kent playing cricket; played in the losing team of the 1875 FA Cup Final in football; ran the family bank; was the inaugural president of the UK's Institute of Bankers; chairman of the London County Council; a privy councillor to the Queen; president of the Royal Statistical Society; vice chairman of the Royal Society; and president of the Anthropological Institute. In addition to these roles, he somehow found the time to research and write several well-received books. Some were whimsical, like his two-volume *The Pleasures of Life*, in which he expounded on the importance of rest, work, sport and nature. Some, like his meticulously researched treatises on British flora and insects, were scientifically rigorous and judiciously argued. Others were more ambitious still, and none more so than his most well-known work, *Pre-historic times, as illustrated by ancient remains, and the manners and customs of modern savages*, which was published in 1865 and for which he was awarded a string of honorary degrees and other awards.

Reading Lubbock's collected works, it is hard to avoid the conclusion that he viewed banking and politics as odious duties but considered his scientific work a worthy indulgence. It is also hard to avoid the sense that his views on the relationship between work and leisure were shaped by the fact that, had he chosen to, he could have lived in idle comfort, being waited on by the brigades of liveried footmen, maids, cooks, gardeners and butlers who kept in good order the grand Italianate mansion and extensive ornamental gardens at the 250-acre family estate, High Elms, just outside London. Indeed, it takes a special form of privilege to be able to devote several intensive months, as Lubbock once did, to trying to teach his beloved pet poodle, Van, how to read.

Lubbock was not unusual in this regard. Like Darwin, Boucher de Perthes, Benjamin Franklin, Adam Smith, Aristotle and even the frenetic Frederick Winslow Taylor, Lubbock's most important achievements were only possible because he was wealthy enough to afford to do exactly what he wanted to. If he'd had to work the same hours as the staff who maintained High Elms or the thousands of men, women and children labouring on farms and in the factories, he wouldn't have had the influence to push the Bank Holiday Act through Parliament, nor the time or energy to study archaeology, play sports or carefully document the habits of garden insects.

When John Lubbock shepherded his Bank Holiday Act through the committee chambers of Parliament in 1871, working conditions in British factories and mills were unregulated, trade unions were banned and, under the Master and Servants Act, workers who were disrespectful to their managers or who agitated for industrial action were subject to criminal prosecution and potentially a lengthy spell in one of Her Majesty's Prisons. The only substantive regulations dealing with workers' rights were those in the Factory Act of 1833, which limited the working week for women and for children under the age of eighteen to sixty hours per week, but imposed no restrictions on the number of hours that men might be required to work. After the Bank Holiday Act had been passed in 1871, it would take another 128 years and the implementation of the European Union's Working Time directive in the late 1990s before any restrictions on male working hours would enter Britain's statute books. Even so, by 1870, the working week for most men and women employed in many factories had already declined from around seventy-eight hours per week to around sixty, based on six ten-hour shifts.

In a rare moment of self-pity, Lubbock wrote that great 'wealth entails almost more labour than poverty, and certainly more anxiety'.[6] It was one of several statements he made in his collected works suggesting that, like many others of his background, he didn't really understand the long hours the working classes actually laboured for, or how unpleasant much of their work was. There is after all a considerable difference between spending a day nodding off in one of the committee rooms of the House of Commons interrupted by a four-course lunch with the Institute of Bankers, and spending a fourteen-hour shift choking on sulphur and phosphorus fumes while gluing boxes together in a freezing matchstick factory. In other words, most people were grateful to Saint Lubbock not because he had won them a little extra time to pursue their individual interests or hobbies, but because he secured them an extra day a few times a year in which they might rest their work-worn bodies and do as little as possible.

The passing of the Bank Holiday Act 1871 signalled a sea change in attitudes regarding time off for workers. This process was hastened by the legalisation of trade unions later the same year, and, in 1888, the first successful legal strike in British history, when the 'matchgirls' working for one of Britain's largest match producers, Bryant and May, took to the streets to protest about their toxic working conditions and demand an end to fourteen-hour shifts.

Despite unions progressively growing in power and influence, working hours still remained high and most people worked a six-day, fifty-six-hour week until after the First World War came to an end in 1918. Then, courtesy of a shift in social attitudes shaped by the carnage men witnessed on the battlefields of the Somme, Ypres and Passchendaele, as well as technological advances and a surge in productivity as a result of the widespread adoption of Winslow Taylor's scientific management techniques, working hours declined quickly to around forty-eight hours per week. Before another decade passed, with Henry Ford – who by then employed close to 200,000 in his American factories, and nearly as many again at his factories in European capitals, Canada, South Africa, Australia, Asia and Latin America – leading the way, the forty-hour week, based on five eight-hour shifts and weekends off, became the norm in most big manufacturing industries.

The Great Depression put further downward pressure on working hours as companies cut production. This process spurred an embryonic 'shorter hours movement', and very nearly persuaded the Roosevelt administration to introduce the thirty-hour working week into law in the form of the Black-Connery 30-Hours Bill, which sailed through the Senate in 1932 with a fifty-three to thirty majority. Pulled at the last minute when President Roosevelt got cold feet, the bill was abandoned, and as the worst of the Depression passed, hours crept steadily upwards again. By the time Hitler's panzers rolled into Poland in the autumn of 1939 most employed Americans were working thirty-eight-hour weeks again.

Apart from a rise in working hours during the Second World War, between 1930 and 1980 the average working week in the United States remained fairly consistently between thirty-seven and thirty-nine hours per week. This was two or three hours shorter than in almost every other industrialised country. But in the last decades of the twentieth century, they started to creep slowly upwards again, while total hours worked in most other industrialised countries slowly declined. Since 1980, average weekly working hours in the United States have been broadly aligned with those of Western European economies, but because of less generous provisions for annual leave, most Americans work several hundred more hours over the course of a year than people in equivalent jobs in countries like Denmark, France and Germany.

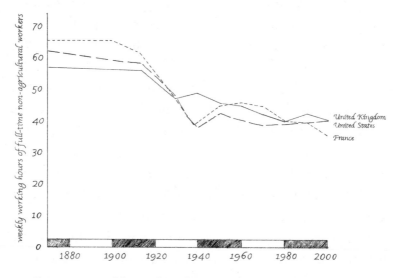

Changes in weekly working hours in the UK, USA and France
1870–2000

John Maynard Keynes's belief that 'the standard of life in progressive countries' in 2030 would be between 'four and eight times as high' as it was in 1930 was based on the assumption that economic growth would increase at a steady rate of around 2 per cent every year. In 2007, Yale economist Fabrizio Zilliboti revisited Keynes's predictions. He calculated that, based on growth rates, a fourfold increase in living standards had already occurred by 1980, and that, assuming growth trends continued, by 2030 we would witness a '17 fold increase in the standard of living, amounting to more than double Keynes's upper bound'.[7] As unevenly distributed as wealth and income are, most people in industrialised economies probably now meet something resembling the basic living standards that Keynes had in mind when he imagined that 'absolute needs' would be adequately met. In the United States, for instance, median net wealth of households in 2017 was $97,000 (£78,600).[8] That is three times higher than it was in 1946 but a good deal less than it was in 2006, just before the subprime crisis sent the global economy into a tailspin. Median household wealth then was in the region of six times higher than 1946.[9] Tellingly, it is also only roughly one-seventh of the average household net worth in the United States, a number skewed upwards by high levels of inequality.

But working hours have not declined as Keynes predicted. Indeed, despite labour productivity in industrialised nations having risen roughly four- or five-fold since the end of the Second World War, average weekly working hours everywhere have continued to gravitate towards an average of just under forty hours per week, and then remain stubbornly stuck there.

Economists have long debated why working hours have remained so stubbornly high, but most agree that one part of the answer is reflected in the story of what remains the world's bestselling cereal brand.

———

Every year an estimated 128 billion bowls of Kellogg's breakfast cereals are fed into hundreds of millions of hungry mouths. The Kellogg's brand is synonymous with a cast of cheerful spoon-wielding cartoon characters who grin from its packaging and commercials. None of these characters much resemble their founding ancestor, John Harvey Kellogg, a Seventh-Day Adventist with a rebellious streak, a passion for healthy living and a pathological hatred of anything to do with sex. An advocate for universal circumcision because he believed it might dissuade boys from masturbating, he invented a small range of breakfast cereals designed specifically to curb the passions of the patients who attended the Battle Creek Sanatorium, the vegetarian 'wellness' retreat he established in 1886.

His cereals were not intended to be particularly tasty. John Harvey Kellogg was of the view that spicy, rich and sweet food induced unwanted sexual urges but that plain food calmed them. Corn flakes, which he patented in 1895, were developed specifically as a sexual turn-off.

It turned out that Kellogg's sanatorium patients liked his crispy cereals anyway. They were a welcome relief from the austere plates of unsalted vegetables they were served for their other meals. But John Harvey Kellogg wasn't interested in commercialising his cereals. It was left to one of his adopted sons, Will Kellogg, who did not share his father's puritanical views, to transform Kellogg's cereals into a globally recognised brand. He added some sugar to the old man's recipes and then in 1906 began to mass-produce his cereals. He also added some sugar to the marketing campaign. To dispel any lingering idea that his product might curb his customers' sex drive, his first big campaign for corn flakes encouraged young men to wink suggestively at pretty grocers.

Over the next forty years, Will Kellogg revolutionised food production in the United States. A serial innovator, he experimented with and applied all the latest trends in management, production and marketing, including Taylorism. By the 1920s, his company and its principal product was a household name in the USA and it would not take long before it expanded internationally.

When the Great Depression struck in 1929, Kellogg's was already a big employer. At the time, its only real rival in the mushrooming breakfast cereal market was Post, who did what many other businesses still do in times of economic uncertainty. They cut back on all non-essential spending and took inventories of paper clips, staples and ink as part of the effort to maximise cash. Kellogg took a very different approach. He doubled his advertising and ramped up production. It was a successful strategy. It turned out that people liked to eat cheap, sugary, crunchy grains soaked in milk when times were hard and his profits soared while shareholders in Post learned not to hold their breath waiting for any dividends.

Kellogg did something else that was unusual. He cut full-time working hours at his factories from an already reasonable forty hours a week to a comfortable thirty hours a week, based on five six-hour shifts. By doing this, he was able to create an entire shift's worth of new full-time jobs in a period when up to a quarter of Americans were unemployed. It seemed a sensible thing to do for other reasons too. By the 1930s, American workers were already lobbying for shorter working hours after companies like Henry Ford's had successfully introduced weekends and five-day weeks with no noticeable dip in productivity (if anything, there was an increase in profitability), and so Kellogg believed that his thirty-hour week was putting him on the right side of a historical trend. It turned out to be the right thing to do for Kellogg's bottom line as well. Production-halting work-related accidents became far more infrequent, and his operating overheads declined so much that in 1935 Kellogg boasted in a newspaper article that 'we can [now] afford to pay as much for six hours as we formerly paid for eight'.

Until the 1950s, the thirty-hour week remained the norm at Kellogg's factories. Then, somewhat to the surprise of management, three-quarters of Kellogg's factory staff voted in favour of returning to eight-hour shifts and a forty-hour week. Some of the workers explained that they wished to return to an eight-hour day because the six-hour shifts meant they spent too much time getting under the feet of irritable spouses back at home. But most were clear: they wanted to work longer hours to take home more money, to purchase more or better versions of the endless procession of constantly upgraded consumer products coming on to the market during America's affluent post-war era.[10]

In the late 1940s and early 1950s, war-weary Americans set about building Chevrolet Bel-Airs instead of tanks, converting their accumulated munitions piles into nitrogen-based fertilisers, and repurposing their radar technology into microwave ovens. This nourished a newly reconfigured American dream set against a background of ice cream in the home freezer, TV dinners and fast-food-fuelled annual interstate vacations. Labour union membership was at an all-time high and the peace dividend from 'the war to end all wars' was nurturing an ever-expanding and more prosperous middle class.

This prosperity convinced John Kenneth Galbraith, the Canadian-born Professor of Economics at Harvard, that advanced economies like the United States' were already sufficiently productive to meet the basic material needs of all their citizens and hence that the economic problem as defined by John Maynard Keynes had, more or less, been solved. He expressed this sentiment in his most famous book, *The Affluent Society*, which was published to great acclaim in 1958.

Galbraith was a towering figure of American economic history and not just because, at six foot eight, he rarely encountered anyone who could stare him in the eye. By the time of his death in December 2007, in addition to his decades-long professorship at Harvard he was the most widely read economist of the twentieth century, having sold more than 7 million books. He also served as the editor of *Fortune* magazine for several years, and assumed a variety of high-profile roles in the Roosevelt, Kennedy and Clinton administrations. But Galbraith did not consider himself an economist in the traditional mould. Neither did he hold his chosen field of study in particularly high esteem. Galbraith, who once described economics as principally being 'extremely useful as a form of employment for economists', accused his colleagues of using unnecessary complexity to disguise the banality of their art, especially when it came to matters like monetary policy.[11] The son of a farmer, his entry into economics came by way of his early ambitions to run the biggest and best shorthorn cattle ranch in his home province of Ontario. To that end he acquired two degrees in agricultural economics. Along the way he also developed forthright views about the fundamental relationship between primary production, like agriculture, and the rest of the economy.

In *The Affluent Society*, Galbraith sketched out a picture of post-war America in which material scarcity had already ceased to be the primary driver of economic activity. The United States, he observed, had become so productive since the war that 'more die ... of too much food than of too little'. Nevertheless, he reckoned that the USA was not making particularly good use of its wealth. 'No problem has been more puzzling to thoughtful people than why, in a troubled world, we make such poor use of our affluence,' he wrote.

One of the main reasons that Galbraith took this view was post-war Americans' seemingly limitless appetite for purchasing things they didn't need. Galbraith believed that by the 1950s most Americans' material desires were as manufactured as the products they purchased to satisfy them. Because most people's basic economic needs were now easily met, he argued, producers and advertisers conspired to invent new artificial needs to keep the hamster wheel of production and consumption rolling rather than investing in public services. Real scarcity, in other words, was a thing of the past.

Galbraith may have considered advertising a modern phenomenon, but the manufacture of desire is at least as old as the first cities. In ancient metropolises, advertising took many forms familiar to us now, from the seductive pornographic tableaus that decorated the walls of brothels in Pompeii to elegantly printed handbills and flyers emblazoned with cute logos and snappy slogans distributed by craftspeople in Song Dynasty China. But until recently advertising was something most people did for themselves. That all changed with mass-circulation newspapers.

In the United States, the birth of advertising as a revenue-generating industry in its own right is now often credited to none other than Benjamin Franklin. In 1729, after purchasing the *Pennsylvania Gazette*, Franklin struggled to turn a profit through sales alone, and wondered whether he might defray the costs by selling space in the paper to local traders and manufacturers wanting to drum up new business. His plan did not work at first, as no one was convinced that forking out good money to a local newspaper would be of much use. Cash-strapped, Franklin tried a different approach and prominently advertised one of his own inventions, the Franklin Stove, to see if that would help. Doing so won him a double victory. Sales of the Franklin Stove surged and other tradesmen soon took notice and purchased advertising space in the *Pennsylvania Gazette*, so earning Franklin a new income stream and an esteemed place in America's Advertising Hall of Fame.[12] Other newspapers and magazines quickly followed Franklin's lead, but it would take another century before the first proper advertising agencies – businesses focused purely on designing and then placing adverts in newspapers on behalf of clients – would be formed.

The exalted position of advertising in global commerce was ultimately enabled by industrialisation. For much of the century after Franklin's marketing experiments, most adverts were dull, informative and aimed exclusively at local people. But this changed with the embrace of mass production, as entrepreneurs with grand ambitions realised that if they were to access markets beyond their home towns they would need to advertise. They also realised that they needed to differentiate themselves from local suppliers of similar products, with the result that advertisers began to focus more and more on catching readers' eyes with snappy slogans in different fonts, and on adding pictures. By the 1930s, advertising was as important to marque brands like Kellogg's and Ford as any part of their operations. As Henry Ford famously commented, 'Stopping advertising to save money is like stopping your watch to save time.'

In making the case that America's affluence was being squandered by the alliance between manufacturers and advertisers, Galbraith was not setting his sights on the likes of Kellogg's or even the Ford Motor Company. To his mind, they at least made useful products. His animosity was towards those he believed were manipulating people's aspirations, exploiting their anxieties about status and exalting their 'relative needs'.

When Galbraith published *The Affluent Society*, the long-lunch and lounge-suit era of advertising was shifting up a gear as advertisers realised the unprecedented power of television to pump messages directly into people's homes and workplaces. It was just over a decade since the agency N. W. Ayer had come up with what is now widely regarded as the most influential advertising tagline in United States' history, a 'diamond is forever'. This almost single-handedly created the association between eternal love and diamonds in the world's richest luxury market, established the convention of men marking their engagements with the gift of a diamond solitaire ring to their fiancée, and in doing so created sustained demand for a product that hardly anyone before 1940 cared much about at all. By the late 1950s, diamond rings became so ubiquitous that Galbraith remarked, 'Once a sufficiently impressive display of diamonds could create attention even for the most obese and repellent body, for they signified membership in a highly privileged caste. Now the same diamonds are afforded by a television star or a talented harlot.'

For Galbraith, advertising served another counter-intuitive purpose beyond keeping the cycle of production and consumption rolling. He thought it made people worry less about inequality because, as long as they were able to purchase new consumer products once in a while, they felt that they were upwardly mobile and so closing the gap between them selves and others.

'It has become evident to conservatives and liberals alike,' he noted drily, 'that increasing aggregate output is an alternative to redistribution or even to the reduction of inequality.'[13]

This should have all changed in the 1980s, after what some analysts now refer to as the 'Great Decoupling' took effect.

It didn't.

For much of the twentieth century, there was a relatively stable relationship between labour productivity and wages in the United States and other industrialised countries. This meant that as the economy grew and labour output increased, the amount of money people took home in their wage packets grew at a similar rate. While this meant that richer people took home a larger net slice of the profits, at least everybody felt that as the companies employing them got richer, so did they.

In 1980, though, that relationship broke down. In the 'Great Decoupling', productivity, output and gross domestic product all continued to grow, but wage growth for all but the highest paid stalled. Over time, many people started to notice that their monthly wages didn't stretch as far as they used to, despite the fact that they were doing the same jobs they had in the same, profitable, businesses.

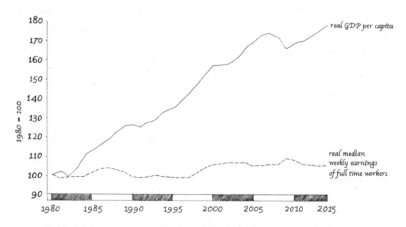

Graph showing real GDP per capita in the USA nearly doubles between 1980 and 2015 but real median incomes stagnate[14]

350

The Great Decoupling killed off any lingering down-ward pressure on the length of the working week. Most people simply couldn't afford to maintain their lifestyles by working fewer hours. Many took on lots more personal and household debt, which conveniently enough at the time was very cheap. Among the better paid segments of the workforce, it encouraged a net rise in hours worked, as the potential rewards for 'top achievers' suddenly went through the roof.

It is not yet clear what caused the Great Decoupling. Some economists even dispute that it happened. They argue that the stark graphs indicating a clear divergence between productivity and median real wages are inaccurate because they don't account for the rising costs of incidental benefits paid to US employees, mainly in the form of ballooning health insurance bills, and because standard methods for measuring inflation don't capture the real picture.

For many others, though, the Great Decoupling was the first clear evidence that technological expansion was cannibalising the workforce and concentrating wealth in fewer hands. They point out that in 1964, the tele-coms giant AT&T was worth $267 billion in today's dollars and employed 758,611 people. This works out at roughly one employee to every $350,000 of value. Today's communications giant, Google, by contrast, is worth $370 billion and has only around 55,000 employees, which works out at roughly $6 million of value per employee.

The process was facilitated by a series of important pol-itical developments. There was the deregulation of markets and 'trickle-down economics' championed by Thatcher and Reagan, as well as, later, the collapse of Communism and the embrace of oligarchy capitalism in the former Soviet Republics, and the rise of the South East Asian 'tiger economies' spurred by China's embrace of state capitalism.

When John Maynard Keynes plotted the course to his economic promised land, he imagined that it would be the 'strenuous purposeful money-makers' – the ambitious CEOs and moneymen – who would pilot us all there. But he also believed that as soon as we arrived, 'the rest of us will no longer be under any obligation to applaud and encourage them'.

In this, he was wrong.

In 1965, chief executives in the top 350 US firms took home roughly twenty times the pay of an 'average worker'.[15] By 1980, CEOs in the same top bracket of firms took home thirty times the annual salary of an average worker, and by 2015, that number had surged to just shy of three hundred times. Adjusted for inflation, most US workers gained a modest 11.7 per cent rise in real wages between 1978 and 2016, while CEOs typically enjoyed a 937 per cent increase in remuneration.

The surge in senior executives' pay was not only a US phenomenon. In the two decades before the Great Recession in 2007, big companies everywhere were persuaded that to attract and retain 'top talent' they had to offer exorbitant pay packages.

It was the global consultancy firm McKinsey & Company who started the hysteria. In 1998, they introduced the word 'talent' to the ever growing lexicon of corporate speak when

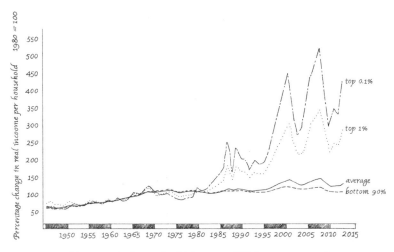

Changes in household income USA 1945–2015[16]

they headlined one of their *Quarterly* briefings to clients and potential clients 'The War for Talent'.[17] These windy, slogan-ridden advertorials were designed to persuade businesses to spend hard cash on soft services they usually didn't need. Most sat unread in executive inboxes or merited, at most, a casual scan in a washroom cubicle.

Aware of the short attention span of most of their readers, McKinsey peppered their briefings with eye-catching subheadings. On this particular advertorial, these would not have been out of place in dispatches from a journalist in a war zone.

'There is a war on talent, and it will intensify,' proclaimed one. 'All are vulnerable,' warned another.

Typically condescended to as junior partners by their peers in charge of 'core' corporate functions such as finance, supply chains and marketing, unloved and under-appreciated human resources directors in the world's big companies found this briefing manna from heaven. It offered them something they could happily put in front of their colleagues, boards and CEOs that wouldn't induce them to roll their eyes and yawn, because this briefing said the difference between good and bad companies was not the processes they followed or how efficient they were, but the clever people steering those businesses. Senior executives just like them.

The beating heart of the briefing was a graph, which McKinsey labelled ominously 'Exhibit 1'. It indicated that some demographers associated with the United Nations guessed that in two years' time the number of thirty-five to forty-four-year-olds in the United States would start to stabilise at some 15 per cent lower than its anticipated peak. In hindsight, this prediction was hokum. But the conclusions that they drew from it – that the boards of top businesses ought to be scrapping ruthlessly with one another to retain the talents of a handful of competent senior executives – was an outrageous stretch at best. It took no cognisance of trends in education, or the fact that every year more graduates and MBAs were entering the job market. Nor did it mention immigration, or that in the ever more globalised marketplace for senior executives, talent could be sourced from almost anywhere regardless of local demographic trends.

To future historians, the 'war for talent' may appear to be one of the most elaborate corporate conspiracies of all time. Future economists might simply regard this as a market bubble as irrational and inevitable as any that came before or since. But others, who recognise that most of the rest of us are also suckers for flattery, may view it more sympathetically. After all, those who benefited from the surge in remuneration greatly appreciated the reassurance that they were worth every penny they were paid. Indeed, like urban elites through history who justified their elevated status relative to others in terms of their noble blood, their heroism or their proximity to the gods, these 'masters of the universe' were convinced they were where they were because of merit.

The team from McKinsey & Company who drafted the viral *Quarterly* sniffed another opportunity. They promptly transformed it into a resoundingly hollow but nevertheless top-selling business book, unsurprisingly enough also titled *The War for Talent*. Other big consultancy firms soon got in on the act and human resources managers everywhere watched their departments transform from dull administrative service providers into bells-and-whistles, make-or-break, core corporate functions that merited seats at the top table of the world's great firms.

It did not take very long for some observers to declare the talent narrative to be nonsense. Jeffrey Pfeffer, Professor of Organizational Behavior at Stanford's Graduate School of Business, published an article called 'Fighting the war for talent is hazardous to your organization's health'.[18] In it he made the seemingly obvious point that businesses succeed because they are collaborative, and that overvaluing individuals was likely to create a corrosive culture. Soon afterwards, in a 2002 issue of the *New Yorker*, Malcolm Gladwell delivered an eviscerating critique on what he dubbed 'The Myth of Talent'. He took the view that the whole thing had been kicked off by overpaid McKinsey executives buying into the myth of their own brilliance. He also implicated McKinsey and their talent mindset in creating the toxic culture that brought down one of their favoured clients,

Enron – which had filed for bankruptcy in 2001 and was keeping the fraud investigators who would later send some of the executives to prison very busy.[19]

As persuasive as they were, Pfeffer's and Gladwell's protests were drowned out by the sounds of tills ringing as stock markets and commodity prices surged everywhere. This, however, had very little to do with the 'top talent'. Rather it was made possible by a billion new customers in South East Asia embracing consumerism, and because, in the United States and Europe, recently deregulated and rapidly expanding banks had persuaded themselves and governments that the clever algorithms they used to fragment and then bury rotten assets had finally brought an end to 'boom and bust economics' – the cycle of collapses and recessions that punctuated the upward trajectory of economic growth over the course of the twentieth century. And even if they couldn't quite understand how they managed this, they nevertheless flooded the market with cheap debt so that people could carry on spending even when their bank balances were deep in the red.

———

When over the course of 2008 and 2009 stock markets collapsed, industrial commodity prices tumbled, and panicked Central Banks started to frantically print trillions of dollars to recapitalise teetering economies, it seemed for a brief moment that the inflated salaries and stupendous bonuses won by senior executives in big corporations were a bubble due to burst in spectacular fashion. It also appeared the public would lose faith in the brilliance of 'top talent' when the financial crisis revealed that their Midas touch only ever produced mountains of fool's gold.

But the bubble didn't burst. The talent narrative was by then so deeply embedded in the institutional fabric of even the most vulnerable businesses that, as they started retrenching staff and closing operations to cut costs, many simultaneously dipped into their meagre cash reserves to allocate large retention bonuses to their senior leadership team, on the assumption that only they would be able to navigate a way through the newly treacherous waters.

Even if many of those at the very top somehow managed to engineer greater rewards for themselves, the crash did precipitate a sharp decline in public confidence in economists. If the so-called experts hadn't seen the crisis coming, then there was good cause to question their expertise. The problem was that because economics had masqueraded as a science for so long, people quite reasonably began to treat expertise in general with more scepticism, even in far more solidly grounded sciences like physics and medicine. As a result, among the more unexpected casualties of the financial crisis was the once near-universal confidence in people like climate scientists warning of the dangers of anthropogenic climate change and epidemiologists trying to explain the benefits of immunisation.

The only disciplined message put out by the impromptu coalition of dreamers and discontents who 'occupied' Wall Street and other global financial capitals in the wake of the financial crisis was something along the lines of 'burn the rich'. But their efforts to highlight inequality didn't do much to change public perceptions. Numerous subsequent research projects have revealed that people in the most unequal countries routinely underestimate the levels of inequality, while those in countries where the bulk of national wealth is in the hands of large middle classes tend to be more accurate and occasionally even overestimate inequality.[20] The gap between reality and perception is particularly extreme in the United States where material inequality is the most acute it has been for half a century.[21] There, surveys revealed that even after the crash most laypeople underestimated the pay ratio between bosses and unskilled workers by more than a factor of ten.[22]

The enduring public illusion of greater material equality in places like the United States and the United Kingdom is in part a testament to the perseverance of the idea that there is a clear, even meritocratic, correspondence between wealth and hard work. Thus, while those who are very wealthy like to believe that they are worthy of the financial rewards they have accrued, many poorer people don't want to mess with the dream that they too might achieve such riches if only they work hard enough. For them to concede that perhaps the system was stacked against them – that money had become far better at begetting more money than working long hard shifts – would be tantamount to abandoning their sense of agency and their cherished beliefs that what made their countries different was that anyone who worked hard enough could be whatever they wished to be.

Perceptions about inequality and its causes in places like the United States now cleave closely to whether people identify themselves as progressives or conservatives. Thus following their 2019 survey on attitudes to wealth and welfare, the Cato Institute notes that 'strong liberals say the top drivers of wealth are family connections (48%), inheritance (40%), and getting lucky (31%) and strong conservatives say the top drivers of wealth are hard work (62%), ambition (47%), self-discipline (45%), and risk-taking (36%)'.[23]

Indeed, it is hard to escape the conclusion that at least some of the anxiety and social media-amplified polarisation over the past decade is attributable to people coalescing around different schools of thought about how to manage the extraordinary economic and social changes automation is visiting upon us. Thus on one side, there are those who advocate nativism, economic nationalism and a return to what they consider to be transcendent virtues based variously on religious dogma and ideas like hard work. On the other side, there are progressives embracing a far more transformative agenda, even if it is not yet clear what that is.

But political polarisation is by no means the only growing pain exacerbated by anxieties about the future in urban, industrialised economies, where for many the boundaries between our professional and personal lives have all but disappeared.

14

The Death of a Salaryman

Among the small group of newspaper correspondents, stringers and freelancers who get a buzz documenting life and death in war zones, the risk of catching a stray bullet, being kidnapped by shouty people in balaclavas or blown up are all part of the job. Journalists who work to expose (or bury) the dirty secrets of the powerful, who dig into the dark hearts of criminal networks, or who traffic in opinions intended to provoke, upset and outrage, also accept that there is a chance their work might put them in harm's way. But for most, journalism is meant to be a safe profession. No journalist, for example, expects to die in the course of reporting on traffic congestion, the ebb and flow of financial markets, when reviewing the latest gadgetry and fashion trends, or while documenting the dull battles that shape city-hall micro-politics.

Tragically, this expectation was confounded for Miwa Sado, a reporter for NHK, Japan's public broadcaster. Her beat was local government and on 24 July 2013, while covering the metropolitan elections in Tokyo, she died in the line of duty and her body was found with her mobile phone still clasped in her hand.

Doctors soon established that Miwa Sado died as a result of congenital heart failure. But following an investigation by Japan's Ministry of Labour, the official cause of her death was changed to 'karoshi': death by overwork. In the month preceding her death, Sado had clocked an exhausting 159 hours of official overtime. That was equivalent to working two full eight-hour shifts every weekday over a four-week period. Unofficially, the number of hours of overtime probably exceeded that. In the weeks following her death, her grieving father trawled through her phone and computer records. He calculated that she had worked at least 209 hours of overtime in the month preceding her death.

Sado's death was one among many similar reported that year. The Japanese Ministry of Labour officially recognises two categories of death as a direct consequence of overworking. *Karoshi* describes such a death as a result of cardiac illness attributable to exhaustion, lack of sleep, poor nutrition and lack of exercise, as in Sado's case. *Karo jisatsu* describes when an employee takes their own life as a result of the mental stresses arising from overworking. At the end of the year, the Ministry of Labour certified that 190 deaths occurred over the course of 2013 as a result of either *karoshi* or *karo jisatsu*, with the former outnumbering the latter two to one. This was roughly in line with the average annual numbers for the preceding decade. But Japan's Ministry of Labour will only ever declare a death by *karoshi* or *karo jisatsu* under exceptional circumstances, and when it can be proved beyond doubt that the worker has dramatically exceeded reasonable limits for overtime, and that there were no other significant contributing factors (like severe hypertension). As a result, some, like Hiroshi

Kawahito, the secretary general of Japan's National Defence Counsel for Victims of Karoshi – one of a host of anti-*karoshi* organisations in Japan – insists that the government is reluctant to embrace the true scale of the problem.[1] He takes the view that the real numbers are ten times higher. Unsurprisingly, the numbers of people who suffer severe mental or health disorders as a result of overwork in Japan are thought to be many orders of magnitude higher again. As are the numbers of people who cause workplace accidents as a consequence of being exhausted while on the job.

In 1969, the first case of *karoshi* was officially acknowledged after a twenty-nine-year-old clerk in the shipping department of a major Japanese newspaper keeled over and perished at his desk after logging eye-watering amounts of overtime. The term soon entered the popular lexicon and increasingly became a prominent part of the national conversation as more and more deaths were attributed directly to overwork. It was added to an already growing vocabulary of work-related ailments specific to Japan, most notably '*kacho-byo*' which translates to 'manager's disease' and was coined to describe the overwhelming stress felt by middle managers over promotions, letting down their team, shaming themselves and their families or, worse still, disappointing their bosses and weakening the company. But where *kacho-byo* is a problem that only afflicts white-collar workers, *karoshi* is an equal-opportunity killer that preys as eagerly on blue-collar workers as it does on managers, teachers, healthcare workers and CEOs.

363

Japan is not the only South East Asian country where the potentially fatal consequences of overwork are contemplated by stressed-out employees hastily eating lunch at their workstations. South Koreans, who work on average 400 more hours per year than Britons or Australians, have adopted a form of the Japanese word *karoshi*[2] to describe the same phenomenon. So too have the Chinese. Since China's cautious embrace of 'state capitalism' in 1979, their economy has grown at breakneck speed and doubled in size roughly every eight years. And while technology has played a big role, China's growth has been catalysed by a disciplined and affordable labour force that has hoovered up manufacturing operations from businesses across the globe, and transformed China into the world's largest producer and exporter of manufactured goods. But one of the unintended consequences of this has been a surge in the number of people whose deaths have been attributed to overwork. In 2016, CCTV, the state broadcaster, which usually only resorts to hyperbole when they have good news to share, announced that more than half a million Chinese citizens die from overworking every year.[3]

According to official statistics, working hours in South Korea, China and Japan have declined considerably over the last two decades, with the greatest strides being taken in South Korea. This shift has been credited in part to the advocacy of anti-*karoshi* groups pushing for a more harmonious work–life balance. In Japan in 2018, for example, the average worker officially clocked around 1,680 hours of work, 141 hours fewer than in 2000. This is close to 350 more hours per year than German workers but 500 less than Mexican workers. It is also below the average for the world's elite club of nations nominally committed to free trade, the Organisation for Economic Co-operation and Development.[4] But there is also a well-established culture of under-reporting working hours in Japan, China and South Korea, and survey data of employees suggest that for many work remains as all-dominating as it ever was. Nothing perhaps reveals this better than the fact that despite a well-funded government campaign in Japan to persuade people to go on holiday once in a while, since the turn of the millennium most Japanese workers still take fewer than half the total days of fully paid leave offered them.[5]

China's Department of Population and Employment Statistics[6] reported in 2016 that urban workers routinely perform close to an hour of overtime every day, with around 30 per cent of workers exceeding the baseline forty-hour week by at least eight hours. Among the hardest working of this group were 'business service personnel' and 'production, transport, equipment operators', with over 40 per cent clocking in more than forty-eight hours of labour every week. But the likelihood is that the real figures are much higher than reported.

While those living in largely rural areas still work to a more manageable rhythm, for the private-sector workers in buzzing urban hubs like Guangzhou, Shenzhen, Shanghai and Beijing, long hours are now par for the course. This is especially so for those working in China's frenetic high-technology sector, led by companies like Baidu, Alibaba, Tencent and Huawei. They now order their working lives according to the mantra '996'. The two 9s refer to the requirements to put in twelve-hour days, from 9 a.m. to 9 p.m., and the 6 refers to the six days of the week that employees with ambitions to get anywhere are expected to be at their workstations.

———

The stress fractures and thickening of the work-worn bones of farming peoples show that ever since some of our ancestors substituted their bows and digging sticks for ploughs and hoes, death by overwork has been a thing. Besides the many who through history have died while 'trying to save the farm', there are the countless souls who were worked to death under whips held by others: the slaves that ancient Romans dispatched to their mines and quarries; the descendants of the men and women stolen from Africa who led hard, abbreviated and brutalised lives in the cotton and sugar plantations of the Americas; the tens of millions who perished in twentieth-century gulags, labour colonies, prisons and concentration camps as a result of committing crimes or finding themselves on the wrong side of one or another -ocracy, -ism or ego; and those who, like the rubber harvesters in King Leopold's Congo or along the Putamoyo River in Colombia at the turn of the twentieth century, were viewed as little more than a disposable mass of cheap labourers.

But what makes the individual stories of *karoshi* and *karo jisatsu* different from these is the fact that what drove the likes of Miwa Sado to lose or take their lives was not the risk of hardship or poverty but their own ambitions refracted through the expectations of their employers.

The convergence of the modern pursuit of riches with a Confucian ethic of responsibility, loyalty and honour may account for the high numbers of deaths by overwork in cities like Seoul, Shanghai and Tokyo, but death by overwork is not a phenomenon that is unique to late twentieth- and early twenty-first-century South East Asia. Indeed, what is perhaps unique about the Confucian belt economies in this respect is not that death by overwork is more common there than anywhere else, but the fact that people there are more willing to engage with it as a problem.

In Western Europe and North America, deaths by overwork are usually attributed to individual failings rather than the actions or failings of an employer or their government. As a result, they don't form part of the national conversation, or feature in news headlines, or result in grieving relatives demanding abject apologies from employers or action by governments. Even so, occasionally the problem has generated some profile. Over the course of the last decade, for instance, the CEO of France Telecom was forced to step down and several senior managers were put on trial charged with 'moral harassment', as a consequence of the toxic working culture they instilled at the company and which prosecutors insisted contributed to thirty-five suicides among staff members over the course of 2008 and 2009.

There is now much more discussion about mental-health issues in the workplace in countries like Britain and the USA. And for good reason if the statistics are anything to go by. In Britain, the Health and Safety Executive reported in 2018 that close to 15 million work days were lost as a result of workplace-related stress, depression and anxiety, and that among a total workforce of 26.5 million, nearly 600,000 individuals self-reported suffering from work-related mental health issues that year.[7] But it is hard to tell from this data whether the reason more mental-health issues in the workplace are diagnosed is because in many countries there is now a trend to pathologise what were once considered to be perfectly normal stresses and anxieties. And one particularly important manifestation of the tendency to pathologise is the now widespread acceptance that 'workaholism' is a real, diagnosable condition with potentially fatal consequences.

―――――――

Born in Greenville, South Carolina, in 1917, Pastor Wayne Oates made the best of an impoverished childhood in the care of his grandmother and older sister, while his mother worked long shifts at a local cotton mill to make ends meet during the Great Depression. But his deeply held Christian faith taught him to count his blessings, and later gave him the resolve to dedicate his energy to reconciling the very secular world of psychiatry and psychology with his religious convictions. A prolific author who penned fifty-three books in addition to forging a distinguished career as a lecturer at the Southern Baptist Theological Seminary in Louisville, Kentucky, he saw something of his own 'compulsion . . . to work incessantly' in the behaviour of some of the alcoholics he counselled, and coined the words 'workaholic' and 'workaholism' to describe it. First published in 1971, *The Confessions of a Workaholic* is now out of print and its avuncular advice is largely forgotten, but his neologism 'workaholic' was instantly ushered into our everyday vocabulary.

Soon after he introduced the term, workaholism became a hotly contested niche field in psychology, albeit one marked by an absence of agreement about how to either define or measure it, let alone treat it. Some insist that it is an 'addiction' like gambling or shopping; some a pathology like bulimia; others a behaviour pattern; and others still a syndrome, born of the unhappy union of 'high-drive' and 'low work satisfaction'.

In the absence of a widely agreed definition for workaholism, there are very few useful statistics indicating its prevalence. The only place where any systematic statistical work has been conducted is Norway, where researchers at the University of Bergen developed an assessment methodology they called the Bergen Work Addiction Scale.[8] Reminiscent of the pop-psychology quizzes in the lifestyle magazines of waiting rooms, the Bergen assessment involves allocating numerical scores based on standardised responses to seven simple statements, like 'You become stressed if you are prohibited from working' or 'You prioritise working over hobbies and leisure activities'. If you respond 'always' or 'often' to a majority of these questions, then, the test's authors reason, you are probably a workaholic. The Bergen research group used data from 1,124 survey responses and cross-referenced these with a series of other personality tests. At the end of it all, they concluded that 8.3 per cent of Norwegians were 'workaholics', and that workaholism was most prevalent among adults between eighteen and forty-five years old, and was far more likely to afflict people who were generally 'agreeable', 'intellectually motivated' and/or 'neurotic'. They also noted that the prevalence rate was sufficiently high for it to merit concern as a public health problem.

In much the same way that John Lubbock considered careful scientific research and writing lengthy monographs to be leisure, for many of us the only distinction between work and leisure is whether we are paid to do an activity or whether we are doing it by choice – and, often enough, actually paying cash earned in regular jobs to do it.

Taking into account time spent getting to and from the workplace and doing essential household activities like shopping, housework and childcare, working a standard forty-hour week does not leave a great deal of time for leisure. Unsurprisingly, most people in full-time employment use the bulk of their pure leisure time for restful, passive activities like watching TV. But unlike in the early days of the Industrial Revolution, most employees have weekends to themselves as well as several weeks of paid annual vacation. And many people choose not to spend these precious hours resting but instead use them for doing work of their choice.

Beyond those who disappear into computer games (which often involve activities that mimic actual work), many of the most popular hobbies people choose to spend their free time on involve doing forms of work that in the past we might have been paid to do or that other people are still paid to do. Thus while fishing and hunting were work for the foragers, they are now expensive but very popular leisure activities; where growing vegetables or gardening was viewed as odious labour by farmers, for many it is now a deeply satisfying form of pleasure; and where sewing, knitting, pottery and painting were once a source of much needed income, people now find peace in their relaxing, often repetitive rhythms. Indeed, many hobbies and leisure pursuits – among them cooking, ceramics, painting, ironmongery, woodwork and home-engineering – involve the development, refinement and use of the kinds of manual and intellectual skills that we depended upon through our evolutionary history, and that are increasingly absent in the modern workplace.

Another reason that psychologists have struggled to define and measure workaholism is because for as long as people have gathered together in cities, many have viewed their work as far more than simply a means of making a living. When Emile Durkheim contemplated possible solutions to the problem of anomie, he recognised that relationships forged in the workplace might help build the 'collective consciousness' that once bound people into small, well-integrated village communities. Indeed, one of the solutions he proposed for dealing with problems of social alienation in cities was the formation of workers' guilds similar to the hundreds of *collegia* that were formed in ancient Rome.

It was not a flippant suggestion. The Romans' artisan *collegia* were not just trade organisations lobbying on behalf of their members' interests. They played a vital role in establishing the civic identities for the *humiliores* – the lower classes – based on work, and then binding them into the larger hierarchies that bound Roman society. In many respects, the *collegia* operated like autonomous villages within the city. Each had its own customs, rituals, modes of dress and festivals, and its own patrons, magistrates and general assemblies modelled on the Roman Senate, which had the power to issue decrees. Some even had their own private militias. But above all, they were social organisations that bound people together into close-knit micro-communities based on work, values, norms and shared social status, and in which intermarriage was frequent, and members and their families socialised mainly with one another.

Many people are now accustomed to life in big cities with mass-transit systems that allow us to move from one side of town to the other far quicker than Romans ever could. Many are now also accustomed to having a device at their fingertips that allows them to form dynamic, active communities regardless of geography. Even so, most modern city dwellers still tend to embed themselves into surprisingly small and often diffuse social networks, which become their individual communities.

When the palaeoanthropologist Robin Dunbar made the case that gossip and grooming played a central role in the development of our evolutionary ancestors' linguistic abilities, he based his argument partially on an examination of the relationship between brain size and composition of different primate species and the size and complexity of the active social network groups each species typically maintained. He noticed a clear correlation. Extrapolating from the data on various other primate species, Dunbar calculated that based on human brain size most of us would be able to maintain active networks of in the region of 150 individuals, and would struggle to cope with more because the business of keeping track of their interactions and interrelationships was far too complex. When he correlated this with data on village sizes gathered by anthropologists across the world, social network sizes of foragers like the Ju/'hoansi and the Hadzabe, and even numbers of 'friends' people actively engaged with on social media sites like Facebook, it turned out he was broadly right: most of us still only maintain active relationships with around 150 or so people at any one time.[9]

For much of human history, these immediate social networks took the form of multi-generational communities that were rooted in shared geography, expressed through the intimacy of kinship, shared religious beliefs, rituals, practices and values, and were nourished by working and living in the same environments and experiencing similar things. But in densely packed cities, most individuals' extended social networks take the form of complex intersecting mosaics of relationships cobbled together from our involvement in a whole series of sometimes very different interests and hobbies. And, perhaps unsurprisingly, for many of us our regular social networks are made up of people we have worked with or encountered at work.

Beyond the fact that most of us spend considerably more time in the company of colleagues than our families, and structure our daily routines around work obligations, the work we do often becomes a social focal point, which in turn shapes our ambitions, values and political affiliations. It is no coincidence that when we first test the waters with strangers at social gatherings in cities, we tend to ask them about the work they do, and on the basis of their answers make reasonably reliable inferences about their political views, lifestyles and even backgrounds. It is also no coincidence that the only regular survey of romance in the workplace has found that nearly one in three Americans enters into at least one long-term sexual relationship with people they meet through work, and a further 16 per cent meet their spouses there.[10]

This is hardly surprising. Our individual career paths are often determined by our backgrounds, schooling and subsequent choices about training. As a result, we tend to progressively align our world views and expectations with those of both our teachers and co-workers, and also tend to look for work among similar people and, where possible, make use of existing social networks to do so. Thus human resources managers at Goldman Sachs do not have to deal with many job applications from people who view usury as sinful, army recruiters don't get many applications from dyed-in-the-wool pacifists and police recruiters do not have to field job applications from avowed anarchists. And just as importantly, once in work we tend to continue to further align our views of the world with those of our colleagues, as our bonds to them are strengthened in the course of pursuing shared goals and celebrating shared achievements.

But even if work offers people a sense of community and belonging, the kinds of communities that Durkheim imagined might coalesce around the workplace have not materialised to the extent he predicted. Indeed, when Durkheim pictured the city of the future as being made up of a mosaic of work-based communities, he hadn't quite come to grips with the changing nature of employment and work in the industrial era. It was as if he imagined that the trade skills rendered redundant by industrialisation would be straightforwardly substituted for another set of new, enduring useful skills. He did not, for example, imagine workplaces operating according to the 'scientific management' methods developed by Frederick Winslow Taylor, in which actual skills were superfluous to requirements. Nor for that matter did he imagine quite the extent to which technological developments would make the workplace in the modern industrial era one of constant flux, in which cutting-edge skills acquired in one decade would become redundant the next.

———

In 1977, Ben Aronson, a civil servant in the employ of the State of Illinois, collapsed with internal bleeding. He was subsequently diagnosed with severe heart problems that required surgery to remedy. He attributed his illness to work-related stress, and explained to a reporter for the *Florida Times-Union* that he was especially worried because his combined vacation and sick leave entitlement was only four weeks and his doctor insisted he could not return to work in his frail condition.[11]

Aronson was not, however, just one among many suffering the consequences of overwork. The reason why this story briefly merited the attention of journalists was that his heart problems arose as a result of underwork.

A few months before Aronson's collapse, his employers had attempted to lay him off for a second time in a few short years. On both occasions, Aronson sued them for unlawful dismissal and on both occasions the courts found in his favour and ordered his employers to reinstate him. This they duly did, but the second time it happened it was only through gritted teeth. They informed Aronson that while he would still receive his very handsome monthly salary of $1,730 (worth around $7,500, over £6,000, in today's money), he would be given no duties of any kind to perform. They then removed the telephone from his office, instructed the mailroom not to deliver or collect his mail, and instructed other staff to ignore him.

Sadly Aronson's story was not newsworthy enough to merit an additional follow-up, and it is unknown whether he ended up being fired from his non-job as a result of non-attendance due to the ill health he suffered as a result of not having meaningful work to do. But there are many people who will see something of themselves in his strange individual circumstances.

A well-paid job for life with zero responsibilities might be like a dream come true to some. But for others, once the novelty of it all wore off, they would miss the structure, the community and the sense of being useful that they derived from their jobs, regardless of how mundane or how poorly paid they were. And if the job involved skill, they would almost certainly miss the often mute pleasure they gained in performing it too. Included in this group are the thousands of lottery winners and individuals who inherited unexpected wealth from distant relatives and continued to perform their old, often not particularly interesting jobs with the same cheerful diligence as before.

Then there are those who work in the service sector of our economies who relate to Aronson's story because if their office email and intranet accounts were suddenly blocked, their computers and telephones removed and their colleagues instructed to ignore them, they know deep down that their absence would make little difference to the fortunes of their organisation.

According to the UK Office of National Statistics, 83 per cent of working people in Great Britain are now employed in the ever more amorphous 'service' or 'tertiary' sector. Sometimes referred to as the tertiary economy, the service sector includes any job that does not involve producing or harvesting raw materials as in farming, mining and fishing, or the manufacture of actual things, like knives and forks and nuclear missiles, from those raw materials.

Britain is not unusual among the world's richer countries in having such a large proportion of its workforce employed in the service sector. It trails behind states like Luxembourg and Singapore, where pretty much everyone with a job is employed in the service sector in one way or another. But it is way ahead of most developing countries like Tanzania, where the majority of people still farm for a living. It is also some way ahead of countries like China, where despite a recent and ongoing surge in service-sector jobs, more than half the population are still employed in farming, fishing, mining and manufacturing.

The supremacy of the service sector in many economies is a relatively recent phenomenon. Up until the surge in agricultural production across Europe during the sixteenth century, an estimated three-quarters of Britons still made a living as farmers, quarrymen, foresters and fishermen. By 1851, once the Industrial Revolution gathered steam, that number declined to just over 30 per cent, with around 45 per cent of the working population employed in manufacturing and the remaining 25 per cent in services.[12] This ratio remained largely unchanged until after the First World War. Then it climbed slowly upwards again, as homes and industries began to draw energy directly from electricity networks, and new technologies like the internal combustion engine came online, so catalysing the invention and manufacture of a whole range of new things for aspirant households and individuals to consume. This trend continued beyond the end of the Second World War until 1966, when Britain's manufacturing sector went into a steady and steep decline. Where in 1966 an estimated 40 per cent of the workforce was employed in manufacturing, by 1986 this number had dropped to 26 per cent, and by 2006 to 17 per cent. Technology and automation played an important role in transforming what were once labour-intensive manufacturing industries into capital-intensive ones. So too did globalisation, as the most labour-intensive industries progressively began losing out to manufacturers operating in geographies where labour was cheaper than in Britain.

The rapid expansion of the service sector is thought by many economists to follow on inevitably from large-scale industrialisation. It is also now often considered to be the hallmark feature of 'post-industrial societies'. This, at least, was the view of Colin Clark, the economist most closely associated with developing the now well-established 'three sector model' of the economy. Writing in 1940, Clark accurately predicted the subsequent expansion of the service sector in economies like Britain's over the following eight decades. He observed that as the total wealth in an economy increased as a result of capital growth, technological development and improving productivity, so demand for services rose, thus offsetting job losses in fishing, farming and mining (the primary sector).[13]

Clark was a socially minded economist. He believed that in addition to working to create a stable and productive economy, it was an economist's moral duty to help attain 'the just distribution of wealth between individuals and groups'.[14] Even so, his model of post-industrialisation has been heavily criticised since then, in particular by commentators from the economic left, as a model for 'capitalist development' masquerading as a model of human development.

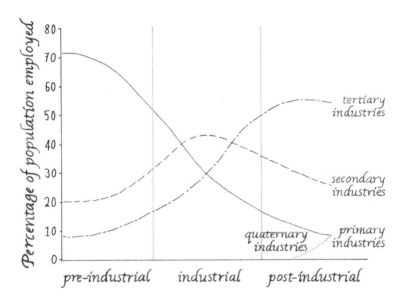

Clark's tri-sector model indicating how service-sector employment offset declines in primary and secondary industries

Clark's famous graphical model depicting the evolving relationship between the three sectors over time is an accurate representation of what has happened in the economies of Western Europe, Japan and the United States.

Other economies, among them China's, also seem to be tacking along the path Clark predicted, with services going steadily upwards in proportion to the decline in agriculture, and with manufacturing progressively declining in importance. But it is hard to account for the massive increase in service-sector professions as a response to actual deep need, or even the efforts of advertisers and influencers to persuade us of their importance.

The other problem with Clark's model is that while the employment of the majority of a national population in the service sector is very clearly a new phenomenon, the sector is as old as the oldest cities, even if the services didn't extend very far beyond the city walls. In even the grandest ancient cities, like Rome, manufacturing was a relatively low-level industry and conspicuous consumption the sole preserve of the wealthiest patricians and merchants. The same was almost certainly true of ancient cities like Uruk, where the majority of the population was made up of priests, administrators, accountants, soldiers and, apparently, bartenders. It is difficult to account for the preponderance of service-sector jobs in ancient cities like Uruk, Memphis, Luoyang or Rome in terms of increasing demand for services on the back of a surge in manufacturing productivity.

Taking a much longer-term perspective on our relationship with work suggests that there are perhaps other ways to interpret the rapid expansion of the service sector, as economies become increasingly 'post-industrialised'.

One is to recognise that many (but by no means all) services are responsive to fundamental human needs, which are also part of our evolutionary inheritance and are not easily met in cities when people are removed from small close-knit social communities. Doctors exist because we like to live and because we dislike pain; artists and entertainers exist to bring us pleasure; hairstylists exist because some of us like to look good or need a sympathetic ear to listen; DJs exist because we like to dance; and bureaucrats exist because even the most passionate anarchists want the buses to run on schedule. Demand for these kinds of services did not increase as a result of improvements in manufacturing. They always existed. Instead, once agriculture and manufacturing were sufficiently productive to enable many people not to focus the bulk of their time and energy producing or making things, these other fundamental needs were amplified.

Another way to interpret the expansion of the service sector is in terms of the culture of work that has become so deeply ingrained in us since the agricultural revolution. This is a culture that makes us intolerant of freeloaders and canonise gainful employment as the basis of our social contract with one another even if many jobs don't serve much purpose other than keeping people busy. This in turn speaks to the fundamental relationship between life, energy, order and entropy. In much the same way that masked weavers and bower birds use their surplus energy to build elaborate and often unnecessary structures, so humans, when gifted sustained energy surpluses, have always directed that energy into something purposeful. From this perspective, the emergence of many ancient service-sector professions was simply a result of the fact that wherever and whenever there has been a large, sustained energy surplus, people (and other organisms) have found creative ways to put it to

381

work. In the human case, this involved the development of a myriad of remarkable and very different skills, the learning and execution of which often brings us great satisfaction. This is why cities have always been crucibles of artistry, intrigue, curiosity and discovery.

Incorporating neurosurgeons, university lecturers, bankers, burger-flippers and quantum-vibration-tantric astrologers, the service sector is now so big and diverse that it has ceased to be particularly useful to analysts trying to understand the ebb and flow of our job markets. Understandably, scholars now consider Clark's division of economic sectors to be obsolete. Some have proposed the addition of another 'quaternary' sector specifically to accommodate computing, coding, research and other cutting-edge hi-tech industries like genomics. But this too is problematic, given the extent to which digital technologies have been transforming other economic sectors. As a result, most analysts prefer to divide the sector up into more granular functions, such as hospitality and tourism, financial services, healthcare and so on.

Others have proposed a more radical reimagining of the service sector and with it the economy as a whole. Some of these ideas hark back to the post-war era in Western economies when governments were more inclined to design good social policies and then work out how to pay for them, rather than make good economic policies and wonder what social goods they might be able to bolt onto them. Central to most is that the way markets allocate value is rarely a fair reflection of the way most people do.

The people who we depend on to educate our children or nurse us when we are ill, for example, are now paid considerably less than those who make a living advising the wealthy how to avoid taxation or who design new ways to spam us with endless unwanted advertising. As a result some analysts argue in favour of disaggregating the service sector to better account for the kinds of non-monetary value – like health or happiness – that different jobs create. No one doubts the non-monetary value that doctors, nurses, teachers, waste collectors, plumbers, cleaners, bus drivers and firemen provide. And while views on what counts as entertainment vary, few people dispute the fact that entertainers, chefs, musicians, tour guides, hoteliers, masseuses and others whose work involves bringing others happiness or stimulating and inspiring them are important too.

One of the most novel approaches to re-categorising roles in the service sector is that proposed by the anthropologist David Graeber. In a brief essay he wrote in 2013,[15] which subsequently went viral and later formed the basis of a book, he differentiated between jobs that were genuinely useful, like teaching, medicine, farming and scientific research, and the apparent efflorescence of other jobs that served no obvious purpose other than giving someone something to do. This latter category of jobs, which he argues includes corporate lawyers, public relations executives, health and academic administrators and financial service providers, he referred to as 'bullshit jobs' and defined as forms 'of employment that is so completely pointless, unnecessary, or pernicious that even the employee cannot justify its existence'.[16]

'It's as if someone were out there making up pointless jobs just for the sake of keeping us all working,' he argued.[17]

For each person in a role which they may think of as a bullshit job, there are of course others in near identical roles who nevertheless find satisfaction, purpose and fulfilment in them. Even so, the fact that workplace surveys consistently find more people are dissatisfied with the work they do, suggests that this is often just a coping mechanism – a characteristic of a species whose evolutionary history has been shaped so profoundly by its need for purpose and meaning.

Graeber was by no means the first to notice the proliferation of pointless jobs in the burgeoning service sectors that characterise post-industrial societies. The tendency for organisational bureaucracies to balloon is now sometimes referred to as Parkinson's Law, after Cyril Northcote Parkinson, who proposed it in a tongue-in-cheek article he published in *The Economist* in 1955. Based on his experiences in the notoriously flabby Colonial Service, Parkinson's Law states that 'work inevitably expands to fill the time available for its completion',[18] and correspondingly that bureaucracies will always generate enough internal work to appear busy and important enough to ensure their continued existence or growth without any corresponding expansion in output. While it was very clearly not Parkinson's intention when writing this article, the language he uses is remarkably reminiscent of that used by scientists like Schrödinger when describing the relationship between work, energy and life.

According to Parkinson's Law, for bureaucracies to stay alive and grow, they must continuously harvest energy, in the form of cash, and do work even if, like energetic masked weavers, the work serves no more purpose than expending energy.

Parkinson's Law may now only occasionally be invoked by CEOs when downsizing and by debt-laden governments sombrely demanding greater austerity, but it is nonetheless something that many in managerial roles are intuitively aware of, even if they haven't a name to give it. After all, in many organisations one of the principal skills required to be recognised as 'top talent' is to be able to bid eloquently for big chunks of budget and more staff to execute grand, but ultimately pointless, projects, just as the quickest route to an undignified exit is to underspend one's budget.

There is evidence of bureaucratic bloat everywhere, but the scale of it only becomes clear when looking at how it has afflicted organisations and institutions like universities, whose basic purpose has not changed substantially for centuries.

In the United States, where the oldest university, Harvard, was established in 1736, student tuition fees, adjusted for inflation, are now on average between two and three times what they were in 1990.[19] In the United Kingdom, where the oldest universities date from the twelfth century, tertiary education was not only free for British residents until 1998, but most students were provided with means-tested maintenance grants by their local authorities that were generous enough for them to be able to live in relative comfort without having to seek paid work during term times to make ends meet. Since their introduction in 1998, tuition fees have risen 900 per cent. In both the the United States and United Kingdom, all but the wealthiest prospective students recognise that on graduation they will likely be saddled with debts that will take decades to settle. While the huge increases in fees in the UK have been accelerated by some external economic factors, the principal justification for their escalation is the need to finance ever more bloated administrative functions. At California State University, for instance, the total number of managerial and professional administrators employed rose from 3,800 in 1975 to 12,183 in 2008, while the total number of teaching positions only rose from 11,614 to 12,019. This is equivalent to an increase in the number of teaching staff of 3.5 per cent versus 221 per cent in administrative staff. Notably, almost all of the administrative staff expansion was in office-based bureaucratic roles. In fact, over the same period the number of clerical, service and maintenance jobs declined by almost a third.[20]

Some of the new administrative roles in universities, and many other organisations, are important and useful. All functioning bureaucracies are also incubators of policy wonks, technical specialists and experts, people who find deep satisfaction in the arcana of their roles and without whom everything would grind to a halt. But it is also hard to avoid the suspicion that many of them are important only because their incumbents are good at persuading themselves and others that they are important, or because they exist only to observe, measure and evaluate somebody else doing something important.

This is certainly the view of many academics. Rather than freeing them up to spend more time doing research and teaching, they now almost universally report spending a considerably higher proportion of their working week doing administration than was the case two decades ago. They also note that while many administrative roles are less specialised than academic ones, and considerably less competitive, they often merit much higher salaries. In the UK, for example, four in ten academics in 2016 were reported to be contemplating quitting the jobs they consider to be vocational and that they had worked for years to secure.[21]

There is no doubt that many people – among them some of those employed in 'nonsense' roles – find satisfaction in their work, or at the very least enjoy the companionship and structure it brings to their lives. Even so, the problem is that the overwhelming majority of workers across the world don't get a great deal of satisfaction out of their jobs. In the most recent iteration of Gallup's annual *State of the Global Workplace* report, it is revealed that only very few people find their work meaningful or interesting. They note soberly that 'the global aggregate from Gallup data collected in 2014, 2015 and 2016 across 155 countries indicates that just 15% of employees worldwide are engaged in their job. Two-thirds are not engaged, and 18% are actively disengaged.' They do, however, note some significant differences in engagement across different geographies. The US and Canada, where 31 per cent and 27 per cent respectively of the workforces are engaged by their jobs, are the world leaders in 'workplace engagement'. By contrast, only 10 per cent of Western European workers are engaged, but at least they are happier than workers in Japan, China, South Korea, Hong Kong and Taiwan where only between five and seven out of every hundred workers are stimulated by their work.[22]

The rise and rise of the service sector may be a testament to our collective creativity when it comes to inventing new jobs to accommodate those ejected from the production lines in the ever more automated and efficient manufacturing sector. But we clearly aren't that clever when it comes to creating (or rewarding) jobs people are likely to find meaningful or fulfilling. Even more importantly, it is now far from certain whether or not the service sector will be able to accommodate all of those whose work will be determined superfluous to requirements by the next tide of automation, whose waves are already licking against the shores of this last refuge of working men and women in the post-industrial age.

15

The New Disease

'We are being afflicted with a new disease of which some readers may not yet have heard the name, but of which they will hear a great deal in the years to come – namely, technological unemployment,' warned John Maynard Keynes when describing his post-work utopia. 'This means unemployment due to our discovery of means of economising the use of labour outrunning the pace at which we can find new uses for labour,' he added. It was a sensible clarification for his 1930s audience. People had worried about the possibility of their trades or livelihoods being elbowed out by new technologies and ways of working ever since the Industrial Revolution shifted into second gear. But few saw quite as vividly as Keynes the extent to which the drive to even greater efficiency and automation would cannibalise demand for human labour.

In hindsight, Keynes underestimated the extent to which ballooning service sectors in 'advanced economies' almost effortlessly soaked up people ejected from farms, mines, fisheries and increasingly automated production lines. The rapid expansion of services is also why despite the widespread automation of many once commonplace roles in many countries, from ticket sellers at train stations to checkout attendants in supermarkets, until recently discussion about the potential of automation to cannibalise the workplace remained largely confined to a few technology hubs, corporate boardrooms and academic journals.

That all changed in September 2013, when Carl Frey and Michael Osborne from Oxford University published the results of a research project to assess the accuracy of John Maynard Keynes's predictions about technological unemployment.[1]

The reason that the Oxford study caused such a stir was because Frey and Osborne concluded that not only were robots already queuing at the factory gates but that they had fixed their beady little robot-eyes on nearly half of all existing jobs in the United States. Based on a survey of 702 different professions, they reckoned that 47 per cent of all current jobs in the USA had 'high risk' of being automated out of existence by as early as 2030. The other thing they noted was that the people who were most at risk tended not to be those who were bloating up bureaucracies or middle management, but those with the more hands-on roles usually associated with lower levels of formal education.

A flood of similar studies followed. Governments, multi lateral organisations, think tanks, gilded corporate clubs like the World Economic Forum and, inevitably, the big management consultancy firms all got in on the act. While each deployed slightly different methodologies, their findings all added layers of detail to Frey and Osborne's gloomy assessment.

A study conducted by the club of most of the world's biggest economies, the Organisation for Economic Co-operation and Development (OECD), for instance, concluded that the impacts of automation were likely to be geographically varied both within and across member states. Some regions, like West Slovakia, they anticipated might experience job attrition rates of 40 per cent, while others, like Norway's capital Oslo, would barely notice anything with fewer than 5 per cent of roles being automated. 'Top talent' at McKinsey and Company's Global Institute suggested that between 30 and 70 per cent of jobs were vulnerable to partial automation over the course of the next fifteen to thirty-five years, and another big consultancy firm, PricewaterhouseCoopers, suggested that 30 per cent of jobs in the United Kingdom, 38 per cent of jobs in the United States, 35 per cent in Germany and only 21 per cent in Japan were vulnerable.[2]

All these studies agreed that some subsectors were considerably more vulnerable to automation than others, because the technology was already affordable enough for businesses to realise a relatively quick return on any investments they made in technology. They noted that the most vulnerable subsectors, those with more than half of existing roles on the chopping board, were 'water, sewerage and waste management' and 'transportation and storage'. These were closely followed by 'wholesale and retail' as well as manufacturing subsectors, which are likely to reduce their labour forces by between 40 and 50 per cent in the near future.[3]

They also noted that some professions appeared to be largely immune from automation, at least in the short term. Among these were those that depended on the slippery arts of persuasion, like public relations; those that demanded a high degree of empathy, like psychiatry; those that required

391

creativity, like fashion design; and those that demanded a high degree of manual or finger dexterity, like surgeons.

But any reassurances they offered were only tentative. Considerable investment is being poured into creating machines with human-like or better levels of dexterity, as well as others that are capable of mimicking social intelligence and creativity. As a result, what appeared to be impossibly distant milestones in automation just a couple of years ago are now looming large. In 2017, for instance, Xiaoyi, a robot developed by Tsinghua University in Beijing, in collaboration with a state-owned company, sailed through China's National Medical Licensing Examination, and Google's AlphaGO thrashed the world's best human Go players. This was considered a particularly important milestone because, unlike chess, Go cannot be won using information-processing power alone. In 2019, an austere black column, the IBM Debater, which had been practising sharpening its tongue arguing in private with IBM employees for several years, put in a losing but persuasive and 'surprisingly charming' performance arguing in favour of pre-school subsidies against a one-time grand finalist from the World Debating Championships.[4] More than this, with technology to generate deep-fake videos now accessible to everybody with an Internet connection and machines getting ever better at interpreting human language and making creative use of it, there is a palpable sense that no one's job is entirely safe. It was thus no surprise when in 2018 Unilever announced it was farming out part of its recruitment functions to an automated AI system, saving the company 70,000 person-hours of work per year.[5]

Another reason organisations like the OECD are uncertain about the potential of AI and machine learning is because those working to design these systems are uncertain as well. They note that some machine learning and AI protocols look like dead ends and that investing additional time into them may be throwing good money after bad. Even so, new models, many drawing on neuropsychology, are being developed all the time, and the trend is moving in only one direction.

Many assessments of the potential capabilities of robotics and AI to cannibalise the job market are curiously reticent to engage with some of the easier to predict but profound economic implications. Indeed, most cheerfully assert that automation will usher in a wonderful new world of even greater productivity, efficiency and ever grander dividends for shareholders.

This is perhaps understandable for the likes of McKinsey and Co. After all, addressing some of the other implications demands venturing down a wormhole in which they will be forced to contemplate a top-to-toe rebuild of the economic system that keeps them in wagyu steaks and flying in the front of the plane. One of these is the final demise of any lingering pretence that there is proportional correspondence between human labour, effort and reward. Another is the closely related question: who will benefit from automation and how?

***

Even if many people still routinely underestimate the extent of material inequality in their home countries, a growing body of research suggests that in some places politicians only do so at their peril. And while this research addresses the sometimes very high differentials in income characteristic of both advanced economies like the United States' and rapidly growing ones like China's, they now focus increasingly on differentials in net wealth. After all, since the Great Decoupling, asset ownership has proved a far more lucrative way of generating additional wealth than hard work.

At first, from the late 1980s through to the early 2000s, the widespread adoption of increasingly affordable digital technologies helped drive substantial reductions in inequality between countries. It did this in particular by helping poorer countries to compete for and then capture a growing proportion of the global manufacturing industry. Now increased automation looks likely to halt or even reverse the trend. By taking labour ever more out of the equation, automation removes any advantage countries with lower wage demands might have, because the costs of technology, unlike labour, are pretty much the same everywhere.

However, automation is not only likely to entrench further structural inequality between countries. Without a fundamental shift in the way economies are organised, it will dramatically exacerbate inequality within many countries as well. It will do this firstly by diminishing opportunities for unskilled and semi-skilled people to find decent employment, while simultaneously inflating the incomes of those few who continue to manage what are largely automated businesses.[6] As importantly, it will increase returns on capital rather than labour, so expanding the wealth of those who have cash invested in businesses, rather than those who depend on taking cash from them in exchange for labour. This means straightforwardly that automation will generate further wealth for the already wealthy, while further disadvantaging those who do not have the means to purchase stakes in companies and so free-ride off the work done by automata. Of course, this would not be as much of a challenge were it not the case that since the Great Decoupling, the wealthiest 1 per cent of people globally has captured twice as much of the new wealth generated by economic growth as the rest of us. The richest 10 per cent of people on earth now own an estimated 85 per cent of all global assets,[7] and the richest 1 per cent own 45 per cent of all global assets.

Many automata and AI already do indispensable work. Among them are the clever algorithms on which the genome researchers and epidemiologists now depend, a whole host of new digital diagnostic tools available to medical practitioners, and increasingly sophisticated climate and meteorological models. Just as importantly, without them we lack the capability to manage our ever more complex cities and the digital and physical infrastructure that sustains them. However, most autonomously intelligent machine systems will be put to work with a single purpose in mind: generating wealth for their owners with none of the obligations that come from having other humans do that work (even if they could). Indeed, in parallel with the Great Decoupling, there has been a progressive transfer of wealth from public to private hands. Where private wealth relative to national income has doubled in most wealthy countries over the last thirty years, national income relative to private wealth in most rich countries has plummeted. In China, for instance, the value of public wealth has declined from 70 per cent of the value of all national wealth to 30 per cent over this period, and in the United States and the United Kingdom, net public wealth has moved into negative territory since the financial crisis.[8]

Fully automated production lines do not work for free. Their basic energy needs are often even greater than those of people. They also require periodic upgrades and running repairs. But unlike employees, they don't strike, and when they are no longer fit for purpose they don't demand redundancy packages or expect to be supported by pension schemes. More than this, replacing or recycling them incurs no moral costs, with the result that no CEO is going to lose sleep before having them uninstalled and dispatched for recycling or scrap.

When John Maynard Keynes imagined his utopian future, he did not dwell on automation's potential to exacerbate inequality. His utopia was one where, because everybody's basic needs were easily met, inequality had become an irrelevance. Only the foolish did more work than they needed to. Almost like a foraging society, his utopia was a place where anyone who pursued wealth for wealth's sake invited ridicule rather than praise.

'The love of money as a possession – as distinguished from the love of money as a means to the enjoyments and realities of life – will be recognised for what it is, a somewhat disgusting morbidity, one of those semi-criminal, semi-pathological propensities which one hands over with a shudder to the specialists in mental disease,' he explained. 'I see us free, therefore, to return to some of the most sure and certain principles of religion and traditional virtue – that avarice is a vice, that the exaction of usury is a misdemeanour, and the love of money is detestable.'

He believed that the transition to near full automation signalled not just the end of scarcity but of all the social, political and cultural institutions, norms, values, attitudes and ambitions that had congealed around what once seemed the eternal challenge of solving the economic problem. He was, in other words, calling time on the economics of scarcity, demanding its replacement with a new economics of abundance, and calling for the future demotion of economists from their hallowed position in society to something more akin to 'dentists' who might be called on occasionally to perform minor surgery when needed.

Nearly thirty years later, John Kenneth Galbraith made a similar argument when he insisted that the economics of scarcity was sustained by desires manufactured by wily advertisers. Galbraith was also of the view that the transition to an economics of abundance would be organic and shaped by individuals relinquishing the pursuit of wealth in favour of worthier work. He also believed that this transition was already happening in post-war America and that at its vanguard was what he called the 'New Class' – those who chose their employment not for the money but rather the other rewards it yielded, among them pleasure, satisfaction and prestige.

Maybe Galbraith and Keynes were right and this transformation is already taking place. On the one hand, millennials in industrialised countries now routinely insist on finding work they love rather than learning to love the work they find. There is also a clear trend towards offering employees greater flexibility in terms of how they execute their jobs. In many countries, men as well as women are now often offered parental leave and, courtesy of digital communications, an ever increasing number of people do their jobs from home a few days every week or work flexible hours.

But working hours remain stuck around the forty-per-week mark and many essential workers who do not have the option of working flexibly endure long and expensive commutes to work, having been priced out of inner cities. More than this, only 15 per cent of people globally say they are engaged in their jobs, and many of those who Galbraith considered to be part of his New Class, like academics and schoolteachers, are being tempted into the private sector. At the same time, like the weeds that followed crops such as wheat into new continents and new ecosystems, the malady of infinite aspiration has found a new home. It has colonised and proliferated across a whole host of digital ecosystems, from Instagram to Facebook, to which it is supremely well adapted.

Were Keynes still alive today, he may well conclude that he just got the timing wrong and that the 'growing pains' of his utopia were indicative of a far more persistent, but ultimately curable, condition. Alternatively, he may conclude that his optimism was unfounded and that our desire to keep solving the economic problem was so strong that even if our basic needs were met, we would continue to create often pointless emplacements that would nevertheless structure our lives and provide purposeful moneymakers with the opportunity to outdo their neighbours.

Keynes was an active member of London's Malthusian Society, a group of enthusiastic birth-control advocates convinced that overpopulation was the greatest potential threat to any future prosperity. Therefore, it is possible he would zero in on another, far more pressing problem altogether, which suggested that it was the medicine Keynes prescribed for curing the economic problem – technologically led economic growth – that was making the patient sick.

In 1968, a group of industrialists, diplomats and academics came together to form what they later called the 'Club of Rome'. Troubled by the fact that the benefits of economic growth tended to be unevenly distributed, and alarmed by some of the obvious environmental costs associated with rapid industrialisation, they wanted to better understand the long-term implications of unbridled economic growth. To this end, they commissioned Dennis Meadows, a management specialist at the Massachusetts Institute of Technology, to provide them with some answers. Armed with a generous budget courtesy of the Volkswagen Foundation, Meadows first offered a job to Donella Meadows, a brilliant biophysicist from Harvard, who also happened to be his spouse. The two of them then set about recruiting a diverse team of experts in systems dynamics, agriculture, economics and demography. Once his squad had been assembled, he informed the Club of Rome that, all being well, he would report back to them with his team's findings in a couple of years.

Making use of the number-crunching power of the fancy new mainframe computers recently installed at MIT, Meadows and his team developed a series of algorithms to model the dynamic relationship between industrialisation, population growth, food production, the use of non-renewable resources and environmental degradation. They then used these to run a series of scenario-based simulations to model how our short-term actions might impact us in future.

The results of this ambitious exercise were first presented to the Club of Rome in private and then published, in 1972, in a book, *The Limits to Growth*. The conclusions Meadows and his team reached were very different from Keynes's utopian dream. They were also not what the Club of Rome, nor anyone else for that matter, wanted to hear.

Aggregating the outcomes of the various scenarios they fed into their mainframes showed unequivocally that if there were no significant changes to historical economic and population growth trends – if business continued as usual – then the world would witness a 'sudden and uncontrollable decline in both population and industrial capacity' within a century. In other words, their data showed that our continued preoccupation with solving the economic problem was the starkest problem facing humankind and that the likeliest outcome if things continued was catastrophe.

But their message wasn't all bleak. They believed that not only was there time to take action but that it was well within our capabilities to do so. It just required accepting that we needed to abandon our preoccupation with perpetual economic growth. Despite some minor reservations about the methodology and the fact that the model made few allowances for us to innovate miracle cures that might chase the problem away, the Club of Rome were persuaded by Meadows's team's findings.

'We are unanimously convinced that rapid, radical redressment of the present unbalanced and dangerously deteriorating world situation is the primary task facing humanity,'[9] they warned ominously, and insisted that the window of opportunity to act was closing alarmingly fast and that this was not a problem that could be kicked down the road for the next generation to deal with.

The world was not ready to embrace such a gloomy vision of the future and no one wanted even to contemplate the weighty responsibilities that, if true, it imposed on them. Nor was anyone ready to contemplate the idea that the very virtues that defined human progress – our productivity, ambition, energy and hard work – might lead us to perdition. 'Garbage in, garbage out,' snorted the *New York Times* in a scathing review that declared *The Limits of Growth* to be 'an empty and misleading work'.[10]

The *New York Times* set the tone for a quarter of a century of vicious criticism. Economists lined up to declare *The Limits to Growth* 'foolishness or fraud'.[11] They insisted that the report underestimated human ingenuity and so should be dismissed as a ham-fisted assault on the very foundations of their noble profession. Demographers contemptuously compared it to Robert Malthus's dire warnings of global catastrophe. For a while, it seemed almost everyone wanted to twist another knife into *The Limits to Growth*. When the Catholic Church declared it an assault on God and the endlessly bickering left-wing movements of Europe and

America declared the book propaganda for an elitist conspiracy, who intended to deprive the working classes and the impoverished citizens of Third World countries of a future of material plenty, Meadows had good reason to feel despondent.

With so few institutional supporters, governments, businesses and international organisations simply chose to ignore it because the authors could not account for things like oil deposits that had yet to be discovered.

In 2002, the Meadows and two other members of the original team revisited their original projections. They also ran a series of new simulations in which they included data from the intervening period.[12] They showed that despite the antiquated computer hardware they used in 1972, their algorithms had done a remarkably good job of anticipating the changes that had occurred over the preceding thirty years. They also showed that updated simulations based on the new data only reaffirmed their initial conclusions that our preoccupation with growth might lead us to oblivion. The only real difference, they explained, was that in the intervening period, a critical threshold had passed. Dialling down economic growth was no longer enough. It needed to be dialled back.

Their update was far more pessimistic than the first book. By then, a rapidly growing body of scientific research pointed to a whole series of ominous environmental issues that Meadows and his team had not taken into account in their original projections. In modelling the potential impacts of pollutants, for example, the team had not thought to consider the plastics that now glut the seas and that ensure the sterility of landfill sites the world over. The original study had briefly mentioned a potential link between carbon dioxide emissions and possible atmospheric warming, but not that the planet was already undergoing a particularly rapid period of climate change as a result of the accumulation of greenhouse gases coughed into the atmosphere by two centuries of rapidly expanding industrial and agricultural output.

Since 2002, the models developed by *The Limits to Growth* team have been reappraised and updated many times, often by third parties. Even so, this once landmark study has been overtaken by a tidal wave of newer studies documenting humankind's unfolding impact on our environment and the anticipated consequences of it. There is now far more evidence than there was in 1972 or even 2002, and computers are capable of spitting out simulations many orders of magnitude larger and more complex. The evidence is now so overwhelming that debate within the scientific community on the scale of human impact on our planet has shifted to asking whether the current geological era merits being redubbed the Anthropocene – the human era.

In John Maynard Keynes's economic utopia, there was no anthropogenic climate change. Nor was there ocean acidification or large-scale biodiversity loss. But if there were, it would almost certainly be under better control than it is now. His utopia was, after all, a place where the scientific method was respected, scientists were admired, and laypeople paid serious heed to their warnings. But more importantly, it was a place where meeting the energy-expensive 'relative needs' that animate our urge to consume had diminished to the point that people were no longer inclined to periodically upgrade and replace everything they owned simply to keep the wheels of commerce turning.

It may be the case that we are well on our way to achieving Keynes's utopia; that we are just shy of crossing a critical threshold that will change everything, or that we are so caught up in the hurly-burly of it all that it is difficult to get a clear sense of its trajectory. The problem is, though, that we no longer have the luxury of waiting to find out.

To be sure, the ominous prospect of a rapidly changing climate has thus far spurred lots of talk and some action. The breezy rhetoric of 'sustainability' now routinely perfumes the annual reports, policies and plans of international organisations, governments and businesses alike. Yet, despite increasing public pressure, there remains obstinate resistance to even contemplating the substantial steps the Club of Rome recommended were appropriate back in 1972. Indeed, a huge number of people have found it easier to question the integrity of hard science, rather than ask the challenging questions about soft economics that sustainability raises.

It is unsurprising, however, that many initiatives aimed at addressing anthropogenic climate change and biodiversity loss have had to try to justify their existence in terms of the very principles of the economics responsible for them in the first place. Thus well-heeled hunters gun down lions, elephants and a host of other wildlife, persuaded that they are supporting a handful of jobs that wouldn't otherwise exist while simultaneously raising revenues used to protect these species; marine biologists argue for efforts to restore bleached coral reefs by reference to the economic impacts likely to be associated with their destruction; environmentalists debate the fate of functioning ecosystems with politicians by invoking the 'services' these ecosystems undertake on our behalf; and climatologists find themselves trying to make the 'business case' for reducing carbon emissions or mitigating climate change impacts.

Perhaps those who do not remember history are doomed to repeat the mistakes of the past. But there are no obvious precedents for some of the potentially existential challenges that confront us now. After all, never before in human history have there been 7.5 billion people each capturing and expending roughly 250 times the energy that our individual forager forebears did. Fortunately, computing, artificial intelligence and machine language have given us tools that enable us to model potential futures far more accurately than any holy men and soothsayers ever could. As imperfect as these tools may be, they are improving all the time and so are shifting our conceptual horizons about cause and effect and about the consequences of our actions now ever further into the future. Where foragers, with their immediate-return economies, invested their labour effort to meet their spontaneous needs, and farmers, with their delayed-return systems, invested theirs to support themselves for the following year, we are now obliged to consider the potential consequences of our work over a much longer time span. One that recognises that most of us can expect to live longer than at any time in the past and that is cognisant of the legacy we leave our descendants. This in turn imposes complex new trade-offs to be made between short-term gains and longer-term consequences that may transform those gains into losses.

The inadequacy of history as a guide to the future was one of the principal points that John Maynard Keynes made when he imagined that by 2030 technological advancement, capital growth and improvements in productivity would lead us to a land of 'economic bliss'. As far as he was concerned the future won by automation was uncharted territory, and successfully navigating it would require imagination, openness, and a historically unprecedented transformation in our attitudes and values.

'When the accumulation of wealth is no longer of high social importance,' he concluded, 'there will be great changes in the code of morals,' as a result of which we shall have no choice but to discard 'all kinds of social customs and economic practices, affecting the distribution of wealth and of economic rewards and penalties'.

Keynes's sense that the changes brought about by auto-mation would catalyse a fundamental revolution in the way people lived, thought and organised themselves, echoed that of many other early twentieth-century thinkers who had voyaged into the future. In this sense, he was not so different from people like Karl Marx and Emile Durkheim, both of whom believed that, in the end, history would somehow sort itself out, even if they had very different views about how that would happen. While Keynes could not have imagined the scale and risks associated with anthropogenic climate change and biodiversity loss because of our efforts to solve the economic problem, being a fan of Robert Malthus he would have understood it immediately.

Where history is a better guide to the future is on the nature of change. It reminds us that we are a stubborn species: one that is deeply resistant to making profound changes in our behaviour and habits, even when it is clear that we need to do so. But it also reveals that when change is forced upon us we are astonishingly versatile. We are able to quickly adapt to new, often very different ways of doing and thinking about things and in a short time become as habituated to them as we were to those that preceded them. This being so, while automation and AI have made it possible for us to embrace a profoundly different future, it is unlikely that it will be the catalyst that causes the dramatic changes in 'social customs and economic practices' that Keynes envisaged. Far more likely catalysts take the form of a rapidly changing climate, like that which spurred the invention of agriculture; anger ignited by systematic inequalities like those that stirred the Russian revolution; or perhaps even a viral pandemic that exposes the obsolescence of our economic institutions and working culture, causing us to ask what jobs are truly valuable and question why we are content to let our markets reward those in often pointless or parasitic roles so much more than those we recognise as essential.

Conclusion

When in the 1960s anthropologists began to work with contemporary forager societies like the Ju/'hoansi, BaMbuti and Hadzabe, they did so in the hope that their work might shed some light on how our ancestors lived in the deep past. Now it seems that this same body of work might offer some insights about how we might organise ourselves in an automated future constrained by severe environmental limits.

We now know, for instance, that the Ju/'hoansi and other Kalahari foragers are the descendants of a single population group who have lived continuously in southern Africa since the first emergence of modern *Homo sapiens* possibly as long as 300,000 years ago. We also have good reason to believe that they organised themselves economically in similar ways to how the Ju/'hoansi lived in the 1960s. If the ultimate measure of sustainability is endurance over time, then hunting and gathering is by far the most sustainable economic approach developed in all of human history, and the Khoisan are the most accomplished exponents of this approach. Hunting and gathering is, of course, not an option for us now, but these societies offer hints into some aspects of what a society no longer beholden to the economic problem might look like. They remind us that our contemporary attitudes to work are not only the progeny of the transition to farming and our migration into cities, but also that the key to living well depends on moderating our personal material aspirations by addressing inequality so that, in the words of John Maynard Keynes, we might 'once more value ends above means and prefer the good to the useful'.

Reflecting the growing uncertainty about our automated future and the sustainability of our environments, there has been a recent efflorescence of manifestos and books proposing how we should or could organise things in the future. Some have sought to map out a path in broadly economic terms. Among the most influential have been the many that propose various models of 'post-capitalism', or those that insist we take economic growth down from its hallowed pedestal and recognise that the market is at best a poor arbiter of value, and when it comes to things like our living environment, a destroyer of it. The most interesting of these have been the ones that seek to diminish the importance we give to accumulation of private wealth. These include proposals like granting a universal basic income (apportioning free money to everyone whether they work or not) and shifting the focus on taxation from income to wealth. Other interesting approaches propose extending the fundamental rights we give to people and companies to ecosystems, rivers and crucial habitats.

Others still have taken a more optimistic approach, based largely on the idea that automation and AI will organically usher in a level of such great material luxury that we will find ways of surmounting whatever obstacles get in the way of our path to an economic utopia. These echo the idyllic future imagined by Oscar Wilde in which we are free to spend our time in pursuit of cultivated leisure, perhaps 'by making beautiful things, or reading beautiful things, or simply contemplating the world with admiration and delight'.

There has also been a resurgence of interest in models of organising our future based on dogma or idyllic fantasies of the past. And while these have little in common with the visions of more technically minded utopians, they are no less influential in shaping the opinions and attitudes among a significant proportion of the global population. The recent rise in many countries of the toxic nationalism that the architects of the United Nations hoped would be banished after the horrors of the Second World War is a reflection of this, as is the trend to greater theological conservatism in many places, and the willingness of many to defer complicated choices back to the imagined teachings of ancient gods.

Beyond channelling the spirits of the thousands of generations of makers and doers, who as faithful servants of that trickster god entropy have found satisfaction through giving their idle hands and restless minds work to do, the purpose of this book is somewhat less prescriptive. One aim is to reveal how our relationship to work – in the broadest sense – is more fundamental than that imagined by the likes of Keynes. The relationship between energy, life and work is part of a common bond we have with all other living organisms, and at the same time our purposefulness, our infinite skilfulness and ability to find satisfaction in even the mundane are part of an evolutionary legacy honed since the very first stirrings of life on earth.

The principal purpose, however, has been to loosen the claw-like grasp that scarcity economics has held over our working lives, and to diminish our corresponding and unsustainable preoccupation with economic growth. For by recognising that many of the core assumptions that under-write our economic institutions are an artefact of the agri-cultural revolution, amplified by our migration into cities, frees us to imagine a whole range of new, more sustainable possible futures for ourselves, and rise to the challenge of harnessing our restless energy, purposefulness and cre-ativity to shaping our destiny.

Notes

INTRODUCTION

1 Adam Smith, *An Inquiry into the Nature and Causes of the Wealth of Nations*, Metalibri, Lausanne, 2007 (1776), p. 12, https://www.ibiblio.org/ml/libri/s/SmithA_WealthNations_p.pdf.

2 Oscar Wilde, 'The Soul of Man Under Socialism', *The Collected Works of Oscar Wilde*, Wordsworth Library Collection, London, 2007, p. 1051.

CHAPTER I

1 Gaspard-Gustave Coriolis, *Du calcul de l'effet des machines*, Carilian-Goeury, Paris, 1829.

2 Pierre Perrot, *A to Z of Thermodynamics*, Oxford University Press, 1998.

3 'The Mathematics of the Rubik's Cube', *Introduction to Group Theory and Permutation Puzzles*, 17 March 2009, http://web.mit.edu/sp.268/www/rubik.pdf.

4 Peter Schuster, 'Boltzmann and Evolution: Some Basic Questions of Biology seen with Atomistic Glasses', in G. Gallavotti, W. L. Reiter and J. Yngvason (eds), *Boltzmann's Legacy (ESI Lectures in Mathematics and Physics)*, European Mathematical Society, Zurich, 2007, pp. 217–41.

5 Erwin Schrödinger, *What is life?*, Cambridge University Press, 1944.

6 Ibid., pp. 60–1.

7 T. Kachman, J. A. Owen and J. L. England, 'Self-Organized Resonance during Search of a Diverse Chemical Space', *Physics Review Letters*, 119, 2017.

8 J. M. Horowitz and J. L. England, 'Spontaneous fine-tuning to environment in many-species chemical reaction networks', *Proceedings of the National Academy of Sciences USA* 114, 2017, 7565, https://doi.org/10.1073/pnas.1700617114; N. Perunov, R. Marsland and J. England, 'Statistical Physics of Adaptation', *Physical Review* X, 6, 021036, 2016.

9 O. Judson, 'The energy expansions of evolution', *Nature Ecology & Evolution* 1, 2017, 0138, https://doi.org/10.1038/s41559-017-0138.

CHAPTER 2

1 Francine Patterson and Wendy Gordon, 'The Case for the Personhood of Gorillas', in Paola Cavalieri and Peter Singer (eds), *The Great Ape Project*, New York, St. Martin's Griffin, 1993, pp. 58–77, http://www.animal-rights-library.com/texts-m/patterson01.htm.

2 https://www.darwinproject.ac.uk/letter/DCP-LETT-2743.xml.

3 G. N. Askew, 'The elaborate plumage in peacocks is not such a drag', *Journal of Experimental Biology* 217 (18), 2014, 3237, https://doi.org/10.1242/jeb.107474.

4 Mariko Takahashi, Hiroyuki Arita, Mariko Hiraiwa-Hasegawa and Toshikazu Hasegawa, 'Peahens do not prefer peacocks with more elaborate trains', *Animal Behaviour* 75, 2008, 1209–19.

5 H. R. G. Howman and G. W. Begg, 'Nest building and nest destruction by the masked weaver, Ploceus velatus', *South African Journal of Zoology*, 18:1, 1983, 37–44, DOI: 10.1080/02541858.1983.11447812.

6 Nicholas E. Collias and Elsie C. Collias, 'A Quantitative Analysis of Breeding Behavior in the African Village Weaverbird', *The Auk* 84 (3), 1967, 396–411, https://doi.org/10.2307/4083089.

7 Nicholas E. Collias, 'What's so special about weaverbirds?', *New Scientist* 74, 1977, 338–9.

8 P. T. Walsh, M. Hansell, W. D. Borello and S. D. Healy, 'Individuality in nest building: Do Southern Masked weaver

(Ploceus velatus) males vary in their nest-building behaviour?',
Behavioural Processes 88, 2011, 1–6.

9 P. F. Colosimo, et al., 'The Genetic Architecture of Parallel Armor
Plate Reduction in Threespine Sticklebacks', *PLoS Biology* 2 (5),
2004, e109, https://doi.org/10.1371/journal.pbio.0020109.

10 Collias and Collias, 'A Quantitative Analysis of Breeding
Behavior in the African Village Weaverbird'.

11 Lewis G. Halsey, 'Keeping Slim When Food Is Abundant: What
Energy Mechanisms Could Be at Play?', *Trends in Ecology &*
Evolution, 2018, DOI: 10.1016/j.tree.2018.08.004.

12 K. Matsuura, et al. 'Identification of a pheromone regulating
caste differentiation in termites', *Proceedings of the National*
Academy of Sciences USA 107, 2010, 12963.

13 Proverbs 6:6–11.

14 Herbert Spencer, *Principles of Ethics*, 1879, Book 1, Part 2,
Chapter 8, section 152, https://mises-media.s3.amazonaws.com/
The%20Principles%20of%20Ethics%2C%20Volume%20I_2.
pdf.

15 Herbert Spencer, *The Man versus the State: With Six Essays on*
Government, Society, and Freedom, Liberty Classics edition,
Indianapolis, 1981, p. 109.

16 Charles Darwin, *On the Origin of Species by Means of Natural*
Selection, or The Preservation of Favoured Races in the Struggle
for Life, D. Appleton, New York, 1860, p. 85.

17 Ibid., p. 61.

18 Roberto Cazzolla Gatti, 'A conceptual model of new hypothesis
on the evolution of biodiversity', *Biologia*, 2016, DOI: 10.1515/
biolog-2016-0032.

CHAPTER 3

1 R. W. Shumaker, K. R. Walkup and B. B. Beck, *Animal Tool*
Behavior: The Use and Manufacture of Tools by Animals, Johns
Hopkins University Press, Baltimore, 2011.

2 J. Sackett, 'Boucher de Perthes and the Discovery of Human
Antiquity', *Bulletin of the History of Archaeology* 24, 2014,
DOI: http://doi.org/10.5334/bha.242.

Notes

3 Charles Darwin, Letter to Charles Lyell, 17 March 1863, https://www.darwinproject.ac.uk/letter/DCP-LETT-4047.xml.

4 D. Richter and M. Krbetschek, 'The Age of the Lower Paleolithic Occupation at Schöningen', *Journal of Human Evolution* 89, 2015, 46–56.

5 H. Thieme, 'Altpaläolithische Holzgeräte aus Schöningen, Lkr. Helmstedt', *Germania* 77, 1999, 451–87.

6 K. Zutovski, R. Barkai, 'The Use of Elephant Bones for Making Acheulian Handaxes': A Fresh Look at Old Bones', Quaternary International, 406 (2016), pp. 227-238.

7 J. Wilkins, B. J. Schoville, K. S. Brown and M. Chazan, 'Evidence for Early Hafted Hunting Technology', *Science* 338, 2012, 942–6, https://doi.org/10.1126/science.1227608.

8 Raymond Corbey, Adam Jagich, Krist Vaesen and Mark Collard, 'The Acheulean Handaxe: More like a Bird's Song than a Beatles' Tune?', *Evolutionary Anthropology* 25 (1), 2016, 6–19, https://doi.org/10.1002/evan.21467.

9 S. Higuchi, T. Chaminade, H. Imamizu and M. Kawato, 'Shared neural correlates for language and tool use in Broca's area', *NeuroReport* 20, 2009, 1376, https://doi.org/10.1097/WNR.0b013e3283315570.

10 G. A. Miller, 'Informavores', in Fritz Machlup and Una Mansfield (eds), *The Study of Information: Interdisciplinary Messages*, Wiley-Interscience, New York 1983, pp. 111–13.

CHAPTER 4

1 K. Hardy et al., 'Dental calculus reveals potential respiratory irritants and ingestion of essential plant-based nutrients at Lower Palaeolithic Qesem Cave Israel', *Quaternary International*, 2015, http://dx.doi.org/10.1016/j.quaint.2015.04.033.

2 Naama Goren-Inbar et al., 'Evidence of Hominin Control of Fire at Gesher Benot Ya`aqov, Israel', *Science* 30, April 2004, 725–7.

3 S. Herculano-Houzel and J. H. Kaas, 'Great ape brains conform to the primate scaling rules: Implications for hominin evolution', *Brain, Behavior and Evolution.* 77, 2011, 33–44; Suzana Herculano-Houzel, 'The not extraordinary human brain', *Proceedings of the National Academy of*

Sciences 109 (Supplement 1), June 2012, 10661–8 DOI: 10.1073/pnas.1201895 10.

4 Juli G. Pausas and Jon E. Keeley, 'A Burning Story: The Role of Fire in the History of Life', *BioScience* 59, no. 7, July/August 2009, 593–601, doi:10.1525/bio.2009.59.7.10.

5 See Rachel N. Carmody et al., 'Genetic Evidence of Human Adaptation to a Cooked Diet', *Genome Biology and Evolution* 8, no. 4, 13 April 2016, 1091–1103, doi:10.1093/gbe/evw059.

6 S. Mann and R. Cadman, 'Does being bored make us more creative?', *Creativity Research Journal* 26 (2), 2014, 165–73; J. D. Eastwood, C. Cavaliere, S. A. Fahlman and A. E. Eastwood, 'A desire for desires: Boredom and its relation to alexithymia', *Personality and Individual Differences* 42, 2007, 1035–45; K. Gasper and B. L. Middlewood, 'Approaching novel thoughts: Understanding why elation and boredom promote associative thought more than distress and relaxation', *Journal of Experimental Social Psychology* 52, 2014, 50–7; M. F. Kets de Vries, 'Doing nothing and nothing to do: The hidden value of empty time and boredom', INSEAD, Faculty and Research Working Paper, 2014.

7 Robin Dunbar, *Grooming, Gossip and the Evolution of Language*, Faber & Faber, London, 2006, Kindle edition.

8 Alejandro Bonmatí et al., 'Middle Pleistocene lower back and pelvis from an aged human individual from the Sima de los Huesos site, Spain', *Proceedings of the National Academy of Sciences* 107 (43), October 2010, 18386–91, DOI:10.1073/pnas.1012131107.

9 Patrick S. Randolph-Quinney, 'A new star rising: Biology and mortuary behaviour of Homo naledi', *South African Journal of Science* 111 (9–10), 2015, 01–04, https://dx.doi.org/10.17159/SAJS.2015/A0122.

CHAPTER 5

1 Carina M. Schlebusch and Mattias Jakobsson, 'Tales of Human Migration, Admixture, and Selection in Africa', *Annual Review of Genomics and Human Genetics*, Vol. 19, 405–28, https://doi.

Notes

org/10.1146/annurev-genom-083117-021759; Marlize Lombard, Mattias Jakobsson and Carina Schlebusch, 'Ancient human DNA: How sequencing the genome of a boy from Ballito Bay changed human history', *South African Journal of Science* 114 (1–2), 2018, 1–3, https://dx.doi.org/10.17159/sajs.2018/a0253.

2   A. S. Brooks et al., 'Long-distance stone transport and pigment use in the earliest Middle Stone Age', *Science* 360, 2018, 90–4, https://doi.org/10.1126/science.aao2646.

3   Peter J. Ramsay and J. Andrew G. Cooper, 'Late Quaternary Sea-Level Change in South Africa', *Quaternary Research* 57, no. 1, January 2002, 82–90, https://doi.org/10.1006/qres.2001.2290.

4   Lucinda Backwell, Francesco D'Errico and Lyn Wadley, 'Middle Stone Age bone tools from the Howiesons Poort layers, Sibudu Cave, South Africa', *Journal of Archaeological Science*, 35, 2008, pp. 1566–80; M. Lombard, 'Quartz-tipped arrows older than 60 ka: further use-trace evidence from Sibudu, KwaZulu-Natal, South Africa' *Journal of Archaeological Science*, 38, 2011.

5   J. E. Yellen et al., 'A middle stone age worked bone industry from Katanda, Upper Semliki Valley, Zaire', *Science* 268 (5210), 28 April 1995, 553–6, doi:10.1126/science.7725100. PMID 7725100.

6   Eleanor M. L. Scerri, 'The North African Middle Stone Age and its place in recent human evolution', *Evolutionary Anthropology* 26, 2017, 119–35.

7   Richard Lee, *The !Kung San: Men, Women, and Work in a Foraging Society*, Cambridge University Press, 1979, p. 1.

8   Richard B. Lee and Irven DeVore (eds), *Kalahari Hunter-Gatherers*, Harvard University Press, Cambridge, Mass., 1976, p. 10.

9   Richard Lee and Irven DeVore (eds), *Man the Hunter*, Aldine, Chicago, 1968, p. 3.

10 *What Hunters do for a Living or How to Make Out on Scarce Resources* in Richard B. Lee and Irven DeVore (eds), *Man the Hunter*, Aldine, Chicago, 1968.

11 Michael Lambek, 'Marshalling Sahlins', *History and Anthropology* 28, 2017, 254, https://doi.org/10.1080/02757206. 2017.1280120.

12 Marshall Sahlins, *Stone Age Economics*, Routledge, New York, 1972, p. 2.

Notes

CHAPTER 6

1 Colin Turnbull, *The Forest People: A Study of the Pygmies of the Congo*, London, Simon & Schuster, 1961, pp. 25–6.

2 J. Woodburn, 'An Introduction to Hadza Ecology', in Richard Lee and Irven DeVore (eds), *Man the Hunter*, Aldine, Chicago, 1968, p. 55.

3 James Woodburn, 'Egalitarian Societies', *Man, the Journal of the Royal Anthropological Institute* 17, no. 3, 1982, 432.

4 Ibid., 431–51.

5 Nicolas Peterson, 'Demand sharing: reciprocity and pressure for generosity among foragers', *American Anthropologist* 95 (4), 1993, 860–74, doi: 10.1525/aa.1993.95.4.02a00050.

6 N. G. Blurton-Jones, 'Tolerated theft, suggestions about the ecology and evolution of sharing, hoarding and scrounging', *Information (International Social Science Council)* 26 (1), 1987, 31–54, https://doi.org/10.1177/053901887026001002.

7 Charles Darwin, *On the Origin of Species by Means of Natural Selection, or The Preservation of Favoured Races in the Struggle for Life*, London, Murray, 1859 p. 192.

8 Richard B Lee, *The Dobe Ju/'hoansi*, 4th edition, Wadsworth, Belmont CA, p. 57.

9 M. Cortés-Sánchez, et al., 'An early Aurignacian arrival in south-western Europe', *Nature Ecology & Evolution* 3, 2019, 207–12, doi:10.1038/s41559-018-0753-6.

10 M. W. Pedersen et al., 'Postglacial viability and colonization in North America's ice-free corridor', *Nature* 537, 2016, 45.

11 Erik Trinkaus, Alexandra Buzhilova, Maria Mednikova and Maria Dobrovolskaya, *The People of Sunghir: Burials, bodies and behavior in the earlier Upper Paleolithic*, Oxford University Press, New York, 2014, p. 25.

CHAPTER 7

1 Editorial, *Antiquity*, Vol. LIV, no. 210, March 1980, 1–6, https://www.cambridge.org/core/services/aop-cambridge-core/content/view/C57CF659BEA86384A93550428A7C8DB9/S0003598X00042769a.pdf/editorial.pdf.

Notes

2 Greger Larson, et al., 'Current Perspectives and the Future of Domestication Studies', *Proceedings of the National Academy of Sciences* 111, no. 17, 29 April 2014, 6139, https://doi.org/10.1073/pnas. 1323964111.

3 M. Germonpre, 'Fossil dogs and wolves from Palaeolithic sites in Belgium, the Ukraine and Russia: Osteometry, ancient DNA and stable isotopes', *Journal of Archaeological Science*, 36 (2), 2009, 473–90, doi:10.1016/j.jas.2008.09.033.

4 D. J. Cohen, 'The Beginnings of Agriculture in China: A Multiregional View', *Current Anthropology*, 52 (S4), 2011, S273–93, doi:10.1086/659965.

5 Larson, et al., 'Current Perspectives.

6 Amaia Arranz-Otaegui et al., 'Archaeobotanical evidence reveals the origins of bread 14,400 years ago in northeastern Jordan', *Proceedings of the National Academy of Sciences* 115 (31), July 2018, 7925–30, DOI: 10.1073/pnas.1801071115.

7 Li Liu et al., 'Fermented beverage and food storage in 13,000-year-old stone mortars at Raqefet Cave, Israel: Investigating Natufian ritual feasting', *Journal of Archaeological Science*, Reports, Vol. 21, 2018, pp. 783–93, https://doi.org/10.1016/j.jasrep.2018.08.008.

8 A. Snir et al., 'The Origin of Cultivation and Proto-Weeds, Long Before Neolithic Farming', *PLoS ONE* 10 (7), 2015, e0131422. https://doi.org/10.1371/journal.pone.0131422.

9 Ibid.

10 Robert Bettinger, Peter Richerson and Robert Boyd, 'Constraints on the Development of Agriculture', *Current Anthropology*, Vol. 50, no. 5, October 2009; R. F. Sage, 'Was low atmospheric CO_2 during the Pleistocene a limiting factor for the origin of agriculture?', *Global Change Biology* 1, 1995, 93–106, https://doi.org/10.1111/j.1365-2486.1995.tb00009.x

11 Peter Richerson, Robert Boyd, and Robert Bettinger, 'Was agriculture impossible during the Pleistocene but mandatory during the Holocene? A climate change hypothesis', *American Antiquity*, Vol. 66, no. 3, 2001, 387–411.

12 Jack Harlan, 'A Wild Wheat Harvest in Turkey', *Archeology*, Vol. 20, no. 3, 1967, 197–201.

13 Liu et al., 'Fermented beverage and food storage'.

14 A. Arranz-Otaegui, L. González-Carretero, J. Roe and T. Richter, '"Founder crops" v. wild plants: Assessing the plant-based diet of the last hunter-gatherers in southwest Asia', *Quaternary Science Reviews* 186, 2018, 263–83.

15 Wendy S. Wolbach et al., 'Extraordinary Biomass-Burning Episode and Impact Winter Triggered by the Younger Dryas Cosmic Impact ~12,800 Years Ago. 1. Ice Cores and Glaciers', *Journal of Geology* 126 (2), 2018, 165–84, Bibcode:2018JG....126 ..165W. doi:10.1086/695703.

16 J. Hepp et al., 'How Dry Was the Younger Dryas? Evidence from a Coupled Δ2H–Δ18O Biomarker Paleohygrometer Applied to the Gemündener Maar Sediments, Western Eifel, Germany', *Climate of the Past* 15, no. 2, 9 April 2019, 713–33, https://doi.org/10.5194/cp-15-713-2019; S. Haldorsen et al., 'The climate of the Younger Dryas as a boundary for Einkorn domestication', *Vegetation History Archaeobotany* 20, 2011, 305–18.

17 Ian Kuijt and Bill Finlayson, 'Evidence for food storage and predomestication granaries 11,000 years ago in the Jordan Valley', *Proceedings of the National Academy of Sciences* 106 (27), July 2009, 10966–70, DOI: 10.1073/pnas.0812764106; Ian Kuijt, 'What Do We Really Know about Food Storage, Surplus, and Feasting in Preagricultural Communities?', *Current Anthropology* 50 (5), 2009, 641–4, doi:10.1086/605082.

18 Klaus Schmidt, 'Göbekli Tepe – the Stone Age Sanctuaries: New results of ongoing excavations with a special focus on sculptures and high reliefs', *Documenta Praehistorica* (Ljubliana) 37, 2010, 239–56.

19 Haldorsen et al., 'The Climate of the Younger Dryas as a Boundary for Einkorn Domestication', *Vegetation History and Archaeobotany* 20 (4), 2011, 305.

20 J. Gresky, J. Haelm and L. Clare, 'Modified Human Crania from Göbekli Tepe Provide Evidence for a New Form of Neolithic Skull Cult', *Science Advances* 3 (6), 2017, https://doi.org/10.1126/sciadv.1700564.

1 M. A. Zeder, 'Domestication and Early Agriculture in the Mediterranean Basin: Origins, Diffusion, and Impact', *Proceedings of the National Academy of Sciences USA* 105 (33), 2008, 11597, https://doi.org/10.1073/pnas.0801317105.

2 M. Gurven and H. Kaplan, 'Longevity among Hunter-Gatherers: A Cross-Cultural Examination', *Population and Development Review* 33 (2), 2007, 321–65.

3 Andrea Piccioli, Valentina Gazzaniga and Paola Catalano, *Bones: Orthopaedic Pathologies in Roman Imperial Age*, Springer, Switzerland, 2015.

4 Michael Gurven and Hillard Kaplan, 'Longevity among Hunter-Gatherers: A Cross-Cultural Examination', *Population and Development Review*, Vol. 33, no. 2, June 2007, pp. 321–65, published by Population Council, https://www.jstor.org/stable/25434609; Väinö Kannisto and Mauri Nieminen, 'Finnish Life Tables since 1751', *Demographic Research*, Vol. 1, Article 1, www.demographic-research.org/Volumes/Vol1/1/ DOI: 10.4054/DemRes.1999.1.

5 C. S. Larsen et al., 'Bioarchaeology of Neolithic Çatalhöyük reveals fundamental transitions in health, mobility, and lifestyle in early farmers', *Proceedings of the National Academy of Sciences USA*, 2019, 04345, https://doi.org/10.1073/pnas.1904345116.

6 J. C. Berbesque, F. M. Marlowe, P. Shaw and P. Thompson, 'Hunter-Gatherers Have Less Famine Than Agriculturalists', *Biology Letters* 10: 20130853 http://doi.org/10.1098/rsbl.2013.0853.

7 D. Grace et al. *Mapping of poverty and likely zoonoses hotspots*, ILRI, Kenya, 2012.

8 S. Shennan et al., 'Regional population collapse followed initial agriculture booms in mid-Holocene Europe', *Nature Communications* 4, 2013, 2486.

9 See Ian Morris, *Foragers, Farmers, and Fossil Fuels: How Human Values Evolve*, Princeton University Press, Princeton, NJ, 2015, and *The Measure of Civilization: How Social Development Decides the Fate of Nations*, Princeton University Press,

Princeton, NJ, 2013; Vaclav Smil, *Energy and Civilization: A History*, MIT Press, Boston, 2017.

10 Ruben O. Morawick and Delmy J. Díaz González, 'Food Sustainability in the Context of Human Behavior', *Yale Journal of Biology and Medicine*, Vol. 91, no. 2, 28 June 2018, 191–6.

11 E. Fernández et al., 'Ancient DNA Analysis of 8000 B.C. Near Eastern Farmers Supports an Early Neolithic Pioneer Maritime Colonization of Mainland Europe Through Cyprus and the Aegean Islands', *PLoS Genetics* 10, no. 6, 2014, e1004401; H. Malmström et al., 'Ancient Mitochondrial DNA from the Northern Fringe of the Neolithic Farming Expansion in Europe Sheds Light on the Dispersion Process', *Royal Society of London: Philosophical Transactions B: Biological Sciences* 370, no. 1660, 2015; Zuzana Hofmanová et. al., 'Early Farmers from across Europe Directly Descended from Neolithic Aegeans', *Proceedings of the National Academy of Sciences* 113, no. 25, 21 June 2016, 6886, https://doi.org/10.1073/pnas.1523951113.

12 Q. Fu, P. Rudan, S. Pääbo and J. Krause, 'Complete Mitochondrial Genomes Reveal Neolithic Expansion into Europe', *PLoS ONE* 7 (3), 2012, e32473; doi: 10.1371/journal.pone.0032473.

13 J. M. Cobo, J. Fort and N. Isern, 'The spread of domesticated rice in eastern and southeastern Asia was mainly demic', *Journal of Archaeological Science* 101, 2019, 123–30.

CHAPTER 9

1 Benjamin Franklin, Letter to Benjamin Vaughn, 26 July 1784.

2 'Poor Richard Improved, 1757', *Founders Online*, National Archives, accessed 11 April 2019, https://founders.archives.gov/documents/Franklin/01-07-02-0030. [Original source: *The Papers of Benjamin Franklin*, vol. 7, *October 1, 1756 through March 31, 1758*, ed. Leonard W. Labaree, Yale University Press, New Haven, 1963, pp. 74–93.]

3 Benjamin Franklin, *The Autobiography of Benjamin Franklin*, Section 36, 1793, https://en.wikisource.org/wiki/The_Autobiography_of_Benjamin_Franklin/Section_Thirty_Six.

4 Adam Smith, *An Inquiry into the Nature and Causes of the Wealth of Nations*, Metalibri, Lausanne, 2007 (1776), p. 15,

https://www.ibiblio.org/ml/libri/s/SmithA_WealthNations_p.
pdf.

5 Ibid.

6 G. Kellow, 'Benjamin Franklin and Adam Smith: Two Strangers
and the Spirit of Capitalism', *History of Political Economy* 50
(2), 2018, 321–44.

7 This federation, which comprised the Mohawk, the Seneca,
the Oneida, the Onondaga, the Cayuga and the Tuscarora, was
of interest to Franklin and was one of the models used by the
Founding Fathers when drafting the United States Constitution.

8 Benjamin Franklin, letter to Peter Collinson, 9 May 1753, https://
founders.archives.gov/documents/Franklin/01-04-02-0173.

9 David Graeber, *Debt: The First 500 Years*, Melville House,
New York, 2013, p. 28.

10 Caroline Humphrey, 'Barter and Economic Disintegration', *Man*
20 (1), 1985, p. 48.

11 Benjamin Franklin, *A Modest Inquiry into the Nature and
Necessity of a Paper Currency*, in *The Works of Benjamin
Franklin*, ed J. Sparks, Vol. II, Boston, 1836, p. 267.

12 Austin J. Jaffe and Kenneth M. Lusht, 'The History of the Value
Theory: The Early Years', *Essays in honor of William N. Kinnard,
Jr.*, Kluwer Academic, Boston, 2003, p. 11.

CHAPTER 10

1 All quotes from Mary Shelley, *Frankenstein*, CreateSpace
Independent Publishing Platform, 2017 (1831 edn).

2 L. Janssens et al., 'A new look at an old dog: Bonn-Oberkassel
reconsidered', *Journal of Archaeological Science* 92, 2018, 126–38.

3 There is some speculation that a 33,000-year-old set of bones
found in Siberia's Altay Mountains may also be from a domestic
dog, but too many doubts remain regarding its pedigree for
archaeologists to be certain.

4 Laurent A. F. Frantz et al., 'Genomic and Archaeological
Evidence Suggest a Dual Origin of Domestic Dogs', *Science* 352
(6290), 2016, 1228.

5 L. R. Botigué et al., 'Ancient European dog genomes reveal continuity since the Early Neolithic', *Nature Communications* 8, 2017, 16082.

6 Yinon M. Bar-On, Rob Phillips and Ron Milo, 'The Biomass Distribution on Earth', *Proceedings of the National Academy of Sciences* 115 (25), 2018, 6506.

7 Vaclav Smil, *Energy and Civilization: A History*, MIT Press, Boston, Kindle Edition, 2017, p. 66.

8 René Descartes, *Treatise on Man*, (Great Minds series), Prometheus, Amherst, 2003.

9 Aristotle, *Politics*, Book I, part viii. http://www.perseus.tufts.edu/hopper/text?doc=Perseus%3Atext%3A1999.01.0058%3Abook%3D1

10 Ibid.

11 Hesiod, *Works and Days*, ll. 303, 40–6. http://www.perseus.tufts.edu/hopper/text?doc=Perseus%3Atext%3A1999.01.0132

12 Orlando Patterson, *Slavery and Social Death: A Comparative Study*, Harvard University Press, Cambridge, Mass., 1982.

13 Keith Bradley, *Slavery and Society in Ancient Rome*, Cambridge University Press, 1993, p. 63.

14 Mike Duncan, *The Storm Before the Storm: The Beginning of the End for the Roman Republic*, PublicAffairs, New York, 2017.

15 Chris Wickham, *The Inheritance of Rome: Illuminating the Dark Ages, 400–1000*, Penguin, New York, 2009, p. 29.

16 Stephen L. Dyson, *Community and Society in Roman Italy*, Johns Hopkins University Press, Baltimore, 1992, p. 177, quoting J. E. Packer, 'Middle and Lower Class Housing in Pompeii and Herculaneum: A Preliminary Survey', in *Neue Forschung in Pompeji*, pp. 133–42.

CHAPTER 11

1 David Satterthwaite, Gordon McGranahan and Cecilia Tacoli, *World Migration Report: Urbanization, Rural-Urban Migration and Urban Poverty*, International Organization for Migration (IOM), 2014, p. 7.

2 UNFPA, *State of World Population*, United Nations Population Fund, 2007.

3 All data from Hannah Ritchie and Max Roser, 'Urbanization', published online at OurWorldInData.org, 2020. Retrieved from: https://ourworldindata.org/urbanization.
4 Vere Gordon Childe, *Man Makes Himself*, New American Library, New York, 1951, p. 181.
5 J.-P. Farruggia, 'Une crise majeure de la civilisation du Néolithique Danubien des années 5100 avant notre ère', *Archeologické Rozhledy* 54 (1), 2002, 44–98; J. Wahl and H. G. König, 'Anthropologisch-traumatologische Untersuchung der menschlichen Skelettreste aus dem bandkeramischen Massengrab bei Talheim, Kreis Heilbronn', *Fundberichte aus Baden-Württemberg* 12, 1987, 65–186; R. Schulting, L. Fibiger and M. Teschler-Nicola, 'The Early Neolithic site Asparn/Schletz (Lower Austria): Anthropological evidence of interpersonal violence', in *Sticks, Stones, and Broken Bones*, R. Schulting and L. Fibiger (eds), Oxford University Press, 2012, pp. 101–20.
6 Quoted in L. Stavrianos, *Lifelines from Our Past: A New World History*, Routledge, London, 1997, p. 79.

CHAPTER 12

1 B. X. Currás and I. Sastre, 'Egalitarianism and Resistance: A theoretical proposal for Iron Age Northwestern Iberian archaeology', *Anthropological Theory*, 2019, https://doi.org/10.1177/1463499618814685.
2 J. Gustavsson et al., *Global Food Losses and Food Waste*, Food and Agriculture Organisation (FAO), Rome, 2011, http://www.fao.org/3/mb060e/mb060e02.pdf
3 Alexander Apostolides et al., 'English Agricultural Output and Labour Productivity, 1250–1850: Some Preliminary Estimates' (PDF), 26 November 2008), retrieved 1 May 2019.
4 Richard J. Johnson et al., 'Potential role of sugar (fructose) in the epidemic of hypertension, obesity and the metabolic syndrome, diabetes, kidney disease, and cardiovascular disease', *American Journal of Clinical Nutrition*, Vol. 86, issue 4, October 2007, 899–906, https://doi.org/10.1093/ajcn/86.4.899.
5 I. Théry et al., 'First Use of Coal', *Nature* 373 (6514), 1995, 480–1, https://doi.org/10.1038/373480a0; J. Dodson et al., 'Use

of coal in the Bronze Age in China', *The Holocene* 24 (5), 2014, 525–30, https://doi.org/10.1177/0959683614523155.

6   Dodson et al., 'Use of coal in the Bronze Age in China'.

7   P. H. Lindert and J. G. Williamson, 'English Workers' Living Standards During the Industrial Revolution: A New Look', *Economic History Review*, 36 (1), 1983, 1–25.

8   G. Clark, 'The condition of the working class in England, 1209–2004', *Journal of Political Economy*, 113 (6), 2005, 1307–40.

9   C. M. Belfanti and F. Giusberti, 'Clothing and social inequality in early modern Europe: Introductory remarks', *Continuity and Change*, 15 (3), 2000, 359–65, doi:10.1017/S0268416051003674.

10 Emile Durkheim, *Ethics and Sociology of Morals*, Prometheus Press, Buffalo, New York, 1993 (1887), p. 87.

11 Emile Durkheim, Le Suicide: Etude de sociologie, Paris, 1897, pp. 280–1.

CHAPTER 13

1   Frederick Winslow Taylor, *Scientific Management, Comprising Shop Management: The Principles of Scientific Management [and] Testimony Before the Special House Committee*, Harper & Brothers, New York, 1947.

2   Daniel Bell, *The End of Ideology: On the Exhaustion of Political Ideas in the Fifties*, Harvard University Press, Cambridge, Mass., 2001 (1961), p. 232.

3   Peter Drucker, *Management: tasks, responsibilities, practices*, Heinemann, London, 1973.

4   Samuel Gompers, 'The miracles of efficiency', *American Federationist* 18 (4), 1911, p. 277.

5   John Lubbock, *The Pleasures of Life*, Part II, Chapter 10, 1887, Project Gutenberg eBook, http://www.gutenberg.org/ebooks/7952.

6   Ibid., Part I, Chapter 2.

7   Fabrizio Zilibotti, 'Economic Possibilities for Our Grandchildren 75 Years after: A Global Perspective', IEW – Working Papers 344, Institute for Empirical Research in Economics, University of Zurich, 2007.

8 Federal Reserve Bulletin, September 2017, Vol. 103, no. 3, p. 12.

9 https://eml.berkeley.edu/~saez/SaezZucman14slides.pdf.

10 Benjamin Kline Hunnicutt, *Kellogg's Six-Hour Day*, Temple University Press, Philadelphia, 1996.

11 John Kenneth Galbraith, *Money: Whence it Came, Where it Went*, Houghton Mifflin, Boston, 1975.

12 Advertising Hall of Fame, 'Benjamin Franklin: Founder, Publisher & Copyrighter, Magazine General', 2017, http://advertisinghall.org/members/member_bio.php?memid=632&uflag=f&uyear=.

13 John Kenneth Galbraith, *The Affluent Society*, Apple Books.

14 All Data sourced from US Bureau of Economic Analysis, US Bureau of Labor Statistics and FRED Economic Data, St Louis Fed.

15 L. Mishel and J. Schieder, 'CEO pay remains high relative to that of typical workers and high-wage earners', Economic Policy Institute, Washington, 2017, https://www.epi.org/files/pdf/130354.pdf.

16 All data from the World Inequality Database, https://wid.world and compiled on https://aneconomicsense.org/2012/07/20/the-shift-from-equitable-to-inequitable-growth-after-1980-helping-the-rich-has-not-helped-the-not-so-rich/.

17 McKinsey & Co., *McKinsey Quarterly: The War for Talent*, no. 4, 1998.

18 Jeffrey Pfeffer, 'Fighting the war for talent is hazardous to your organization's health', *Organizational Dynamics* 29 (4), 2001, 248–59.

19 Malcolm Gladwell, 'The Myth of Talent', *New Yorker*, 22 July 2002, https://www.newyorker.com/magazine/2002/07/22/the-talent-myth.

20 O. P. Hauser and M. I. Norton, '(Mis)perceptions of inequality', *Current Opinion in Psychology* 18, 2017, 21–5, https://doi.org/10.1016/j.copsyc.2017.07.024.

21 United States Census Bureau, 'New Data Show Income Increased in 14 States and 10 of the Largest Metros', 26 September 2019, https://www.census.gov/library/stories/2019/09/us-median-household-income-up-in-2018-from-2017.

html?utm_campaign=20190926msacos1ccstors&
utm_medium=email&utm_source=govdelivery.

22 S. Kiatpongsan and M. I. Norton, 'How Much (More) Should
    CEOs Make? A Universal Desire for More Equal Pay',
    Perspectives on Psychological Science, 9 (6), 2014, 587–93,
    https://doi.org/10.1177/1745691614549773.

23 Emily Etkins, 2019, 'What Americans Think Cause Wealth
    and Poverty', Cato Institute, 2019, https://www.cato.org/
    publications/survey-reports/what-americans-think-about-
    poverty-wealth-work.

CHAPTER 14

1   'Death by overwork on rise among Japan's vulnerable workers',
    Japan Times (Reuters), 3 April 2016.

2   Behrooz Asgari, Peter Pickar and Victoria Garay, 'Karoshi
    and Karou-jisatsu in Japan: causes, statistics and prevention
    mechanisms', *Asia Pacific Business & Economics Perspectives*,
    Winter 2016, 4(2).

3   http://www.chinadaily.com.cn/china/2016-12/11/con-
    tent_27635578.htm.

4   All data from OECD.Stat, https://stats.oecd.org/Index.
    aspx?DataSet Code=AVE_HRS.

5   'White Paper on Measures to Prevent Karoshi, etc.', Annual
    Report for 2016, Ministry of Health, Labour and Welfare,
    https://fpcj.jp/wp/wp-content/uploads/.../8f513ff4e9662ac515d
    e9e646f63d8b5.pdf.

6   China Labour Statistical Yearbook 2016, http://www.mohrss.
    gov.cn/2016/indexeh.htm.

7   http://www.hse.gov.uk/statistics/causdis/stress.pdf.

8   C. S. Andreassen et al., 'The prevalence of workaholism: A
    survey study in a nationally representative sample of Norwegian
    employees', *PLOS One*, 9 (8), 2014, doi: https://doi.org/10.1371/
    journal.pone.0102446.

9   Robin Dunbar, *Gossip Grooming and the Evolution of Language*,
    Harvard University Press, Cambridge, Mass, 1996.

10 http://www.vault.com/blog/workplace-issues/2015-office-
    romance-survey-results/

11 Aronson's story is recounted in W. Oates, *Workaholics, Make Laziness Work for You*, Doubleday, New York, 1978.

12 Leigh Shaw-Taylor et al., 'The Occupational Structure of England, c.1710–1871', Occupations Project Paper 22, Cambridge Group for the History of Population and Social Structure, 2010.

13 Colin Clark, *The Conditions of Economic Progress*, Macmillan, London, 1940, p. 7.

14 Ibid., p. 17.

15 https://www.strike.coop/bullshit-jobs/.

16 David Graeber, *Bullshit Jobs: A Theory*, Penguin, Kindle Edition, 2018, p. 3.

17 https://www.strike.coop/bullshit-jobs/.

18 *The Economist*, 19 November 1955.

19 *Trends in College Pricing*, Trends in Higher Education Series, College Board, 2018, p. 27, https://research.collegeboard.org/pdf/trends-college-pricing-2018-full-report.pdf.

20 California State University Statistical Abstract 2008–2009, http://www.calstate.edu/AS/stat_abstract/stat0809/index.shtml. Accessed 22 April 2019.

21 *Times Higher Education*, University Workplace Survey 2016, https://www.timeshighereducation.com/features/university-workplace-survey-2016-results-and-analysis.

22 Gallup, *State of the Global Workplace*, Gallup Press, New York, 2017, p. 20.

CHAPTER 15

1 Carl Frey and Michael Osborne, *The Future of employment: How susceptible are Jobs to Computerisation*, Oxford Martin Programme on Technology and Employment, 2013.

2 McKinsey Global Institute, *A Future that Works: Automation Employment and Productivity*, McKinsey and Co., 2017; PricewaterhouseCoopers, *UK Economic Outlook*, PWC, London, 2017, pp. 30–47.

3 PricewaterhouseCoopers, *UK Economic Outlook*, p. 35.

4 'IBM's AI loses to human debater but it's got worlds to conquer', CNet News, 11 February 2019, https://www.cnet.com/

news/ibms-ai-loses-to-human-debater-but-remains-persuasive-technology/.

5 'The Amazing Ways How Unilever Uses Artificial Intelligence To Recruit & Train Thousands Of Employees', *Forbes*, 14 December 2018, https://www.forbes.com/sites/bernardmarr/2018/12/14/the-amazing-ways-how-unilever-uses-artificial-intelligence-to-recruit-train-thousands-of-employees/#1c8861bc6274.

6 Sungki Hong and Hannah G. Shell, 'The Impact of Automation on Inequality', *Economic Synopses*, no. 29, 2018, https://doi.org/10.20955/es.2018.29.

7 World Inequality Lab, *World Inequality Report 2018*, 2018, https://wir2018.wid.world/files/download/wir2018-full-report-english.pdf.

8 Ibid., p. 15.

9 D. Meadows, R. Randers, D. Meadows and W. Behrens III, *The Limits to Growth*, Universe Books, New York, 1972, p. 193, http://donellameadows.org/wp-content/userfiles/Limits-to-Growth-digital-scan-version.pdf.

10 *New York Times*, 2 April 1972, Section BR, p. 1.

11 J. L. Simon and H. Kahn, *The Resourceful Earth: A Response to Global 2000*, Basil Blackwell, New York, 1984, p. 38.

12 D. Meadows, R. Randers and D. Meadows, *The Limits to Growth: The 30-Year Update*, Earthscan, London, 2005.

Acknowledgements

Many of the main ideas that have shaped this book found their genesis while I was living and working in Kalahari where foragers, traditional pastoralists, missionaries, freedom fighters, bureaucrats, policemen, soldiers and modern commercial farmers merged and clashed. There are too many individuals there who shaped my approach and thinking to mention and in singling out my Ju/'hoan name-father 'Oupa' Chief !A/ae Frederik Langman, who navigated strange frontier with such assured wisdom, I am extending my gratitude to you all.

A book that spans such huge time horizons is by its nature derivative. It would not have been possible were it not for the countless hours of research and analysis by a veritable army of scientists, archaeologists, anthropologists, philosophers and others whose diligence, intelligence, creativity and hard work continues to refresh and add detail to our sense of the past, present and future. I hope I have not done your insights a disservice in representing them here and placing them alongside what may sometimes seem unlikely bed fellows.

Writing is ultimately a solitary task. But the kind of isolation it demands places strains on those closest to you. So to my children Lola and Noah, my thanks and love for being kind to your preoccupied Papa and reminding me of the folly of working too hard on a book about working less . And to Michelle, my love and gratitude for everything, not least for using your magic to transform some of the clumsier ideas in this book into wonderful images.

This was far more work than I imagined it would be when various voices, the loudest of which belonged to my agent Chris Wellbelove, encouraged me to write it. My fate was subsequently sealed when editors Alexis Kirschbaum at Bloomsbury in London and William Heyward at Penguin Press in New York backed it with terrifying enthusiasm and publishers from all corners of the earth also piled in. I blame them for endless hours of hard labour and the anxiety I endured writing it, and am deeply grateful for the confidence they showed in backing someone whose premise was that we all should take a far more relaxed approach to work.

Index

Index

A Note on the Author

James Suzman is an anthropologist specialising in the Khoisan peoples of southern Africa. A recipient of the Smuts Commonwealth Fellowship in African Studies at Cambridge University, he is now the director of Anthropos Ltd, a think tank that applies anthropological methods to solving contemporary social and economic problems. He has written for publications including the *New York Times*, the *Observer*, the *Guardian*, the *New Statesman* and the *Independent*. He lives in Cambridge.

A Note on the Text

The text of this book is set in Linotype Stempel Garamond, a version of Garamond adapted and first used by the Stempel foundry in 1924. It is one of several versions of Garamond based on the designs of Claude Garamond. It is thought that Garamond based his font on Bembo, cut in 1495 by Francesco Griffo in collaboration with the Italian printer Aldus Manutius. Garamond types were first used in books printed in Paris around 1532. Many of the present-day versions of this type are based on the *Typi Academiae* of Jean Jannon cut in Sedan in 1615.

Claude Garamond was born in Paris in 1480. He learned how to cut type from his father and by the age of fifteen he was able to fashion steel punches the size of a pica with great precision. At the age of sixty he was commissioned by King Francis I to design a Greek alphabet, and for this he was given the honourable title of royal type founder. He died in 1561.